TALL SHADOWS

Interviews with Israeli Arabs

Smadar Bakovic

Hamilton Books
A member of
The Rowman & Littlefield Publishing Group
Lanham · Boulder · New York · Toronto · Oxford

Copyright © 2006 by
Hamilton Books
4501 Forbes Boulevard
Suite 200
Lanham, Maryland 20706
Hamilton Books Acquisitions Department (301) 459-3366

PO Box 317
Oxford
OX2 9RU, UK

All rights reserved
Printed in the United States of America
British Library Cataloging in Publication Information Available

Library of Congress Control Number: 2005932168
ISBN 0-7618-3289-0 (paperback : alk. ppr.)

∞™ The paper used in this publication meets the minimum
requirements of American National Standard for Information
Sciences—Permanence of Paper for Printed Library Materials,
ANSI Z39.48—1984

To my family

What is needed, rather than running away or controlling or suppressing or any other resistance, is understanding fear; that means, watch it, learn about it, come directly into contact with it. We are to learn about fear, not how to escape from it....
So when you are listening to somebody, completely, attentively, then you are listening not only to the words, but also to the feeling of what is being conveyed, to the whole of it, not part of it.

–Krishnamurti

Table of Contents

Foreword	iii
Arab Citizens of Israel	iv
Political Ambience: Colonial Ideology & Colonial Condition	vi
Current Arab Muslim Rhetoric	vii
Left Wing Voices in Israel	ix
Historical Roots of Anti-Jewish Sentiment in Islam	xi
Historical Attempts by Others to Define Jews	xi
Anti-Jewish Sentiment: Past and Present	xiii
Origins of Ethnic and Religious Hatred	xiv
An Articulated Dream is the First Step	xv
Preface	xix
Conventions	xxi
Acknowledgements	xxiii
Introduction	xxv
Religion	xxv
Demographics: Israeli Arabs	li
1 Israeli Arabs and the Jewish State	**53**
Education: the Competition for the Human Mind	53
Media: the Competition for the Human Soul	62
Interviews with Adults	73
Interviews with Children	117
Media: Interviews with Adults	130
Media: Interviews with Children	156
Education: Interviews with Adults	163
Education: Interviews with Children	178
2 Israeli Arabs and the Palestinians	**187**
Living in the Middle: an Identity Crisis	187
Interviews with Adults	196
Responses from Children	237
3 Suicide Bombings and Shaheeds	**250**
Children in Paradise: Qur'anic Verses	250
Responses from Adults	259
Responses from Children	272
Epilogue	**283**
Notes	300
Select Bibliography	**311**
Index	**312**
About the Author	**314**

Foreword

Mishael M. Caspi

Professor of Religion, Bates College

Writing an introduction to this collection of interviews conducted by Ms. Smadar Bakovic was a very difficult task. It required me to utilize words of reconciliation, words of hope and words that will allow me to see the light beyond the darkness that this work and that our present world present. It required me to avoid using any stereotypes that could promote hatred. I needed to create an introduction that is focused on the topics of peace and respect. I can share that I realized that Ms. Bakovic faced many difficulties as she wrote this book and that, happily, she met many hospitable and friendly people in the process. However, after reading her chapters which detail a project that I was involved with from its inception, I sadly realized that I cannot offer many words of hope to the reader about the future of a Muslim-Jewish reconciliation.

While writing this introduction I had to remind myself of the way ethnic and religious hatred is transmitted from one generation to the next. A young child first learns of hatred by word of mouth, often at home, and that learning is often followed by exposure to written works that are shared at school. During the second half of the 20th century, hatred was also displayed to children on the most popular media: television. Once we accept the depth and breadth of the transmission of ethnic and religious hatred, we can begin to explore the hatred that was expressed by Arab children and collected in Ms. Bakovic's work. For example, when the author began her interview with the people in the Arab village in *"The Triangle"*, the author initially thought she would be taking a journey to a world where she would see the practice of a religion that differed from her own. But she also felt assured that her journey was taking her to a place that was governed by law and order. She knew from what she had read that her journey was taking her to a country where the citizens were covered by a robust national health policy, where public education was free, and where social welfare was a common practice. However, once she arrived, she realized she had landed in a world that she had not expected. She discovered she had come to a place where the idea of a reciprocal relationship of a citizen to his or her country was a foreign and rejected concept. She had arrived in a land where the citizens had a multitude of advantages but where those same citizens had no desire, or need, to give something back to their country. As an outsider, she found herself welcomed into the homes of many Arab-Muslim citizens. She later came to realize that she had been welcomed by some people only because she was being used as a safe medium to channel the complaints of those people who believed that they were being discriminated against by Israel and who were deeply troubled by their perception that they unjustly held a second-class citizenship. Others unconditionally welcomed and opened their homes and hearts to her.

As I read her discoveries, I realized that I could not refute what she had been told because when the beliefs of any citizen are so strong, then it is vain and useless to attempt to deny them their perceptions. Refutation would serve no purpose. But, I also realized that I had questions that most Arab citizens of Israel would find challenging. I concluded that the best thing I could do in this introduction was to attempt to understand the Israeli Arabs' views that are presented in this book by examining the historical relationship between Muslims and Jews. By sharing this research I hoped that readers would discover the many sources of the Muslims' ethnic and religious hatred for Jews.

Arab Citizens of Israel

Since the founding of Israel, the Arab Muslim community that exists within Israel has deliberately and voluntarily separated itself from the mainstream of the new nation. They did this while maintaining their own political representatives within the Israeli Knesset. The Israeli government collects tax money and then an allocation of this tax money is given to the separate Israeli Arab Muslim community. That allotment of tax money given to the Arab Muslims in Israel was used for the development of their own schools, their own water systems, their community centers, and their religious life. Until the mid-1970's, however, Israel did not assess its Arab

Muslim citizens any income tax, even though this separate community was receiving state support. These citizens also did not participate in the national service required of non-Arabic citizens in Israel. Many Arab Muslims took but they did not give anything back to their country. To worsen matters, Arab Muslim citizens of Israel often ran, and continue to run, summer camps for their children where young children, who were and are citizens of Israel, were, and are now taught by their elders to say and believe biased, anti-Jewish slogans such as, "Let the Jews all go back to where they came from." This Muslim hatred of Jews is even shared today via the Internet. An example of such an Internet message was recently created by a man from the Gaza Strip who was one of the principal leaders of Hamas, Dr. Abd al Aziz Rantisi who wrote:

"Bush (President George W. Bush) believes in the vain idea of the Jewish Torah that they (the Jews) are "the chosen people" of Allah. (Mr. Bush has) offered them the divine covenant and bequested (to) them Palestine forever."

Such a biased and hateful statement calls into question the validity of Dr. Rantisi's standing as a Muslim intellectual. Another example of the deep Arab Muslim hatred of Jews is found in a sermon shared by Dr. Nasar al-Zahrani of Qatar on Friday, March 21, 2003. Among the many things he shared with his listeners in this sermon were many of the myths that the Muslim Imams have allowed themselves to share with Muslim believers, along with their misrepresentations of Islamic texts. Sadly, the Arabic tendency toward hyperbole in their poetry has now been passed along and appears today in their unbalanced and biased rendition of historical data. Dr. al-Zahrani blatantly reported as an historical fact, for example, that during the Crusades the Christians had killed "70,000 Muslims" in the al Aqsa Mosque in Jerusalem, even though in all of Jerusalem, which was then a small town, only a few thousand people lived there at that time. In his great fervor Dr. al-Zahrani made such an incorrect statement publicly that it couldn't be ignored. Personally, I considered the following statement that Dr. al-Zahrani included in his Friday khutba (1) to be false but also a vulgar statement for any self-professed intellectual to make: "In the history of Islam there was never a war which aimed to control the resources of the land." These mistakes in his well-prepared khutba were deliberate. He knew that the best way to captivate his listeners was to feed them dangerous lies.

Political Ambience: Colonial Ideology & Colonial Condition

When we undertake the task of evaluating political ambience, it is equally important to evaluate two concepts of colonialism, its ideology and its condition. First, let's look at colonial ideology. If it is present, it means that there is political and cultural control by the state over another nation and its people. In colonial ideology, force is used to compel the captured people to imitate the culture, language, and literature of the colonial rulers. For example, France was a colonial power that once forced the Algerian people to learn and speak French and also insisted that Algerian students quote and understand French writers and philosophers, such as Victor Hugo and Racine. Some Algerians were even granted French passports, even though the French government officially considered Algerians to be natives who could not become French citizens. The French colonialists took advantage of the natural resources of Algeria and enslaved its citizens. The Belgians did the same thing in the Congo. Today the Belgian Ministry of the Treasury continues to possess the gold and silver resources that Belgian colonists had removed long ago from the Congo. The English and Dutch were leading European forces that colonized much of Asia. All these European colonial powers stated that they intended to transform the native people into "good" citizens who would gladly and eagerly imitate the values and culture of their foreign rulers and would reject their own inferior ways. This was a form of levantinism. As European colonial powers made sure of their complete control of the people in each captured colony, they simultaneously enriched their own national museums with the valuable artifacts and objects of art that they systematically removed from these foreign lands. Today those pilfered treasures remain on display in the famous museums throughout Europe. The irony is that today the political leaders and some intellectuals in France, England, the Netherlands and Belgium are pointing a blaming finger and moralizing the state of Israel on their perception that Israel has now become a modern and evil *colonial* nation. Their rhetoric on this issue is full of anti-Jewish slogans and demonstrates their nations' deep ethnic and religious hatred and biases.

Next, let's examine the concept of colonial condition. This is a *temporary* state that does not intend to control the people, nor does it intend to impose any social, cultural, or religious ideology on them. In fact, it is a condition that requires the power brokers to apply political wisdom to exit this temporary condition they have initiated. Such a necessary and temporary condition exists in Israel today as it continues to deal with its Arab

Muslim citizens following the 1967 War. In Israel today no leader exists who has the capacity or the wisdom to stand up and proclaim the end of Israel's colonial condition. There is no one in Israel today who has the voice of persuasion like Ben Gurion had in 1968 when he spoke to a gathering of some faculty at the College of the Negev. In that speech, Ben Gurion stated that he felt it was in Israel's best interest to leave the conquered land it had attained following its success in the 1967 War. He stated that it was dangerous for Israel to indulge in adopting a colonial condition in its strained relationship with the losers of that war, its Arab Muslim neighbors. Such an indulgence, according to Ben Gurion, was akin to Israel committing "hara-kiri". Such "suicidal action" had been practiced in Jerusalem nineteen hundred years ago when the Jews of that day lost control of the city to the Romans. When Jerusalem was lost to the Muslim invaders in the seventh century, we see the establishment of the harsher realities of Muslim colonial ideology, which the conquerors imposed in the city as its ruling conquerors and we simultaneously witness the quick expansion of Islam. Muslims then became the paradigm of colonial ideology as they went on to conquer Iraq, Egypt, Palestine, the Maghrib, and Spain, and as they forced the conquered people to adopt their language and to choose Islam as their new religion, or to choose death instead. They spared the lives of those they called the "People of the Scripture", the "ahal-al-kitab," but those they spared from death were required to pay a poll tax for their lives. As the Muslims took control of the land and its law, they forced their colonial ideology on these new lands and indigenous people in the name of Allah. Should we, then, blame God for these atrocities carried out in his name, as Muslims aimed to conquer and then Islamize the whole world, creating one Muslim nation on earth? This period of history proves that Dr. al-Zahrani was wrong when he asserted in his sermon that Islam has never aimed to take over the power or wealth of any other nation. Islam has taken these things, and the Muslims have taken them in the name of Allah.

Current Arab Muslim Rhetoric

There is an interesting new development in the rhetoric being used in the Arab world today. Western leaders of democracy are now being compared to Hitler. We are being told that the President of the United States is using the "language of Hitler," that Mr. Bush "reminds us of Hitler's speeches," and that this president "identifies himself with Hitler." Munir Shafik, a Palestinian intellectual, was a communist in his early days and he once sought to overthrow capitalism. Then he became an Islamic extremist who is currently living in Amman, Jordan, where he ironically enjoys and uses the wealth created by that country's capitalist system. He has recently written, "The world today is facing the dangers of Hitler's time. The danger to the world today is from the U.S.A." Although he hasn't compared the President of the United States to Hitler, he has claimed that Ariel Sharon is akin to Hitler and that Zionism is akin to Nazism. This Muslim tendency to throw dirt in the face of opposing leaders is a tendency that was put into practice centuries ago by the prophet Mohammad when he and his followers massacred the Jewish tribe of al Qurayza and eliminated the Jewish population in the city of al-Medina. There were three Jewish tribes in al-Medina (Yathrib): the Qurayza, the Banu'l-Nadhir, and the Banu Qaynuqa'. Two non-Jewish tribes later settled in this city, the Awas and the Khazraj. In his ethnic cleansing campaign in al-Medina, the prophet Muhammad exiled and massacred the three Jewish tribes and declared the city as his own. The Muslims accepted this harsh act of ethnic cleansing because it was seen as an act committed in a war they had fought and won in the name of "God Almighty," who had instructed the prophet to commit these acts of aggression. Once again, on September 11, 2001 the Muslim extremists claimed "God Almighty" instructed the believers led by Muhammad Atta to commit murder in the name of the holy words recorded in the Qur'an. As he acted, Atta did not forget to tell his fellow assassins "the women of Paradise ("banat al-hur") are awaiting, calling out, come, friend of God." Here we witnessed the paradigmatic paganism of a tradition calling itself, according to contemporary interpreters, "the true messengers of God". In truth, the Muslims' twisted interpretation of their role as God's messengers throughout is an insult to humanity and to God.

Today Abu Bakr Bashir is a leading interpreter of the Islamic tradition in Southeast Asia. This distinguished leader, who has many followers, made several statements recently that contradict his publicized position that Islam embraces and is founded on a tradition of love, peace and God's manifestation on earth. These contradictory and inflammatory statements include:

- Israel is the main enemy of Islam. We will fight for the Shari'ah even though Israel opposes us in this struggle.
- Islam is being attacked by the whole world and the greatest terrorists are the Jews and the Americans.
- If Islam is attacked, we will win or die fighting. To protect Islam one should win or die.

As the current Israeli-Palestinian conflict continues to rage, Islamic extremists around the globe have emerged to fan the flames of hatred. Bashir incites Muslims in Manila, while Sheikh Ahmad Yassin incites believers in Gaza. All these extremists see their enemies as the Jews and the Americans. Their narrow-minded focus allows these religious Islamic leaders to seek out justification for continuing this violent conflict by citing their holy Book.

However, there are moderate Islamic leaders who are stating their conviction that Palestine can become a nation state of Muslim believers that can exist in peace, side by side with Israel. In order for this event to occur, these moderate voices within Islam state that Israel will have to withdraw to its 1967 borders and relinquish its colonial condition over Palestinian Arabs now living in refugee camps. I feel Israel needs to take this step as well as to suggest that some areas of *The Triangle* such as Umm el-Fahem, Ara, and Arara (homes and properties included) become a part of a new, independent nation to be named Palestine, as part of a proposed land swap.

Left Wing Voices in Israel

If Israel returns to its 1967 borders, its citizens must be determined that an independent Jewish state will stand firm. The left wing voices in Israel currently advocating for the creation of a bi-national state are undermining the continuance of Israel as an independent Jewish nation. These left wing voices do not understand that Jews living in Muslim controlled states today cannot state freely what the Muslim leader MK (Member of the Knesset) Ahmed Tibi allows himself to state freely in Israel. Had he been living in Palestine, he could not freely say anything negative about Arafat, for example, for fear of being killed or for fear of losing his paycheck. In the independent Jewish nation of Israel all citizens are afforded rights, such as freedom of speech, which are protected in a democratic society. In Israel anyone who identifies himself as an Arab Palestinian can travel with an Israeli passport and simultaneously be as critical of Israel as he wishes, without fear of religious or political reprisals. For the sake of argument, let us ask Mr. Tibi to identify himself, although he is not required by his fellow countrymen, as an Israeli Arab or as an Arab with Israeli citizenship. He is allowed to identify himself as a Palestinian of the clan of Tibi and to claim that he is one of those Palestinians who actually came to this land not long ago but who falsely claims that he had never left it. The Israeli leftists do not care about the problem of national identity and they do not acknowledge the danger within Israel posed by those Muslims who benefit from the state's support but who continue to espouse vile hatred for the Jews. In the midst of this present turmoil, however, while attention is focused on the Arab Muslims who are awaiting the destruction of the state of Israel, the country of Israel and its leaders have lost sight of a loyal Arab faction in their midst. I feel it is a grievous mistake for Israel not to be paying attention to the Bedouins. Being familiar with the culture, state of mind, and the ability of the Arabs to be ambiguous, I have developed a grudge toward the leftists in Israel. Many of them have never visited the homes of their Arab neighbors, yet whenever these same Israeli leftists visit America, they continue to pour fuel on the fire of the Palestinian-Israeli conflict. Some of the Israeli leftists are presenting the thorny issue of the demand by a multitude of refugees to return to their old lands. They do this even though no one knows the correct number of these refugees. After all these years, how many refugees are they talking about? One million? Two million? And who is defined as a refugee? Can I also present my claim to be a refugee from Yemen on my father's side, or as a refugee from Iraq, or Kurdistan, on my mother's side? My maternal grandparents were kicked out of their land in Qara dahg, where they had owned orchards and land. They were forced to flee their home and they fled to Israel. Today that side of my family only numbers 300 to 400 people. Will talk about who's a refugee and what should be done for all refugees continue? Will any good be achieved by this exercise in futility?

Many of the Arabs living today in the refugee camps overseen by the United Nations have become the political pawns of other Arabic states. Today Kofi Annan's mediocre leadership has crippled the U.N. For example, Annan has declared his belief that the occupation of the West Bank by Israel is illegal, but he has not offered a viable solution to this problem. When Annan condemned the suicide bombings by Arab Palestinians in Israel, he also condemned the Israeli army's military response to these terrorist attacks. When the Norwegian diplomat, Terje Roid-Larsen, described the refugee camp in Jenin as "horrific beyond belief," Annan firmly agreed with Larsen. Annan did this in spite of a chorus of voices that called for Larsen's removal. Annan is unable to challenge or control the block of nations that have currently united and now control this hijacked, stagnant, international organization. As a result, the U.N. has presently lost most of its credibility as an objective peace broker around the world.

Historical Roots of Anti-Jewish Sentiment in Islam

In the holy Qur'an we can read this verse, "And we will know those among you who transgressed in the matter of the Sabbath, we say to them, be you apes, despised and rejected." (2:65/64) and this verse, "The Jews say God's hand is tied up and be they accursed..." (5: 62/63).

These verses from the holy Book of Islam, the Qur'an, are said to be the divine word of God. The Iman Muhammad Saiyd Tantawi, who currently holds the most important position in Sunni Islam, recently borrowed these verses from the Qur'an to describe the Jews as the enemies of Allah. Important interpreters on a committee organized by Dr. Jamal al-din Mahmud then presented a kind of childish interpretation by saying that if the Arab Muslims continue to describe Jews so rudely then the Jews will continue to describe the Arab Muslims as worms and vipers. These interpreters of the Qur'an stated that it is "important not to use these descriptions or to curse someone because we suffered and we are still suffering (from) such descriptions from the Jews." Dr. Mahmud then stated that even though crimes were committed by Jews against the prophets, and that this is recorded in the Qur'an, those words today, describing Jews as apes or pigs, are only metaphors. He then stated that these despicable traits recorded in the holy Book are not necessarily traits that are passed down from one generation to the next. These "moderate" voices of Dr. Mahmud and the committee were directly challenged by Inman Muhammad al Rawi, who said that the Qur'an states that God himself, who created the Jews, called them apes and pigs. Muhammad al Rawi questioned how believers of Islam could be asked by Dr. Mahmud and his committee to ignore God's verbatim description of the Jews as it's presented in the holy Qur'an. He did not see why it should be considered wrong to introduce an anti-Jewish sentiment today from the Qur'an, even if that anti-Jewish sentiment was rooted in ancient times.

Historical Attempts by Others to Define Jews

Throughout the long history of the Jewish people, various attempts have been made to define the unique character of this people. These first attempts were made in Alexandria in early Greek times. It was done in the midst of an anti-Jewish climate that Professor Zvi Yavetz has termed it as a "climate of Judeophobia" (2). Hecatacus claimed then that Jews were people who practiced a different religion, even as they lived in the midst of the ancient Egyptians. Jews were defined as foreigners and as a source of trouble. This Greek blamed the Jews for possessing an unsocial and hostile way of life. In the third century B.C.E. the concept of "misoxenia," which is the hatred of "the other," first appeared. Its attendant misanthropy was directed against the Jews. The ancient Greeks described the Jewish exodus from Egypt as an exodus of people who were impious and who believed God had no human form. The Jewish laws were deemed to be very different when compared to the laws of the Egyptians. Soon the anti-Semitic indoctrination that began in Greece became a low-grade cliché.

By Roman times, these clichés were still being used and were joined by more writings that examined the Jewish concept of God. The accusation grew in these Roman works that the Jews refused to share their God with other people. The Jewish belief that God didn't have a human form was also used in Roman times as proof in the validity of the "misoxenia" of the Jews. These Roman works also stated that since the Jews claimed that their God was invisible, then that was proof to the Romans that the Jewish God didn't exist. Ancient Greeks and Romans acknowledged that Jerusalem was the center of the Jewish religion. The Greek and Roman writers often pointed out that non-Jews were forbidden to enter Jerusalem. Hostility that was centered on religious and on socio-political issues grew between the Greeks and the Romans in their dealings with the Jews of their day. In the realm of religion, the Roman idea that Jews worshipped an unseen God was challenged by the story Antioch Epiphanes told after he had invaded Jerusalem. Upon his coming to the inner sanctum of the Jewish Temple in Jerusalem, he discovered a marble statue of a bearded man holding a book and seated on an ass. In the socio-political realm, the Greeks and Romans defined Jews as misanthropes who followed xenophobic laws and preached hostility toward those the Jews considered as foreigners. In the second century Tacitus and Cicero accused the Jews of being superstitious. Then Juvenal accused the Jews of refusing to become integrated within Roman society and he claimed that the Jews had adopted hostile ways of life toward Rome. In fact, these Jews had rejected the culture, the way of life, and religion of the Romans.

In the Christian era, many of the Greek and Roman negative clichés about the Jews had survived and were still in use. In the fourth gospel of John we are introduced to the notion that the Jew is the devil. Heinrich von Treitshke, a 19th century historian, wrote that the Jews were defined as an element of unrest in civilization. Toynbee, a 20th century English historian, claimed that the Jews are the fossilized relics of the ancient Syriac civilization. Non-Jewish intellectuals created very few positive descriptions and definitions of Jews. Alfred Whitehead was an exception. He wrote that Jews are very much alive in the twentieth century and that they are a most able people. However, after surveying western historical texts, it becomes apparent that many western historians had written that Jews were considered a pariah, as a group that lived on the edge of the sword, and a minority that eventually grew dependent on the protection of a sovereign. While a few positive descriptions of Jews can be found dating from the early times and down through the last two millennia of the Christian era, no positive descriptions of Jews have been found, to my knowledge, in any Islamic writings of the past or present. Moreover, the Islamic writers and commentators adopted and adapted all the Greek and Roman and Christian negative and narrow clichés about Jews and placed them in their works in their attempt to prove their cultural and religious superiority.

Anti-Jewish Sentiment: Past and Present

As Arab Muslims are declaring falsely that Israel today as a racial state, these same Muslims are simultaneously claiming that no one should blame them for being anti-Semitic, because they define themselves, as well as the Jews, as being Semitic people. Such a statement not only proves the ignorance of these present day Muslims, but it also demonstrates their fear of the stigma of hatred that exists toward the Jews. This hypocrisy also exists outside the Arab Muslim world. Other nations currently proclaim anti-Israel and anti-Zionist slogans. In the 19th century the newly coined term, "anti-Semitism," was only applied to the Jews. It never targeted the other Semite people, regardless of what kinship Muslim-Arabs are falsely claiming today. Before the 19th century, the prejudicial term against the Jews that was used in Europe was the more unsophisticated but straightforward term, "anti-Jewish." Throughout European history leaders in many European countries struggled to divert the attention of the common people from their miseries and in order to deliberately create a convenient scapegoat for the common people's dire socio-economic conditions. The Jews in Europe were killed for their falsely alleged complicity in the death of Jesus Christ. These persecuted Jews were easy targets for ethnic and religious hate mongers because they were a minority and they were considered a pariah and an unwanted people who were perceived as worshipping the mysterious God of old Israel.

In our time, it is not considered politically correct to make statements against Jews, so the shift has been made to make statements against Israel instead. Not one French, Belgian, or Swedish intellectual will dare to admit the truth that their schools' curricula today do not include the facts on the atrocities that the Jews suffered in the Holocaust of World War II in Europe. At the same time, whenever a Palestinian has been killed in the West Bank, no matter what the circumstances, these same intellectuals and leaders in France Belgium, and Sweden have quickly called upon their national piety and have falsely accused Israel of committing a racially biased atrocity. It appears that France has completely forgotten the real atrocities it committed as a colonial power in Southeast Asia and Africa, where it felt it was also justified when it looted the treasured artifacts of those regions. Those pilfered treasures still reside in its mighty state supported museums. The Belgians have apparently forgotten that their nation accumulated a vast storehouse of gold, silver, and diamonds from its stint as a colonial power in the Congo. Somehow these same nations now feel they have the moral right and responsibility to be the social conscience in world affairs and they continue to falsely target Israel as our world's greatest enemy of peace. These European voices of bigotry that are currently targeting and persecuting Israel are being strengthened by the many bigoted voices emerging from the Muslim world.

Origins of Ethnic and Religious Hatred

At one point in this research project, Ms. Bakovic wondered about the origin of the present ethnic and religious hatred that was evident in her collected interviews. Even after reading the songs that young Muslim children sang for her and after digesting the words uttered by the young, school-aged boys and girls that she had interviewed for this book, it is evident in this book that despite being troubled by the current atmosphere of hatred which Ms. Bakovic had witnessed as a researcher, she is still valiantly searching for the golden paths that could lead new generations of Arab-Muslims and Jews toward peace and harmony. As her quest for the ideal was placed in such vivid contrast with the unrelenting rhetoric of hatred that is presently pouring out of many Islamic centers of power, I began this introduction with a profound sense of discomfort and worry. I feel that my and Ms. Bakovic's hopes for peace in the Middle East may not be realized in the very near future. The roots of my fear are connected to my knowledge that we can't ignore the influence that the Qur'an has had, and continues to have, on Muslim children in their religious studies. We cannot ignore the fact that in the Qur'an Jews are called the enemies of Islam and that the prophet accused the Jews of having forged the Book of Moses. In

Surat al Baqara (Sura 2), Jews are accused of being the slayers of the prophet (2:61/58), and of being idol worshipers (5:60/65), and are even accused of being greedy and cowardice. These and other strong, anti-Jewish strong statements found in the Qur'an accentuate and promote the continued hatred of the believers of Islam toward the Jews. It's interesting to note that the Qur'an that emerged from the seventh century contained an anti-Jewish phrase that was adopted by the Christians in their Prayer of Good Friday. That term, "perfidious Jews," was later removed from the Prayer of Good Friday by Pope John the XXIII in 1963. This happened because these couple of powerful words were eventually recognized and rejected by the Catholic Church as an anti-Jewish statement that had no place in a Catholic prayer. In their sermons and in their teachings today, Muslim clerics, however, continue to use the old ethnic stereotypes against Jews that originated in ancient Greece and Rome. And the vivid smears against Jews that are recorded in the Qur'an continue to exist in today's curricula being taught in many Muslim schools. The Muslim image of the bearded Jew can be traced to the discovery of the marble statue found in the Temple in Jerusalem by Antioch Epiphanes. And yet *nowhere* in Islamic history or commentary is the slaughter in Medina of the Jewish tribe called the Qurayza ever mentioned. Instead, the Muslims invented the concept of the "dajjal," or "the one who opposed the prophecy of Mohammad and who attempted to poison him," and they assigned that role to the Jews.

The combined teachings against Jews found in the Qur'an and in the *"hadith,"* or "the oral Islamic tradition" and in the canonized commentary of the Islamic clerics, have created a monolithic barrier to the establishment of peace and harmony between Muslims and Jews. Young Muslim children continue today to learn the words of hatred toward the Jews and they are being taught that these words of hatred come directly from their God. If God did, in fact, transmit these recorded words of hatred toward the Jews recorded in the Qur'an, then God needs to explain why he committed this terrible act.

An Articulated Dream is the First Step

The aim of this introduction to this important work is not to smear Islam. On the contrary, my introduction is an attempt to ask Muslims to completely reject their mistaken notion that the Jews want to conquer the worlds of others, and to completely reject all ethnic slurs and stereotypes of Jews from past times. My desire is that the common man in any Muslim state will come to realize that he has been misinformed by corrupt regimes of political and religious leaders who have unfairly and unjustly targeted the Jews throughout the world for hundreds of years in an effort to distract the common Muslim citizens from confronting their miserable socioeconomic conditions. I want Muslims to learn that throughout their long history they have been manipulated by different political regimes that had created strong alliances with the Islamic clerics down through the ages. It will be liberating when the common Muslim understands that the blind hatred he has been taught for the Jews is, in fact, an instrument used by Muslim leaders, religious and political alike, to keep the commoners in a deep but troubled slumber, since that is the easiest way their leaders have to control the Muslim commoners.

Arabs living in Europe and North America today are providing healthy links between Muslims living in the west with those living in the Muslim world. And those healthy links are important since alarming statements from the leader of the UK Majahudin have recently emerged, "The Jews are essentially different from other people in the world. I am stating this on the BBC and I am not ashamed. We Muslims are aspiring to dominate the world. We want everyone to be Muslim and to follow Muslim law." This Muslim leader has expressed what I term the "Granada Complex". In January of 1492 when Granada, then the Muslim cultural, religious, and political center of power on the Iberian Peninsula, was captured by the Catholic monarch of Spain, the surviving Muslims were forced to leave their beloved city. The new western rulers of Granada forbade the use of the Arabic language in this newly acquired Spanish city. Muslims then and now lament this loss of Granada so long ago. At the start of the 21st century, their lost Granada has now emerged as the symbol of the Muslim aspiration to eventually dominate the western world. This aspiration's roots are centuries old and run very deep in the Muslim culture. Today the Muslim quest to realize this long held aspiration is being funded by their collective capital and by the mass migration of Muslims to the west. Granada is now a powerful metaphor for the "Muslim comeback" and is seen as a symbolic jumping board that Muslims can use to realize their ancient dream of dominating the west.

Today's Muslim leaders are telling believers that the Muslim era of world rule is well on its way to becoming a reality. Although yesterday's history can often become tomorrow's mystery, I can imagine that a very real possibility exists that by the middle of the twenty-first century the women who will be seen walking along Fifth Avenue in New York City will be veiled and that police with whips will be present on Fifth Avenue and around the world, to enforce the Islamic rule that all female body parts must be covered in public. This is, I realize, a very gloomy prediction. But it is a prediction that I feel is based on ancient evidence, as well as on the alarming evidence currently emerging of a renewed Muslim aspiration for world domination, and of the Muslims' continued use of ethnic hatred of Jews, and of the friends of Jews, to attain its domination of the whole world, east and west, north and south.

Notes:

(1) Khutba is a sermon given during Friday midday prayers, the most significant of the weekly Islamic prayers. Khutba is also given during the holidays of Idu l-Kabir and Idu l-Fitr; such a sermon may also be given during times of hardship. Traditionally, khutba are short; however today's khutbas have become long lectures which may range from Islamic subjects to social and political commentary. In some cases, they have become platforms for incitement against what is perceived as the encroachment of Western ideals on Islam.

(2) All citations are taken from http://www.memri.org.il/. sent to me from Israel by mail unless otherwise noted.

(3) Yavetz, Zvi. "Judeophobia In Classical Antiquity: A Different Approach", JJS. 44 (1993), 1-22.

Preface

Since I wrote the book, certain events have taken place in Israel and in the Palestinian Authority:

- Sheikh Ahmed Yasin and his successor Rantisi, both leaders of the Hamas, were assassinated by the Israeli Army in March 2004.
- Yasser Arafat died on November 11, 2004 at the age of 75.
- The Palestinian Authority held its first democratic elections on January 2, 2005.
- Mahmoud Abbas, also known as Abu Mazen, won the elections with approximately 62% of the votes.
- On February 20, 2005, the Israeli Cabinet gave a final approval to the government's final withdrawal from Gaza, making it illegal for Israelis to be in Gaza and northern West Bank after July 20th. People on both sides are demanding a more mature approach from their politicians who are expected to find new ways to bridge between Israelis and Palestinian and offer new hope for people on both sides.

Smadar Bakovic, Neve Ilan, Israel, April 18th, 2005

Conventions

- Unless otherwise noted, all translations are by the author.
- In the interview sections, the author's comments appear in brackets.
- During the course of the interviews, the same question is often asked of different interviewees. The change in speakers is marked by the lines shown below:

Acknowledgements

In the course of writing this book, there were many times when I felt like giving up. This feeling might be quite natural and might be experienced by all writers. My unique privilege was, however, that I was always surrounded by people who loved me and who pushed me to continue this important and much needed work. This support caused me to believe that giving up was never really an option!

First and foremost I should like to thank my family: Davor, Grania, Naor and Abigeil Bakovic for all of their love, patience and encouragement. I would especially like to thank my mother, Grania, for helping to edit the book.

I would like to thank all the people who let me into their lives at a time where suspicion and mistrust between Jews and Arabs were so widespread in Israel. Although I do not share many of their political and religious views, I respect these views and beliefs and give them a voice in this book. I cannot mention all the people whom I met or to whom I spoke, but would like to personally thank Susu, Buthina, Suaad, Souhad, Samar, Dalal, Samuel, Ibrahim, Muna, Muhammad, Mahnoud, Manar, Adila, Salman, Zohariyye, and so many others who let me into their lives. I respect their request not to be fully identified.

I would also like to thank Mishael and Gila Caspi who were always there to listen to me and to comfort my heart and soul. I would especially like to thank Mishael for coming up with the idea of writing this book and guiding me through the long, complicated, challenging, tiring, but ultimately rewarding process. He is to me a mentor, professor, confidant and friend.

Three people immensely helped shape who I am and the way I view life. Alake Pilgrim from Trinidad and Tobago, Ritika Juneja from India and Stella

Emefa Aniagyei from Ghana were my loyal and trustworthy friends throughout my Bates College experience and after it. They challenged me, made me rethink some of my beliefs, assumptions and prejudices and were always there for me. Although we all held different religious and political beliefs, our friendship and love for each other kept us bonded. I would especially like to thank Alake who helped edit my book, as well as causing me to rethink and at times rewrite certain parts of it. I would also like to thank Erol Kohli, who became my close friend. Last but not least, I would like to thank Shamarie Horn, a true friend who always believed in me and helped edit this book, Jana Buchholz, who helped me with the graphic design aspects of the book and Cara Bereck Levy who prepared the Camera-Ready copy and assisted in editing the book.

I would like to thank Iris Peer and Tsipa Kimmel, old friends back In Israel, who not only supported me in each and every step, but who were compelled to listen to me talk for hours about my experiences in numerous Arab villages and to help me find answers to the most complicated and controversial questions I was writing about.

All this work could not have been done without the help of Bates College and certain unique people whom I met there. I would like first to thank the Phillip Fellowship Committee for deciding to allocate money for my project. I would also like to thank Phyllis Graber Jensen who has done so much in order to make this project possible.

I am who I am, not only because I have worked hard to reach this point, but also because all these people surrounded me with so much love and trust. For that, and much more, I thank them all.

Introduction

Religion

One evening, my host sister took me to the house of one of the members of her family, a man in his thirties who had recently married a woman much younger than himself. He and his wife Salam lived in one of the most beautiful houses I had ever seen—Said had definitely invested his life savings in building it. We all sat outside on the veranda which overlooked the entire village and were enjoying the warm summer night.

A conversation about Judaism, Christianity and Islam began when Said started asking me questions about my religion, Judaism. Initially, I was very excited about the topic of the conversation. Knowing that Islam accepted all of the three monotheistic traditions and their prophets, I was looking forward to an informative and engaging dialogue. I was disappointed. What I discovered was quite to the contrary and recurred many times while I was talking to Muslim Israeli Arabs or to other Muslim people. After only a few minutes it was evident to me that Said, who had proudly exclaimed only a few minutes earlier that his religion accepted my prophets, had never even read the Bible. He had no idea what the Bible really was, what significance it had for Jews or what its message was. All that he and the others had heard about the Bible was that the Jews had distorted the text and changed it to suit their own purposes. And all they knew about the Jewish prophets was that the Jews had betrayed and manipulated them. They were not willing to accept new ideas or at the very least *attempt* to understand my explanation of the significance of the Bible to Jews all over the world. The level of ignorance they exhibited when speaking about Jews and Jewish history (Muslim history is rewritten[1]), coupled with their blind and unquestioning following of the Qur'an, was quite a revelation to me.

I discovered that although Islam theoretically accepts both the Jewish and Christian religions, it in actuality discourages Muslims from reading and studying the Old and New Testaments. It also encourages them to oppose (sometimes violently) every text and/or prophecy which does not view Muhammad as a prophet. I strongly feel that this prohibition to investigate texts which precede the Qur'an, to debate and find different answers to questions, to question the Qur'an and its historical, ideological and literary accuracy is one of the most worrisome aspect of "modern" Islamic culture and tradition. The effect of these prohibitions can be seen all over the world, whether in New York City, Tel Aviv or Riad.

There is no doubt that when I returned to Israel in the summer of 2001 in order to undertake a Phillips Fellowship project, I was not at all prepared for the intensity I was about to encounter. My project was to evaluate the attitudes of the Israeli Arab population[2], a part of Israeli society which is commonly ignored by both national and international bodies, especially in light of the Israeli-Palestinian conflict. I wanted to see how Israeli Arabs felt after Bshara, an Israeli Arab member of the Israeli *Knesset*[3], hinted in a speech in Damascus in the summer of 2000 that the Arab world should oppose Israel. I was also interested to see their reaction after thirteen Israeli Arabs were killed by Israeli police forces in October 2000, when they took to the streets and rioted in response to Ariel Sharon's visit to Al-Haram Al-Sharif [the Temple Mount] in Jerusalem[4]. I had registered for an Arabic course in *Ulpan Akiva*[5] in Netanya and hoped that by the time the course was over, I would have made the necessary contacts for the continuation of my project. From my comfort zone in Lewiston, Maine, where I was attending Bates College at the time, the situation in Israel looked bad, senseless and very far away. When I arrived in Israel, however, I quickly discovered that things were actually much worse than I believed them to be. I noticed that in the midst of all the confusion and chaos, one thing was very clear: Arabs and Jews not only mistrusted one another, but were unequivocally afraid of each other.

It was on one of my trips from Tel Aviv to Jerusalem that I understood, maybe for the first time, the extent to which the mistrust between Arabs and Jews had reached. As I was sitting in an *Egged* bus[6], I noticed two Arab men sitting across the aisle from me. Since I had only recently begun to study the Arabic language, I was fascinated by its lyrical sound. Although I could not understand most of what these two men were saying, I was listening attentively to their conversation, trying to identify a word here and there. At one point a man, clearly Jewish, who was sitting behind the two Arab men, got up, knelt down, looked under their seat and exclaimed, "There's something under your seat." The Arab men looked at one another and one of them knelt down to look. He could not see anything. The Jewish man, once again, this time a bit louder said, "Can't you see that box under your seat?" By this time, most of the other people in the bus were getting interested in the unusual dialogue. Several people, very conspicuously, tried to look under the man's seat. Some people seemed increasingly worried and looked suspiciously at the two Arab men. Weekly suicide bombings had caused people to react to every small incident with suspicion, fright and even panic. The Arab men, somewhat bewildered, suddenly understood what was going on. There was no box under their seat. The Jewish man was "joking" around, by insinuating that an Arab would automatically have a box (a suspicious object which could possibly be a bomb) under his seat. The Arab man then looked the Jewish man in the eye and said, "You are afraid of me, aren't you?" The Jewish man returned the look and said, "Yes, I am, very much."

When I spoke to Jewish people it was obvious that they were afraid of Arabs. When I told one of my orthodox Jewish friends that I was about to meet with Arabs she looked at me with disbelief and said, "When I hear the word 'Arab' I start shaking. All I can think about is that this Arab might want to kill me." The daily terror inflicted by numerous fanatic young Muslim Palestinians echoed in the minds and hearts of many Israelis (Jews and Arabs alike) who genuinely feared for their lives. Walking down a hectic street in Jerusalem, or taking a ten or fifteen minute ride in a local bus was not an activity that was taken lightly by anyone. Many people genuinely felt that boarding a bus or shopping in downtown Jerusalem or Tel Aviv was not only frightening, but life threatening. Everyone remembered the stories in the media of people who happened to be in a bus when it exploded, but somehow survived. Some survivors said that none other than God was protecting them and others simply thought they were extremely lucky. Everyone who was a part of Israeli society, however, remembered the victims' voices, faces and crumpled bodies; bodies that would never again be the same. These images transformed the daily lives of many people living in Israel. As a passenger in a bus, I would stare at people boarding it, looking for "suspicious" people who might be terrorists (but how would a terrorist look like?) and as a passenger boarding the bus, I would feel dozens of eyes staring at me. This was life in Israel. Cafes, bars, restaurants, malls, hospitals, banks and all other public buildings were all heavily guarded. Everyone had to submit to a bodily search, not allowing them to forget, even for a second, that they were living in the midst of a violent conflict. It took time for me to get used to the situation. It was not surprising that the video rental stores were some of the most profitable businesses in Israel at that time—people did not want to leave their homes unless they absolutely had to and preferred staying at home watching television or spending time with their families. By the summer of 2004 most people had already gotten used to the bleak situation and allowed themselves to wander through Jerusalem and Tel Aviv more freely. Still, it was not like in other places—people could not completely detach themselves and forget that in any given moment their lives might change forever.

This reality was a harsh one and people of all ages and backgrounds wondered from time to time whether life in Israel was worth all the hassle. One time, as I was making my way from the Central Bus Station in Tel Aviv to the center of the city, a woman who observed the two cameras I was carrying around with me asked me in a loud voice, "What are you doing with these fancy cameras?" I told her that I was studying at Bates College in the United States and that I had come home for a short visit in order to undertake a project about the Israeli Arab population. She looked at me with a very serious expression and said, "Good for you. Anyone who has where to go should go and never come back. My son and his wife left for England a few months ago and believe me, that if I could leave I would. No one should live in this country the way things are going on now. Don't

INTRODUCTION   xxix

come back here if you can help it." Another person, a woman in her early twenties, responded somewhat differently to my desire to write about Middle Eastern socio-political issues. When I told her what I was doing in Israel that summer she smiled at me and said, "That is great! The media is so unjust to Israel, especially the European media. They hate Jews there. We need more Israelis who are able to get to positions where they can defend Israel and honestly and justly portray Israeli politics to the world!" Two years later, when I was attending meetings in the United Nations in New York City as part of my job I understood more fully what she was saying. While working in New York I discovered a quite hostile United Nations where Israel could not even pass a resolution because of the Arab and Muslim countries' vote and because of an indifferent Europe which always made sure to abstain.

In 2003 Israel tried to pass a resolution in the United Nations for the protection of Israeli children from terrorism. A similar resolution protecting Palestinian children from Israeli "terror" had already been passed. Although the United Nations "passed" the resolution, the Arab and Muslim nations had forced so many amendments to it that Dan Gillerman, Israel's ambassador to the United Nations, withdrew the resolution and said that the United Nations valued the lives of Palestinian children over the lives of Israeli children. He also publicly questioned the credibility of the United Nations when he said that as long as such behavior continues, people should not wonder why the United Nation's credibility is questioned by so many people.[7]

When people heard that I was about to visit Arab villages in *The Triangle*[8] they thought I was either mad or extremely naïve, or maybe both. One religious woman even told me, "Smadar, you are insane. May God help you, because no one else can." Some of my closest friends, who were genuinely concerned about my safety told me, "Smadar, you don't live here and you don't really know what's going on between Arabs and Jews. Please don't put yourself in unnecessary danger." They were right in many ways—I had spent many years in the United States traveling around, attending college, going to classes, meeting friends and engaging in various extracurricular activities. I had seen the suicide bombings and the fright in people's eyes solely through a television screen. There is no doubt that my life was very different from the life of a "full time" Israeli who had to face fear each and every moment. Nonetheless, being a native Israeli who had grown up in Israel and who had gone back for visits at least once every year, I could pick up very quickly on some of the social, political and psychological changes both Jews and Arabs were experiencing. One thing that immediately struck me was that Jews had mostly stopped visiting Arab villages by that time, even Abu Ghosh[9] which is considered to be one of friendliest villages towards the State of Israel.

When I made my way to the village of Arara,[10] where I had arranged to meet a group of women who had agreed to be interviewed, the local Jewish taxi drivers in Hadera[11] were incredulous when they found out where I was heading. One of them, a dark and chubby man named Shaul, called out to his colleague who was busy doing something in the office, "Hey can you believe it? This young girl here wants to go to Arara!" It had been months since any Jew had asked them for a ride to an Arab village, let alone to Arara, situated in a volatile part of *The Triangle*. They both stared at me and tried to talk me out of it for a few minutes, but once it became clear to them that I was a stubborn young woman who was not about to change her plans, they refused to take me there. Five minutes later, standing in the middle of a chaotic street, I asked one of the shop owners in the Hadera market place where I could find an Arab taxi service going to Arara. He was very friendly, directed me to the Arara taxi station, but asked me, "You know it's an Arab village, right?" There was no doubt that he did not think that going to Arara was a very good idea and he did not conceal his feelings of suspicion. The taxi ride went well, although not knowing how people from Arara would feel about a Jewish Israeli person coming to their village, I decided to speak in English and pretend that I was a tourist. A woman in her fifties, wearing a *hijjab*[12] and a long white and green dress, tried to make conversation with me but gave up after a few minutes because her English was not very good. When we entered Arara, she pointed towards a building, said "There, there" in English and assured me it was the *Naamat*[13] Center for Women. My adventure had begun.

In Arara, I never felt afraid or unsafe. I actually felt much safer there than walking down the busy streets of Jerusalem or Tel Aviv and I made this fact clear to my Arab hosts. In spite of this, one evening as I was sitting outside with my hosts drinking tea and eating *maklube*,[14] Muna, a 12 year old girl, grabbed my hand, took me to her room and asked me, "Smadar, please answer me truthfully. Are you afraid when you come to visit us?" I looked at her, took her hand and said, "No, I am not afraid to come and visit you here. I actually feel much more afraid when walking down a busy street in Jerusalem or Tel Aviv." I was convinced that a Jewish person would not come and plant a bomb or explode themselves in the middle of an Arab village. Arab towns and villages (as well as taxi services run by Arab people) were probably some of the safest places in Israel at that time. When she heard this she said to me, "I am glad to hear that. We love having guests here. We don't want war and I wish that Israel felt this way too. It's because of what they are doing to the Palestinians, our brothers and sisters, that we don't like them." The close association many Israeli Arabs had to the Palestinian people became more and more evident to me as time went by. Muna, just like many other Israeli Arabs I would later speak to, referred to Israeli Arabs and Palestinians as "us" and to all other Israelis as "them."

There were two times, however, when I felt somewhat uncomfortable within *The Triangle*. In spite of the fact that I was trying to stay neutral throughout the duration of the project, I was always very aware of who I was and where I had come from. This fact could get me into trouble if I did not pay sufficient attention to social and political realities surrounding me. The first time I felt uncomfortable was during one of my trips from Hadera to Arara when I encountered a woman who showed great verbal animosity towards me. She was making her way to Umm el-Fahem[15] and was not happy about the fact that the taxi driver agreed to take me right into Arara and not just drop me off on the highway. When she found this out, she looked at me with rage and started cursing me in Arabic. Although I could not understand all that she was saying, I could understand the main words and phrases she was using. "The damn Jews," she said, "not only did they take our lands from us, but they also have to constantly harass us. What's her problem? Can't the Jews walk? Do they always have to be taken to the exact spot to which they wish to go? Why should we drive into Arara because of her? And who is she going to see there anyway?" The other passengers in the taxi looked at her somewhat bewildered and then with increasing signs of embarrassment. Occasionally they looked at me, probably in order to see my reaction, but no one said a word. Then, as she was going on and on they quietly whispered to her, probably asking her to stop. I just sat there in a daze, my cheeks becoming redder by the minute, but I knew that there was nothing I could do about it. Although my short and hot temper told me to start shouting back at the lady, I did not even move. After all, I was a guest, an outsider and I was visiting Arab village during a fragile and tragic time. When I left the taxi, I turned around to the other passengers, wished them a good day (in Arabic) and left with my tail between my legs.

The second time I felt uncomfortable was when I was making my way back to Tel Aviv from Arara one summer evening. One of my women friends had dropped me off at the bus stop on the highway after I had attended a party in the *Na'amat* Center for Women. I stood there for a long time, but no bus would stop for me. I started wondering why the buses were not stopping. Were they not supposed to stop there? Or had the drivers decided, on their own judgment, not to stop? Night was falling and it began to get dark. Another half an hour passed and still no bus would stop and no taxi passed by. I started getting somewhat nervous and agitated. After all, it was about 8:15 p.m. and I was standing between three major Arab villages. I knew that the area was very close to Jenin[16] and that some of the residents living in *The Triangle* supported the daily suicide bombings and terrorist attacks against Israeli citizens. Although I tried to persuade myself that I shouldn't be afraid, I was. With shaking fingers I called my father on my cellular phone and he tried to calm me down by assuring me that I had nothing to be afraid of. Just as I was closing the phone, I saw a taxi approaching the bus stop and before I was able to raise my hand and stop it, it came to a halt. A worried looking man rolled down the window and said to me in a concerned voice and in fragmented English, "Tourist? American? English? Lost?" I assured him in Hebrew that I was a native Israeli and that I was heading for Tel Aviv. He stared at me half with disbelief and half in shock and replied in Hebrew, "What the hell are you doing here? Are you crazy?" All that came out of my mouth was, "I was visiting friends." "Friends, here?" he said with amazement, "You must be crazy." He then motioned me towards the back door of the car and said, "Get into the taxi, I'm on my way to Tel Aviv anyway and will take you all the way there for half price or even for free if you don't have any money."

My experiences in Arara and in the other Arab villages I visited were, on the whole, wonderful and enlightening. Although Israeli Arab society was still a mystery to me (and I still don't know everything that there is to know) I was learning so much about it and through it about myself. There is one experience I had in Arara that I will never forget. I was attending a *henna* party[17] given for my hosts' cousin who was about to be married. Several women, including my host sister, exclaimed at the luck of the bride-to-be. "You know," they said, "in our culture, it's rare for a woman in her thirties to get married. The men usually go for the younger women and those who are older usually stay unmarried. She's lucky to have been chosen by him. And you should see the house he built for her!" I looked around me—tens of women dressed up in their best clothes, food, drink, loud Arab music and laughter—what a fabulous occasion. The women started to dance and I was almost immediately dragged into the circle of dancers. I love the traditional Arab *Dabka* music and although I was deeply embarrassed at my poor dancing, the women were encouraging me to go on. Holding hands, the older women formed an outer circle of dancers and the younger women were dancing within. It was a rare moment of extreme happiness and my feet carried me around and around without any effort whatsoever.

At one point, after more than an hour had passed, hardly able to keep up with the other women (of whom many were much older than myself), I sat on a nearby chair, hoping to become a passive spectator. My host sister, Susu, came up to me and said she wanted to introduce me to someone special. She led me to a woman holding a little baby. Next to her sat her two teenage daughters, one of whom was extraordinarily beautiful and even angelic-looking. "This is Dalal," said my host sister, pointing to the mother. "She is a Palestinian from Jenin. She crossed the border to come and celebrate with us tonight." My heart jumped and missed a beat. I had never met a Palestinian woman from Jenin before and I was amazed and even overwhelmed. All I knew about Jenin and the people living there was from television and that was never anything positive. I immediately shook her hand and sat next to her. She told me a bit about herself. She was an English teacher and loved the profession. She taught in one of the high schools located not far from Jenin. She then told me a bit about her family, especially about her newest child, the baby girl she was holding. "In the beginning, I wanted to call her Jenin because she was born during the massacre there," she said. "But then, I realized that if I called her Jenin, she would always have this scar on her and everyone who said her name would remember something terrible. I want peace, and I don't want to think about bad things all my life. So I decided to call her Salha." Salha, on her part, just lay in Dalal's arms and stared into the air, her eyes shutting from time to time. She was so young and had no idea into what reality she was born or what kind of future was awaiting her.

I sat with Dalal for several hours and she seemed eager to tell me about her life. She came from a village near Jenin and before the Second *Intifada* started in October 2000 she used to travel into the city nearly every day. She told me about the poverty in Jenin and about how people there could not afford nice weddings such as Arabs living in Israel can. "People in Jenin don't have money for weddings," she told me, "and they can't afford building a house to live in, so people who get married now live in small rented apartments because they have no other choice. This is contrary to our tradition, where a man is expected to build a house before he can propose marriage to a woman." Talking about Salha again, she told me, "She was born when there was a curfew because the Israeli Army was in Jenin and I couldn't be taken to hospital. My husband was not present because he was not allowed to travel back home from his work place. I gave birth to my daughter at home with the assistance of some friends." We spent the entire evening talking, dancing with the other women and talking again. Rarely have I ever felt such an immediate connection with another person as I did with Dalal.

The next day, the entire family and their guests got together again. This time a big circle of chairs was set up in the backyard and both men and women were present. When my host sister indicated that it was time for us to leave and go back home, Dalal handed her baby-girl to her eldest daughter and approached me. We held hands for a few seconds and looked at each other. I could sense that many pairs of eyes were looking at us and I felt somewhat awkward and uncomfortable. We didn't say a word except "Take care," and "Salam," but I know till this day (and I can still see Dalal's eyes) that what we were really saying to one another was, "Let this horrible conflict end."

The feeling many Jews had towards Arabs came mainly, in my opinion, from the hardships of daily life many Jewish people in Israel were experiencing at the time, hardships due to the frequent suicide bombings. For many Jews it was not necessarily the feeling of hatred of the Arab as an Arab that influenced and dominated their intellect, rationale or emotion, but rather the mistrust and fear that the word Arab implied: maybe a terrorist, or someone who would harm a Jew. The political situation in general and the numerous suicide bombings in particular only contributed to the feelings many Jews had towards Arabs. Even people who had previously never disliked Arabs showed signs of suspicion and fear towards them, not because they necessarily hated Arabs, but because they were afraid. I think that it would be fair to say that real hatred towards Arabs among the majority of Israelis can mostly be found on the personal level among individuals, who were raised to hate in their homes. A small group of about five Jewish settlers, whose activities are all motivated by their hatred of the Arab, sent their children to a short summer camp where they were taught to resist Israeli soldiers and the evacuation of Jewish settlements in Gaza. Other extremists in the West Bank occasionally came out with anti-Arab exclamations. Hate towards the Arabs as a group, however, is not something which is taught or encouraged in the Israeli schools system or in other formal institutions—it is not an Israeli policy. The Israeli school system is mostly if not entirely based on Western, pluralistic and democratic values.

When I spoke to Arab people, Christians and Muslims alike, it was obvious that they, too, were afraid. Prior to undertaking this project I never thought that Arabs living in Israel would have a reason to be afraid of the terrible conflict. "What could possibly happen to them?" I thought to myself. It became more evident to me, however, as time went by, that Israeli Arabs were also getting killed in suicide bombings and that some suicide bombings (even if very rarely) happened in primarily Arab-populated places. Palestinian suicide bombers did not care who they were killing—they viewed Jews as their enemy and Israeli Arabs as collaborators with the Jewish state. No one was safe and each and every person was viewed by the terrorist organizations as a legitimate target. This is what made everything so much more frightening and monstrous—that whatever anyone, Jew or Arab, might do to protect themselves was in vain. Many of my Arab interviewees, especially covered women,[18] told me that after a suicide bombing they were afraid to go to Jewish towns because of the chance of being beaten by a Jewish mob. "They [Jews] can see that we are Arabs," they said, "so we're afraid to be near them." Even a year and a half after my encounter with the women of Arara (many of whom I befriended), some of them were still reluctant to come and visit me in my Jewish home village, Neve Ilan, located in the Judean Hills. "I know that you accept me and who I am, Smadar," Rula, a 40 year-old unmarried artist, once told me, "but how can I know if your neighbors will?"

Throughout the summer I spoke to tens of Jews and Arabs, each in their own communities who rarely made an effort to visit the other side. The separation between Jews and Arabs was more evident than ever and only a few crossed from one side to another for an occasional friendly visit, or a passionate but constructive political discussion. There was a breakdown of trust between Jews and Arabs and persons on each side talked almost exclusively about themselves and about the fear they had of the other. They both assumed what those on the other side thought of them, but were reluctant to engage in a dialogue, not only because they were afraid, but also because they had become disinterested to some extent in everything related to the other side. Rarely did they stop and consider how people on the other side felt or what they were going through. Rarely did one side listen to and then legitimize the fear and concern expressed by people from the other side. Each side was stuck in their own self-victimization, not because they were necessarily selfish, but rather because they were suffering and were sick and tired of the situation. All of them, without exception, were subjects of fear, trying to survive another day in the midst of a bloody conflict.

Before arriving in Israel to begin my project, I did not know exactly where I find the subjects for my interviews. I assumed that I would make some connections while attending the Arabic language course in *Ulpan Akiva*. I was right in my assumption because during the course I met Jews who had Arab friends or acquaintances or who worked with Arabs. Through these people I was able to go to Arab towns and villages (and even to *Masof Carney*[19]), meet the local population and speak to them. All my interviewees, with the exception of one, were people I had never met prior to the summer of 2001. All of them, with the exception of one who knew a bit of English, communicated with me in Hebrew and Arabic. Nearly all of them expressed to me their desire to learn English and did not hide their disappointment at not being able to communicate in this language. Knowing that I was an English major [at Bates College[20]], they all asked me to start a beginners' English class in their villages. Even some mothers said that they would attend if I opened a class and if they could bring their babies with them. Most of my interviewees were very welcoming and friendly when I asked to interview them, although one woman asked me, with no sign of embarrassment, "Are you from the *Mossad*?"[21] Although I was not at all offended by this blunt question, I understood at that moment that I would most probably never be fully accepted into this society and that some people might always be suspicious as to my motives and intentions. After all, not many Jewish Israeli women (or as a matter of fact not many Jews whatsoever) made it a point to go into Israeli Arab villages all alone and interview people at that time. I encountered the same suspicion from other Arab and Muslim people I met in Europe, Turkey and the United States. They could not understand why an Israeli Jewish girl was so interested in learning Arabic and talking to Arabs.

When I was still at Bates College I made a list of the questions I was going to ask people. I tried to read as many articles as I could about the Israeli Arab population. My questions mostly referred to problems I noticed many Israeli Arabs were dealing and struggling with at the time. I knew that in spite of reading endless books and articles, my knowledge of Israeli

Arabs was extremely limited. In this matter I was no different from most other Israeli Jews. My project, I knew already then, would be an incredible and unique educational tool that would enable me to listen and learn from the people themselves, people who were so different from myself. It became more and more clear, as the days went by, that the project was an incredible learning experience for me. Once I got to Israel, many questions were added to the list and others omitted, depending on what interested me or was important for me at the time. The nature of some questions also changed depending on what my interviewees wanted to talk about at the time or what seemed important to them. Many of the questions were added in the course of the interviews and many were spontaneously altered. Once I arrived in Israel, I understood that most of what Israeli Arabs felt and thought was not only unknown to me, but maybe even to the vast majority of Israeli Jewish society.

One thing that stayed the same, however, was that regardless of where the Arabs I interviewed came from or what religion they professed, the killing of thirteen Israeli Arabs by Israeli police in October 2000 could not be forgotten. The fact that Israeli Arabs, citizens of Israel, were killed by Israeli forces was something that their minds and hearts could not forget or forgive. It seemed to me that the killing of these thirteen men created a deep and painful wound in the hearts of Israeli Arabs—a wound which might never fully be healed. All of my interviewees, with the exception of one woman, did not believe that the Israeli police forces which confronted the Arab demonstrators would have shot Jewish demonstrators. This, they believed, was exclusively an anti-Arab phenomenon which was meant to break the spirit of the already oppressed Israeli Arab population. Most interviewees said that they did not trust the *Orr Commission*[22] and that justice would never be done to Israeli Arabs. Nazir Majli,[23] for example, in an article he wrote, strongly criticizing the Israeli Arab leaders "who brought the young [Arab] people out to the streets and watched them block roads, sabotaging private property, burning shops and plundering them, throwing stones at cars, whose drivers were Jewish etc…" reflected on this general feelings when he wrote:

When the Israeli police kill thirteen young Arab men, citizens of the state, it's hard for the Israeli Arab to criticize the Arab side. The police are prohibited from killing anyone, especially citizens, no matter what they might have done. When the number of dead people reaches thirteen in three days, we can understand that this wasn't the consequence of a mistake. Either this was a direct political act, or a consequence of a policy which does not only scorn the rights of the Arab citizen, but also his life."[24]

Several interviewees decided to ask me questions about my life in the United States (especially after the events of September 11th in New York City), my opinions about the Israeli-Palestinian conflict and about Islam in general. They were interested to know how Muslims and Arabs are viewed and perceived in the United States and whether people living abroad know anything about the Prophet Muhammad and about his message, Islam. They were also interested to know if people's views about Islam and about Arabs had changed after September 11th and whether Islam was viewed in a negative way by most people in the United States. Surprisingly to me, not many of them expressed their desire to leave and immigrate to the United States and I think this was influenced by their concern that after the terrorist attack on the World Trade Center they would never be accepted by American society. Some people told me that their family members and friends decided to return to Israel after September 11th. "It's frightening for Arabs there now," said one of my interviewees whose dream to send her son to study in the United States was shattered. Most of them saw a clear division between the United States and the Muslim people and they expressed their fear of being discriminated against as Arabs.

Once a close relationship was formed between a group of Israeli Arab women and me, I was introduced to a new aspect of Muslim tradition and culture. Several times some of these friends suggested that I convert to Islam. They did it out of genuine concern for my present well being and more importantly, for the well being of my soul in the after life. Although they sometimes said it half jokingly, they were very serious about this issue and they were very concerned for my celestial safety. Since they were very fond of me, the thought that I would one day end up in *Jahannem,* Hell, was very painful and disturbing to them. I can remember my friend Tahiyye once telling me, "Come on, Smadar, when will you convert to Islam?" From their perspective, they were trying to save me and spare me the experience of burning in Hell for eternity. Many of the women told me, "Any person who picks up the Qur'an [Koran], reads it and *understands* it, would not hesitate to immediately become a Muslim. If all the people in the world were Muslim and followed the Qur'an and the words of the Prophet Muhammad, peace be upon him, the world would be a much better place." "Look," they said, "all over the world people are converting to Islam. Even in America." Back in the United States, especially when I was living in the

"Bible Belt," many people tried to convert me to Christianity or at least into a Jew for Jesus Christ. It seemed that wherever I went people could not completely accept me as a Jew.

Generally, I tried to (and was sometimes forced to) keep my interviews on the level of a simple conversation so as not to intimidate people or make them feel uncomfortable. One must remember that most Arab people living in *The Triangle* were not used to having Jewish people come to their villages at that time. Most of the interviews were conducted in people's homes and I was usually not able to set a specific time and/or place to conduct them. Many of my informal conversations with people spontaneously evolved into long and informative discussions. In addition, it is important to remember that most of my interviews were conducted between 2001 and 2002. Since then, some things have changed, both politically and socially, within Israeli Arab society, as well as within the Palestinian Authority and the Middle East as a whole. In spite of this, I believe that the ideas and thoughts expressed to me by Israeli Arabs are mostly still the same, even though some changes have occurred.

I interviewed men, women and children. Very few of the interviewees were part of the Israeli Arab intellectual elite. None of these people were politicians and they all showed signs of anger and disgust when I mentioned both the Israeli and Palestinian governments. Some of them also exhibited anger towards the Israeli Arab political parties, which according to them, were "inefficient and corrupt." The people I spoke to were mostly shopkeepers, truck drivers, housewives, hired employees or the owners of small businesses. Each group was notably different from the others and had distinctive characteristics.

When I started my project I did not plan on spending a lot of time interviewing children. In fact, when I arrived in Arara for the first time to find out that the only people I could interview were children (because the older women who were supposed to arrive at the *Na'amat* Center were being detained at a checkpoint which was set up due to recent suicide bombings), I was extremely disappointed. I could not imagine what children could tell me that I didn't already know. I realized in retrospect, however, that children were not only the most fascinating group to interview, but also the most open, straightforward and honest. When I returned to Arara for the second time, a year later, I made it a point to interview mostly children. It was mainly from these children, who tend to say what their parents think and who do not weigh their words before speaking them, that I discovered the true ambience existing within the Israeli Arab village. I also understood that we (namely adults) should pay more attention to children and to what they feel and think if we want to better the future of the Middle East and of the world as a whole—children are the future.

Women were also fascinating and intriguing to speak to, as they seemed to be more expressive and emotional than the men to whom I had spoken. I interviewed women as young as eighteen and as old as seventy. There is no doubt that I connected more easily to younger women (some of whom had children) than to older women, who spoke about times and concepts very foreign to me. It was evident to me, that in a culture that has different sexually defined roles, women felt more comfortable confiding in me and sharing their secrets, some of which they said they had never told anyone before, because they were talking to a woman just like them. In addition to this and quite surprising to me, they were more observant than men of the socio-political climate existing in Israel at that crucial time. They were also more interested in the future of their children and in issues relating to the field of education and culture. They also wanted to talk about the suicide bombers, many of whom were young teenagers the same age as their own children. These women spoke to me, laughed with me, cried with me and most importantly, looked me in the eye when replying to my questions. Even when, as was often the case, we disagreed on fundamental concepts, ideas or political solutions, our womanhood connected us and enabled us to have a productive and constructive dialogue. I shall never forget how my host-mother used to sit me down next to her and tell me about her life before and after 1948 and say to me, "You are like my daughter. My home is your home. You are always welcome here." It was a month later, while I was washing dishes, when I heard my host-father say, "Smadar is part of the family, she can do these things around the house now. She's not a guest anymore," that I understood that I had been accepted, as much as possible, into the family.

The third group, composed mostly of young and middle-aged men, was very different from the two previous groups. Men usually quoted the media (newspapers and television) and spoke about their experiences working outside of the house. Their views, which did not surprise me, often resembled those of politicians. They usually did not speak about their wives and children (unless they spoke about the role of Islam in their wives' lives) and often avoided questions relating to the field of education. I did not always feel comfortable speaking to men, maybe because Israeli Arab society, like much of the Arab world, does not usually encourage men and women (who are not members of the same family) to spend time together, unless there is a chance of marriage between them. I was overwhelmed when one man started talking to me about the sexual intimacy between him and his wife, although the same dialogue with a Jewish man would seem less shocking to me. I generally felt out of place when speaking to men, even though I tried to respect the cultural codes expected of a Muslim woman.

When reading these interviews, one must bear in mind some important things that are essential in order to understand my book and its goal. When I tell people about my project, many of them ask me whether I believe all the things that the Arab interviewees told me when I interviewed them. My answer is always that it is not necessarily a question of believing or disbelieving what I was told, but more of patiently listening to whatever the interviewees chose to say. This point can further be emphasized with several of my experiences. One experience I had happened on the way to a wedding. We were driving there when we suddenly saw clouds of smoke on the left side of the road. We deviated from the road and stopped the car in the parking lot of a marble factory belonging to one of the family members. The fire, which was in one of the fields surrounding the village, was getting closer to the factory and to several houses in its proximity. One of the men immediately pulled out a cellular phone and called the fire department located in Hadera. The city of Hadera is located about ten miles from Arara and it would probably take the fire department approximately fifteen minutes (or even twenty) to get there, especially during rush hour. After about ten minutes, a woman approached me and said, "You see how they treat us, Smadar? Because this is an Arab district, they are taking their time. Had this fire occurred in a Jewish settlement, the fire department would have been here a long time ago." It was obvious to me that she was wrong, because no one could have driven from Hadera to Arara in less than ten minutes. But it was her feeling of discrimination that was interesting—her ingrained belief that she was being discriminated against because of her being an Arab. What was both interesting and troubling was her belief that because she was an Arab, her life was not viewed as equally important as the life of a Jew.

Another time, my friend Butheyna asked me to come with her, her brother and his friend to Umm el-Fahem in order to do some shopping. After I was introduced to the friend, he started telling me about what had happened to him that very same day. "I never hated the Jews," he said, "and I have worked with Jews all my life." I nodded, but was not sure where this conversation was going. "Then, after all these years, I was fired." There was silence in the car, and no one said a word. "Do you know why I was fired?" he asked and looked at me. I shook my head, indicating that I had no idea why. "I was fired because those people are racist and they don't want to work with an Arab," he said. "I was loyal to them all of these years. I always showed up for work, not a minute late. They always counted on me. And now, they fired me because they don't like Arabs. I never did anything bad to a Jew and look what they have done to me." He continued to talk about the subject for the duration of the trip. Although I had never met him before and therefore could not assess his working capabilities, I noticed that in his mind he was fired solely because of the fact that he was an Arab. For him, there was no other possibility, even if in actuality he was fired for a completely different reason. The more I spoke to people, the more I understood that reality did not necessarily matter. What mattered and was important was what people felt in their hearts and transmitted to others.

Additionally, it is important to understand that all the answers I received to my questions in this book are from the perspectives of the interviewees. In my book, I am not trying to prove anything, or preach to Arabs living in Israel. I wrote this book solely in order to give Israeli Arabs[25] the opportunity to express themselves and in order to bring to the surface a problem to which a solution must be found before it is too late. By writing this book, I raise questions about some of the most severe problems Israeli Jews and Arabs are currently facing, but which both sides frequently ignore. Both sides, Jewish and Arab alike, are shutting their eyes and trying to ignore an existing, distorted reality that cannot and should not be tolerated. In my analysis, found in the beginning of each chapter, I try to discover and explain where some of the ideas many of the interviewees had might have come from. When doing this, I turn mainly to events within the Palestinian Authority, as well as within the Arab and Muslim worlds, because of the unique connection that exists between Israeli Arabs and Muslim Arabs living in other countries. I criticize both Jews and Arabs, although it is obvious to me, and this can easily be detected in my book, that each side is facing very different problems and obstacles.

I cannot estimate how much of what was told to me is true and how much is false; how much of it actually happened and how much was fictitious. Muslim Israeli Arabs, like many other Arabs, are bound by their religion, Islam, and by their oral and written traditions. On the whole, I think it would be right to say that parts of Arabic lore and literature to which some Israeli Arabs (and other Arabs) are exposed, mostly reflect a negative attitude towards Jews and other non-Muslim people, one of distrust and suspicion. This is a worldwide phenomenon which can be found in many places where Islam is misinterpreted, manipulated and taken out of context. In his article "From Defensive to Offensive Warfare: The use and abuse of Jihad in the Muslim World" Dr. Abdulaziz A. Sachedina writes about this belief:

More deeply, this belief reflects an even deeper one, one to be exploited to generate perpetual conflict: namely the belief in the absolute superiority of Islam, belief that regards it as the final and perfected message that abrogated the pre-Qur'anic religions like Judaism and Christianity. This sense of spiritual-moral superiority not only serves to instigate interfaith conflicts, it also provides sufficient religiously crafted justification for the mutual condemnation of, and ensuring deadly conflict in, the intra-faith relations between Sunnites and Shi'ites.[26]

It is widely claimed by Muslims (and this was evident in the words of some Israeli Arab children in particular) that from the days of the Prophet Muhammad the Jews were enemies of Islam, both in direct military conflict with the Prophet and in plots to undermine Islam. Several of my Palestinian friends who are currently residing in Turkey told me that in school [in the Gulf states] they used to learn (when learning certain *hadiths*[27]) that the Jews betrayed first their own prophets and then Muhammad and that they had lied and turned their backs to him. I would like to suggest that this belief has, to some extent, penetrated into some Israeli Arab homes and mosques. In addition to this some Israeli Arabs are exposed to anti-Israeli and anti-Jewish propaganda on a daily basis and use many traditionally European anti-Semitic stereotypes when speaking about Israelis and about Jews in general. Some of my interviewees viewed the Jews as liars (just as Europeans who believed that the Jews would stab them in the back, did) or as dangerous people who wanted to take over the Middle East (just as the *Protocols of the Elders of Zion*[28] insinuated that the Jews wanted to take over the world). The answers of some of my interviewees, especially the children, were very much influenced by these variables because many of their attitudes (or those to which they were exposed) towards Jews seemed to emerge from these sources. They rarely differentiated between Jews and

Israelis and usually bunched all the Jews into one group, regardless of where they lived or what their political views might have been. To many of them, all the Jews are the exact same people who came and took their lands in 1948 and this phenomenon can be seen in demonstrations all over the Arab and Muslim worlds where demonstrators yell, "Massacre the Jews" and not, "Massacre the Israelis."

In spite of this, the important thing to remember is that these interviews represent the feelings of Israeli Arabs, regardless of their factual accuracy. It is these feelings that we must consider and not brush aside if Israel is to exist as a country which indeed takes into consideration all of its citizens and treats them equally, regardless of their religious or ethnic background. It is these feelings which must be considered if Israel desires to be a truly democratic state, where all its citizens enjoy the same rights in practice and not just in theory. Israel has to decide whether it wants to be a strictly Jewish state which does not exercise full democracy (because it ignores some of the needs of its minority groups and implements several discriminatory laws), or whether it can successfully combine the existence of a Jewish state with full democratic principals.

There is no doubt that the feelings Israeli Arabs expressed to me came not only from the propaganda to which they were exposed and the misinterpretation of Islam prevalent within some parts of their society (and the Muslim world as a whole), but also from something else. The current political situation between Israel and the Palestinians, the events of 1948 and the fact that many of my interviewees said that they did not feel that they were equal citizens receiving equal rights and that they were being discriminated against by Israeli Jews on a daily basis also contributed to their sentiment towards Israel and Jews in general. Bar Kochva, a retired Israeli Defense Forces general and a Middle East Studies scholar who associates himself with the center-right Israeli political parties, told me about the history of the Israeli Arabs in connection to the Jews:

Today, the Israeli Arabs are no different from the Palestinians. Until 1967 and maybe up to 1970, Israeli Arabs tried to differentiate themselves from the Palestinians living in Gaza. They would say, "We are not a part of them, we are not from Gaza, we are not from the West Bank." But later, slowly but surely, Israeli Arabs identified more and more with the Palestinians. Israeli Arabs and maybe more specifically the Israeli Arab leadership have always been seen as anti-Israeli. This does have some justification in my opinion. The justification is that the ways of the world do not go against human nature. Jews from Eastern Europe came in the 1890s during the First Aliyah[29]. Then, in the beginning of the 20th century, Jews came during the Second, Third and Fourth Aliyah. These Jews had a different culture from the Arabs. They immediately bought land. Then they did something that people who had lived on the land for hundreds of years had never done—they started drying swamps and expanding their agricultural lands. They also brought modern technology of that time from Europe and started developing agriculture in ways that had never been known in these areas before. The Jew suddenly became a farmer. The Jew, who in the Arab world was known to be submissive and scholarly, became connected to the land. This Jew, who was never able to protect himself in the Diaspora, suddenly held a gun and protected himself. Even Jewish women, wearing short pants, a thing which is viewed by Arabs as being disgraceful, were walking around, also holding guns.

The consequences of these events could clearly be detected in the answers of my interviewees. They were genuinely infuriated about the "Jewish invasion" and could not forget that once, not too long ago, they possessed the majority of the land that is now Israel. To them, the course history had taken was distorted and one girl even told me, "The land belongs to the Arabs, not to the Jews. Can you see the injustice?" It seems clear that present social and economic injustices experienced by most, if not all Israeli Arabs, only accentuate and elevate those injustices experienced by them in the past, in this case in 1948. They seem to forget, however, that much of the land was sold legally by Arabs (mostly absentee landlords) to the Jews before 1948 or that many Arabs fled and left their lands at the beginning of the Israeli War of Independence, hoping to return once the Jews were swept into the sea by the Pan-Arab forces. They also seem to forget that most of the land was uninhabited, barren and uncultivated. About the Israeli Arabs and their adjustment to the new reality in which they found themselves, Bar Kochva said:

In 1948 arrived, a certain reality existed. Historical truth does not matter, what matters is how people behave. We [the Jews] destroyed close to 450 Arab villages, villages of which there is now no trace left. We then enforced military rule after most of the Arab inhabitants had fled to Syria, Jordan and Lebanon. It does not matter whether the houses they left here were big and nice, or small and shabby. Young children, women, men and old people were now living in tents in foreign countries, while their houses remained in Israel. Among the Israeli Arabs and Palestinians who live in Israel today there are still some people who lived in pre-1948 Israel. They remember their houses and they cannot accept the reality in which they are living. All the nonsense we Jews have uttered about them gaining a good education and having a better future had no significance for them. The land was the most important thing because the land for the Arab is his soul and this is what was taken in 1948. So, we came and did all of this to these people who had lived here for centuries. And now, fifty some years later, we want them to accept this fact. But this is not natural. It's not human for them to just accept this. It doesn't matter what I personally think and I am by no means a left-wing person. But one has to understand a human being's soul. You can't expect that Arab people who left their lands and homes should just accept us.

Bar Kochva also pointed out that during the fifty years of the existence of Israel not one new Arab town or village has been built, with the exception of Kfar Makhoul which was established by Naim Makhloul in 1952, whilst hundred of Jewish towns have been founded. He portrayed a reality in which Arabs were not able to advance equally and in which many stayed behind, unable or unwilling to integrate into Israeli society. In spite of the fact that he clearly states that there is discrimination against Israeli Arabs, he does point out that this discrimination is not a policy within Israeli society and that a lot of it has been caused by incompetent Israeli governments and to some extent also by the Israeli Arab population itself:

I don't think that this [injustice] was necessarily done on purpose. I do think that it was great stupidity of the Israeli government of that time which caused this situation. You have to remember that most of the Israeli heads of state at that time were Eastern European. They disrespected and looked down on people coming from Middle Eastern countries, even Jews who were Yemenite or Moroccan. The Arab, in particular, was considered inferior. But I told a friend that I don't think that Israeli Arabs are always discriminated against in a special manner. They have internal problems that can be seen in other groups living in Israel, which are not Arab. I think that that Israeli Arabs also have a hand in how things are currently manifested. They contributed to this discrimination too. On the one hand, they have to be understood to a certain extent. Who will Israeli Arabs identify with? With Israel? Why would they identify with Israel? They [the Arabs] say that the flag and the national Israeli anthem don't represent them. Why are people angry with them? The flag and the national anthem really don't represent them. Will the Arabs sing about the 2000 years of yearning to return to Zion while in the Diaspora? Will they sing about the Jewish state? The Israeli Arabs are right in their feelings and why are Jews surprised or angry at this? On the other hand, this is a Jewish state, the State of Israel and you are Israeli, even if you are an Arab. Respect it. You don't have to identify with the flag or the national anthem and I understand you say you can't. It's just like when I lived in Iraq. Did I identify with the Iraqi flag or with the Iraqi anthem? Was I an equal citizen? Of course not. But I respected the Iraqi state and its rule. In the same manner, they should respect the Israeli state.

When I asked Bar Kochva to propose some solutions to some of the problems existing between Israeli Jews and Arabs, he talked of a solution which several other leaders, both Jewish and Arab, have started contemplating in recent years. The idea to connect *The Triangle* with the Palestinian Territories, namely with the West Bank, has been voiced by several people, politicians and civilians alike. Some people believe that since many Israeli Arabs identify themselves as Palestinians and support the Palestinian people more than they do Israel, it would be better for both Israeli Arabs and Israeli Jews if they became Palestinian citizens and were included in the Palestinian state, whenever it is established. Thus, they would be a part of the land swap that has been suggested by some. During January and February of 2004 several articles discussing this controversial issue were published in major Israeli newspapers such as *Maariv* and *Yediot Ahronot*. Several Israeli Arab people were also invited to speak about this idea on radio programs and it seemed that some kind of a debate was slowly but surely emerging. Most Israeli Arabs, however, strongly rejected this idea and one girl even wrote a public letter to Ariel Sharon in which she exclaimed, "If you like Arafat, you go and live with him!" In November 2004 in the article, "Sharon Suggested, Lieberman Promotes,"[30] this issue was introduced to the Israeli public once again; this time more straightforwardly. In the interview with Lieberman concerning the issue of Israeli Arabs he said, "The real problem of Israel is not the Palestinian population but the Israeli Arab one." He concluded his explanation by saying, "The Israeli-Arab conflict existed way before the creation of the State of Israel. Therefore, the solution is complete separation." According to him, the Israeli Arab population should be included (together with its lands and property) in the future Palestinian state and not within the Israeli political borders. Most of my interviewees were very reluctant at accepting such a plan, mainly because of the instability of the Palestinian Authority and its corrupt dictatorial government as well as its downtrodden economy. It seemed that most of them were aware of the fact that their life in Israel was better than it would be under the Palestinian Authority or in Palestine. In Israel, by the mere fact of them being citizens, they receive Social Security services such as medical care, as well as a formal education. They are also entitled to vote in the national Israeli elections and elect their representatives, whether secular or religious, Jewish or Arab. These rights, as some of them stated to me, would most probably not be provided to them if they decided to move to Palestine—a state which might turn out to be non-democratic and maybe even fundamentalist. In spite of this, Bar Kochva believes that geographically connecting *The Triangle* to the West Bank would be a solution that would ultimately satisfy both Jews and Arabs:

Israel today is facing a demographical problem. If we didn't have Jews immigrating from all over the world, we would not be five million Jews living in Israel today. The Arabs have naturally increased their numbers, while we have increased ours by welcoming immigrants from Russia, Ethiopia and now South America and Europe. Now, we have even brought half a million non-Jewish Russians who once upon a time had a Jewish ancestor. The faster we are separated from the Arabs and they from us, the better. We are not used to them and they are not used to us. Give back Taibe and Tira and Umm el-Fahem.[31] Even if they don't want to become a part of Palestine, return those areas. I do not call for expelling them. I am saying that with their lands, with their houses and property, they should become Palestinians, living in Palestine. Is it true that their life with us is miserable? It's true. Is it true that we are unjust to them? It's true. Is it true that they would prefer living without Jews amongst them? It's true. Is it true that this also influences how Jews and Arabs feel in this country? It's true. So, it's very simple: go and live with your brothers and sisters, the ones you support and prefer anyway. Then, from your mosque in Umm el-Fahem, you can support Arafat, Dahlan and Abu Mazen or preach against Sharon and we won't be angry with you. This is exactly what Atatürk did in Turkey. By exchanging Greek and Turkish populations, he solved a lot of Turkey's problems. He exchanged populations by expelling people from their lands. Here, no one has to be expelled or relocated—they can stay in their homes, on their ancestral lands. These areas have a population of about 120,000 people and none of them would be relocated. This would solve some of the long-term problems of both Jews and Arabs.

This idea, often referred to as the 'Transfer' policy, is very controversial and raises many moral and ethical questions as both Jews and Arabs have pointed out. It is an idea which has mostly been theoretically discussed but has not yet become (and will most probably never become) official Israeli policy. Though some Jews and some Arabs support this plan, for different reasons altogether, many view it as racist and unacceptable. On the one hand, one must ask whether it is acceptable to suggest that a part of Israel be transferred to Palestine against the will of its Israeli Arab inhabitants. On the other hand, it is important to look at the quality of life Israeli Arabs enjoy within Israel. Will Arabs ever feel equal in a state which has been internationally recognized as a Jewish state? Can Israel be a democratic, albeit Jewish state or is it doomed to be a Jewish state which is not able to exercise full democracy? Is there a chance that Israeli Arabs will ever be accepted by Israeli Jews as equals or that Israeli Arabs will accept the existence of Israel as a Jewish state, or as a state at all? Will Jews and Arabs really benefit from living in total separation or will this be disastrous and catastrophic for both peoples? Most importantly, what is the future of both Jewish and Arab Israelis, if Arabs continue to be discriminated against and do not therefore feel that they need to contribute to the well being of the state?

Just recently, the findings of the *Orr Commission* have been published after nearly three years of intense investigation into the October 2000 riots. During these three years there have been, on both sides, many speculations as to the conclusions and recommendations of the *Orr Commission*. Most of my interviewees did not believe that the Orr Commission's investigation would bring true justice to Israeli Arab society. Many believed that even if the Commission ruled in favor of the Israeli Arabs, the implementation of its conclusions would be very hard and even impossible. Whether they are right or not in their assumption, the Orr Commission's recommendations go far beyond what many people, Jews and Arabs alike, ever expected. Although it is true that the *Orr Commission* harshly criticized the Israeli Arab leadership who "...did not succeed in directing the demands of an Arab minority into solely legitimate democratic channels," and even ruled that "This radicalization process [of sectors within the Israeli Arab community] was related to the increasing strength of Islamic politics in Israel..." it is important to note that the appalling discrimination against Israeli Arabs was revealed to the public:

[3] The events, their unusual character, and serious results were the consequence of deep-seated factors that created an explosive situation in the Israeli Arab population. The state and generations of its government failed in a lack of comprehensive and deep handling of the serious problems created by the existence of a large Arab minority inside the Jewish state.

Government handling of the Arab sector has been primarily neglectful and discriminatory. The establishment did not show sufficient sensitivity to the needs of the Arab population and did not take enough action in order to allocate state resources in an equal manner. The state did not do enough or try hard enough to create equality for its Arab citizens or to uproot discriminatory or unjust phenomena. Meanwhile, not enough was done to enforce the law in the Arab sector, and the illegal and undesirable phenomena that took root there.

As a result of this and other processes, serious distress prevailed in the Arab sector in various areas. Evidence of the distress included poverty, unemployment, a shortage of land, serious problems in the education system and substantially defective infrastructure. These all contributed to ongoing ferment that increased leading up to October 2000 and constituted a fundamental contribution to the outbreak of the events.[32]

In addition to this, the *Orr Commission* strongly criticized Jewish Israeli policemen and politicians such as Barak and Ben Ami for failing to handle the riots that broke out in October 2000 in a just manner. Although there will always be people who will say that this is not enough or that there is still more to be done (and this is, of course, true), the conclusions of the *Orr Commission* should not be ignored, brushed aside or oversimplified. This small step might be the first step in a much needed social and political transformation.

The fact that an entire Commission was established to investigate the killing of the thirteen Israeli Arab men; that both Jews and Arabs were tried and convicted and that this commission publicly called for change, shows that Israel possesses many of the fundamental freedoms and rights other Middle Eastern countries are still lacking.

What happens now and in the future depends on many social and political factors. It seems that in order to normalize Jewish-Arab relations in Israel, many changes on both sides will have to be made. The Israeli-Palestinian conflict makes things even more complicated because it inevitably polarizes both the Jewish and Arab societies. Each side feels that it is in the midst of an existential struggle. People take sides. People identify. People forget one another's humanity in the midst of chaos and war. Only radical changes and genuine compromises on both sides will bring Israeli Arabs and Jews closer to one another.

Demographics: Israeli Arabs

There are over one million Israeli Arabs living in Israel today. As citizens of Israel, they are entitled to all civil rights, including the right to vote. Arab Israeli citizens composed aapproximately 18% of the total Israeli population in 2003.

The breakdown of the Israeli Arab population into religious groups is approximately as follows:
- Muslim: 1,000,000
- Christian: 117,000
- Bedouins: 170,000
- Druze: 80,000

More that 15% of the Israeli Arab society is under 15 years of age and 70% are under the age of 17. There are 2.2 million children in Israel (ages 0-17); Israeli Arabs compose 27% of this group (around 600,000).

Note that the numbers above do not include:
- Arabs living in East Jerusalem. Largely Muslim, this population numbers approximately 210,000, and are mostly citizens of either Jordan or the Palestinian Authority.
- Arabs living in Ramat HaGolan. Largely Druze, this population numbers approximately 18,000, and are mostly citizens of either Syria or the Palestinian Authority.

These populations are not included because the majority are not Israeli citizens, and are therefore are not entitled to vote in the Israeli elections.

1
Israeli Arabs and the Jewish State

Education: the Competition for the Human Mind

The way an entire society thinks and behaves depends primarily on the education its children receive. Education is the basis for understanding between peoples because it aims at finding a meeting point between one human and another. It is what children learn in schools and in their parents' homes that will later shape the moral and ethical makeup of the society to which they belong. Education, as it occurs in some Israeli Arab elementary schools, mosques and homes, is at times harmful because it presents the otherness of the Jews in a very stereotypical way. Islam claims to be the final word of God and views Judaism and Christianity as deviant and as a human invention contrary to divine dispensation. This is demonstrated by the widespread critique of the Bible by many Muslims. Jews [and Christians] are traditionally charged with tampering and distorting the texts and falsely interpreting them. Islam claims that the Qur'an is the original, ultimate and final word of God to humanity which has never been edited or changed in any way and that the Jews and Christians forged their holy scriptures (the Torah and the New Testament) in fraudulent imitation. The assumption is, therefore, that the Qur'an is the source of all other scriptures.

In many Muslim religious and secular texts, Jews and Christians are grouped under the noun "infidels," even if they are considered by Islam to be a*hal-al-kitab*, People of the Book.[33] Robert S. Wistrich in his study *Muslim Anti Semitism: A Clear and Present Danger* expands on this subject:

The most basic anti Jewish stereotype fostered by the Koran remains the charge that the Jews have stubbornly and willfully rejected Allah's truth. Not only that, but according to the sacred text, they have always persecuted his prophets, including Muhammad, who was eventually obliged to expel two major Jewish clans from Medina and to exterminate the third tribe, the *Qurayza*. The *hadith* (Islamic oral tradition) goes much further and claims that the Jews, in accordance with their perfidious nature, deliberately caused Muhammad's painful, protracted death from poisoning. Furthermore, malevolent, conspiratorial Jews are to blame for the sectarian strife in early Islam, for heresies and deviations that undermined or endangered the unity of the *Umma* (the Muslim nation). The well-enhanced archetype of a "Jewish threat" or a challenge at the very birth of Islam has assumed an increasingly strident and militant form since 1948, especially in the battle against Israel and world Jewry today.[34]

These ideas are being taught to a lesser extent in Israeli Arab schools (which receive their curriculum from the Israeli Ministry of Education and are therefore under close supervision)[35] and to a greater extent in Israeli Arab homes and religious schools and institutions such as the *Madrase*[36] and even in some mosques.[37] There was hardly a child (and some of the children were as young as seven years of age) who did not mention the fact that the Jews faked the Bible and were, therefore, not to be trusted. This belief and the fact that numerous *hadiths* foresee the return of the land (which is now Israel) to the hands of Muslims, is expressed by many of the children and adults to whom I spoke, when they questioned the rights of the Jews to the land. The words "The Jews can't be trusted because they betrayed the Prophet Muhammad," or simply, "the Jews can't be trusted because they faked the Bible" were repeated to me again and again by some children who did not believe that the Jews had *any* historical and/or spiritual connection to the land. One girl even went as far as to say, "The Jews must go back to wherever they came from." When I asked her where that might be, she just stared at me and said, "I don't know and I don't care!"

Some of the children even expressed their desire to become a *shaheed*.[38] They genuinely believe that the Holy Qur'an promises a *shaheed* an eternal life in Paradise. They also wanted to become *shaheeds* in order to redeem the land (which according to them belongs only to the Arabs) from the evil and conniving Jews and return it to the Palestinians[39]. The idea that the land belongs to only one people can also be found in the Jewish tradition where the land (including Judea and Samaria) was ordained to the Jews by God. This is clearly a perception that distances people from one another rather than bringing them together. People on both sides who feel this way are a main obstacle to solving the lingering Israeli-Palestinian conflict, as well as Jewish-Arab unrest in Israel.

There is no doubt that the education many Israeli Arab children to whom I spoke received in their schools and in their homes influenced their worldview tremendously. This worldview has penetrated into Israeli Arab villages mainly from other Arab and Muslim countries, including the Palestinian Authority. Many of the things Israeli Arab children told me closely resembled what Palestinians, living in the Palestinian Authority and in the neighboring Arab states, are exposed to. This worldview can often be seen not only as anti-Israeli, but furthermore as anti-Jewish:

The anti-Jewish poison that rose so naturally to Assad's lips has by now become a staple feature of the Palestinian Authority's educational program. In Palestinian textbooks today, reference to Jews is minimal, except for negative generalizations that attribute to them character traits of trickery, greed and barbarity. They also insinuate that Jews never keep agreements as Muslims do. The Jewish connection to the Holy Land is generally denied or else confined to antiquity and virtually ignored after the Roman period. There is no reference to Jewish holy places or to any special connection of the Jews to the city of Jerusalem. Hebrew is not even considered to be one of the languages of the land, and Zionism is mentioned only in the context of alien intrusion, invasion or infiltration. The State of Israel is not acknowledged at all and its internationally recognized territory is referred to only by terms such as the "interior" or the "1948 lands." By definition, the Jewish state is presented as a colonialist usurper and occupier. Brutal, inhumane and greedy, the Jewish state is held exclusively responsible for obliterating Palestinian national identity, destroying the Palestinian economy, and expropriating Palestinian lands, water and villages.[40]

One evening, as I was sitting on the veranda with some friends in Arara, someone suggested that I record the singing of Mahmoud, my host mother's grandson. Mahmoud was truly an amazing and gifted child, who was unique in many ways. At the age of three, he was already singing songs in Hebrew, Arabic and English and could detect a car's model from afar. He knew the parts of the body in three languages and rarely stumbled. His favorite activity was to stand in the middle of the living room and sing and dance while everyone else was clapping and encouraging him. I pressed the "record" button and Mahmoud's mother encouraged him to sing something for me. He looked at us with an embarrassed smile and the first song that came to his mind started with the words, "*Falastin bladna, wa el Yahoud klabna*," meaning: Palestine is our land and the Jews are our dogs. The song was extremely long and consisted of at least four or five verses. Mahmoud knew all the words by heart and was encouraged by everyone to continue singing, although some people glanced at me to see my reaction. I couldn't believe that a three year old already knew how to sing songs of incitement in which the Jews are depicted as dogs. I could never imagine myself teaching my children a song in which Arabs, or any other groups of people, were depicted as dogs. I was embarrassed, overwhelmed and angry, but I didn't say a thing. Everyone seemed so excited and amused by Mahmoud's song and I was surrounded by laughter. At the end of the song everyone cheered loudly and Mahmoud went to the next song, this time a children's song he had probably learned from some friends.

Unfortunately, when it comes to the field of education, the modern Israeli nation is not paying sufficient attention to two important points. Firstly, the fact that schools must be supported by the Israeli government without any discrimination has been blatantly ignored by the Israeli Ministry of Education. Although, according to Israeli law Jewish and Arab schools should receive equal funding, Israeli Arab schools do not receive the same amount of financial support as do Jewish schools. A short visit to an Israeli Jewish school and then to an Israeli Arab school will easily reveal this inequality. One must also remember, however, that schools in Israel are funded by both the Ministry of Education (an arm of the Israeli government) and by the local municipalities, consisting of local governing bodies. The question, therefore, is not only how much the Israeli government is spending on Israeli Arab public schools and education, but also how much the local Arab municipalities are allocating to them in comparison to what they spend on religious institutions, or on other things such as the *Waqf*.[41] Some of my interviewees emphasized the fact that substantial amounts distributed to Israeli Arab local governing bodies are spent on internal feuding etc. rather than on education and the development of infrastructure. One interviewee even told me, "The only place which is discriminating against me is my own village."

Whether it is the Jews or the Arabs that should be held accountable for the lower quality of the education that Israeli Arabs receive, the fact remains that Arab schools have not received the same funding as have Jewish schools and Arab people have not been able to advance at the same pace as have Jews. Education for all Israeli citizens, irrespective of religion, race or sex is guaranteed by the Israeli Declaration of Independence and must, therefore, be available to all. Proportionately, Israeli Arabs do not do as well in their matriculation exams and only a few make it to university or to other institutions of higher education. Thus, Israeli Arabs almost always find themselves at a disadvantage in comparison to Israeli Jews when it comes to the field of education. This fact has been detrimental to all parts of Israeli society, not only to the Arab sector, which directly suffers from this discrimination. Since a large part of Israeli society is not advancing equally, Israeli society finds itself in a moral and ethical dilemma. This phenomenon can also be seen throughout the world, where women, today composing over 50% of the world's population, are forced to remain poor, uneducated and without equal rights. Until women, or other minority groups, are given freedom and equality, the world as a whole will not truly be free.

Many of the interviewees condemned the poor infrastructure of their schools and the lack of computers and sport facilities. Others pointed out the unfairness of English being taught as a third language in their schools while it is taught as a second language in Israeli Jewish ones. The inequalities were always compared to what the Israeli Jews have, or what they receive. Several mothers who had visited Jewish schools spoke to me with rage about the abundance of equipment to be found there in comparison to that which is found in a typical Israeli Arab school. The main complaint coming from children (and this complaint was also voiced to me by many of the mothers with whom I spoke) was that by the time they take their university entrance exams, Jews are much more advanced in the English language and therefore much more likely to receive better grades and get into university. Altogether, nearly all my interviewees felt that Israel was discriminating against them in the field of education and some even believed that this was an intentional policy.

Secondly, the Israeli Ministry of Education seems not to comprehend the importance of Arabic being taught as a second language in Israeli Jewish schools. Israel, falsely, considers itself to be a European country in all aspects and it makes a great effort to prove this by joining cultural and sporting events such as the European basketball championships and the annual Eurovision Song Contest. Because of this false assumption English is considered to be the second language in Israel. Israeli Jewish children are required to study Arabic, but it is literary, classic Arabic and not spoken, standard Arabic. Arabic, in effect, is being marginalized and taught in some schools as a third language which most Jewish students do not want to learn and even strongly reject. The average Israeli Jewish student, therefore, is not able to carry on a simple conversation in the Arabic language. It is my view that the greatest mistake of the Israeli Ministry of Education is that it has failed to introduce Arabic to Israeli Jewish children as a second language. This is in effect the Achilles heel of Israeli education - its failure to understand that in order to know one's neighbor, one must know their language, literature, religion and traditions. All of this is lacking (to varying degrees) in the Israeli education system where most students are not even required to study the translated poetry and prose of Israeli Arabs such as Nida'a Khouri or Emil Habibi, a winner of the Israel Prize for Literature. Many of the Arab high school students I interviewed complained to me about the fact that most Jewish people (and especially young people) cannot speak Arabic. They did not understand why they had to learn Hebrew, while Jews could graduate from high school without even being able to say "Kif halak" (How are you?) in vernacular Arabic.[42]

I made the effort to ask an acquaintance, a seventeen-year-old Jewish girl who attends a secular high school, about her Arabic class. I asked her whether she is required to take Arabic classes and if she is, how they have been conducted. She told me, "Arabic is the most unpopular subject in our school. People from my class attend Arabic lessons because our head teacher teaches them and we can't escape. But most other people skip Arabic class, and don't take it seriously." When I asked her why she thought students felt this way, she said, "The Arabic we learn is not the spoken form of Arabic, but rather the written one. Even if we learn it for a whole year, we would not be able to speak the language. It just doesn't seem to be an important language to learn. I think that in most schools people can choose to take another foreign language, such as French instead of Arabic, so most people choose this option." She also told me that she hardly ever learned poetry or prose written by Arab people because it was not part of the school's curriculum. I told her that I hoped she would take her Arabic classes more seriously, because they might change her life one day, but I had the feeling that she did not completely comprehend what I meant. I remembered the days when I was being forced to study literary Arabic and was not surprised.

Now that I have learned to speak basic Arabic, I find that I can communicate more freely and effectively with Israeli Arabs and that they make more of an effort to understand me and the political views I hold. Now I understand, more than ever, how language opens channels of communication between peoples, especially in the midst of a painful and senseless conflict. I also realize that speaking Arabic gives me an advantage over Jews who do not speak Arabic and those Arabs who do not speak Hebrew. Having basic Arabic skills further helped me when I attended an Israeli-Palestinian conference in Copenhagen in the summer of 2003. Being able to understand when the Arab participants spoke among themselves and then respond in Arabic contributed immensely to my experience. Language, most certainly, connects people and increases their desire to listen and to understand one another. Knowing a certain language increases the chances that other people who speak that language will try to listen to you more attentively and with more desire to understand what you are trying to communicate. Although it is completely true that Israel has the right to decide that it will not teach Arabic as a second language or that it will not enforce Arabic as a third language in all its schools, I believe that it is wrong and furthermore discriminatory to make such a decision. I will even go further and say that by deciding not to teach Arabic as a second or third language in all Jewish Israeli schools, Israel is in effect contributing to the already existing distance and mistrust between Jews and Arabs.

Education has the unique ability of bringing people together to establish dialogue, which is a pertinent aspect of teaching people how to respect and understand one another. Being adults, we are all immersed in whatever beliefs, assumptions and misconceptions we have been taught. It is the children who will determine how the world in general, and our own society in particular will appear in the future. It is my view that the main obstacle to peace, especially in the Middle East, is religion. It is due to religion and to the way it has been and continues to be interpreted, taught and then used, that we, not only in the Middle East, but in the world as a whole, have been unable to establish a true dialogue between different groups of people. Although it is true that many people use religion in order to do good, it is evident that those who use it in order to do bad are much more successful and influential in a world in which corrupt and deceitful clergy of all faiths are constantly being revealed to the public. It is religion and the fact that different people have different beliefs, which, at the end of the day, brings people into conflict. It is religion which stresses the differences and not the similarities between peoples. The movie "Promises"[43] emphasizes this tragic point when it tries to solve the question of who has sovereignty over this land. A religious Jewish boy pulls out the *Torah*[44] and points to the verse in which God promises the land to Abraham. "This is why," he said, "we *know* the land is ours." A religious Muslim boy then recites an aya (verse) from the Qur'an which, according to him, promises the very same piece of land to the Prophet Muhammad and to Muslims. These two boys, deeply bound by their religious traditions, were the ones who at the end of the movie were not willing to meet with people from the other side and create a constructive dialogue. It was religion that was so forcefully preventing these two boys from seeing the human aspect existing in the other. It seems that until pseudo- religious indoctrination on both sides stops and until people are able to look beyond a written "holy" text, no genuine solution will be found.

In the context of the relations between Jews and Arabs in Israel, it is evident that there are inequalities in the allocation of funds for education with Arabs generally receiving less funds. There also seems to be very little effort in bringing people from both sides together to learn about each other. Israeli Jewish schools do not allow any room, or hardly any room, for Arab literature and tradition to be taught and this is most easily detected in the lack of Arabic language classes. Israeli Jewish schools are not making a sufficient effort to introduce their students to "the otherness of the other." These schools are currently not making any effort in teaching Jewish students about the culture surrounding them on three fronts and are seemingly ignoring the fact that approximately 18% of the Israeli population is Arab. Nazir Majli commented on this issue:

Unfortunately, the situation in Israel is not different. Also here, people don't know the Arab world. There isn't a free and inquisitive access to it, and if there is, the tools needed in order to learn about the other are absent. Besides the political barriers, there's also a language barrier. This is the attitude towards Israeli Arabs. The Jews don't know us. Some of them don't want to know us and they keep their distance from us. And if this continues, the day will come when we'll hear about another dividing fence, that between Arabs and Jews. Especially now, that some Arabs are calling for autonomy. People are talking about cultural autonomy, and I would not be surprised if they soon talk about political autonomy. And I am sure some Jews would embrace this idea too. And if this is not enough, let me add: We [Israeli Arabs] have not learned to know ourselves, just as we have not learned to know the other. It is as *though* we know, as *though* we recognize and even as *though* we exist.[45]

The situation is similar in Israeli Arab secular schools, religious schools and mosques. On the one hand, Israeli Arab schools whose curriculum is dictated to them by the Israeli government, force their students to study Jewish literature and tradition, thus causing many children and teenagers to automatically feel repelled by it. Some of the children I interviewed mentioned their Hebrew language and literature classes and spoke of them in a positive way, but most people spoke of these classes in a negative manner and one woman even told me, "I don't like to speak Hebrew. I wish you spoke fluent Arabic so that we wouldn't have to slip into Hebrew from time to time." On the other hand, these schools, taught mostly by an Arab faculty paid by the Israeli government, do not stress the genuine respect that must be exhibited towards the "otherness of the other," in this case, the Jews amongst whom they are living. The situation seems to be much worse in some religious schools and mosques where Jews are often systematically being dehumanized. If we want an education system that does not teach children only facts and dates, but which also teaches respect for other human beings and their culture, the education which both Jewish and Arab children receive must be immediately reexamined and altered. It is unacceptable that in a country where people live in such proximity to each other, people are not encouraged by their national educational system to know the other, especially those who practice a different religion and who have a different language and set of values and traditions.

Media: the Competition for the Human Soul

"The reality is that complete freedom of information and freedom of speech among Israelis and Jews allows for the widest array of views to be presented, whereas virtually total control over information to most residents of Arab and Muslim states, coupled with extreme sanctions for expressing dissenting views, makes any realistic comparison impossible."

–Alan Dershowitz, author of *The Case for Israel*

We are living in a time in which television seems to be rapidly replacing the newspaper and the book. We can get all the information we want while comfortably sitting in our living room and gazing at our television screen. Unlike reading a book or a newspaper (with the possibility of re-reading a certain article we do not understand or agree with and investigating the text), we do not have time to genuinely rethink something we have seen or heard on television. It is what we hear and see that sticks in our mind. This was especially evident in the painfully selective coverage of the Second Gulf War on American television, where we saw images of American soldiers fighting in the desert, but almost none of dying Iraqi women and children. At the same time, the Iraqi television's only channel (owned by Saddam Hussein's family) was showing Iraqi officials, such as Saddam Hussein and Muhammad Saeed al-Sahaf,[46] the Iraqi minister of information, promising the Iraqi people, even after the actual Iraqi defeat, a swift victory over the American and English armies, calling the invading powers "infidels" and promising the status of a *shaheed* to all those willing to die for Iraq. It was the images which influenced the viewers' opinions. When watching television, we also give up another right we might practice when choosing a book or reading an article in a newspaper—the right to choose what we want to read and what not. We are bombarded with so many images and with so much information that it is often hard to completely escape, even after we have changed channels or turned off the television.

Thus, we often do not have the time to analyze what we hear and see or to filter what reaches our living room.

People in most Arab and Muslim countries all over the Middle East (and even in parts of the Western world) can watch and listen to Syrian, Saudi Arabian, Jordanian, and many other Arab channels on satellite. They can view the suicide bombings occurring in Israel and the speeches of Arab leaders (mostly very anti-Israel and anti-Jewish) from their living room without necessarily making an effort to examine what they hear or to disagree with it. Many people living in the Arab world are exposed solely to the interpretations they see and hear on their television screens, which usually amount to "We in the Arab world are suffering, and one of the main reasons why we are suffering is because of the existence of the State of Israel."[47] The opinion some Jews voiced, I that "even if a housewife in Syria burns the cake she is baking she will say that it is Israel's fault," was not far from being true. Therefore, many Arabs and Muslims conclude that the State of Israel should be annihilated, even if it means killing the last Jew.

Many of my questions to the different interviewees, both adults and children, related to the media and to the influence it has on Israeli Arabs. It was obvious that many people I visited in the Arab villages (especially those situated in *The Triangle*) get most of their information from television. Only rarely was their television on an Israeli news channel or on any other news channel that was not coming from an Arab or Muslim country. It was mostly either on the Saudi Arabian, Palestinian or Syrian channels, or on *Al Jazeera*, a news channel coming all the way from Qatar. Some people to whom I spoke even mentioned the *Al Manar* television channel, the official channel of *Hizballah* (which has been internationally recognized as a terrorist organization by the U.N.) as being a reliable source of information. When asked why they preferred to watch Arab news channels, they all indicated to me that the Arab channels were much more reliable and trustworthy than the Israeli ones. The Israeli news channels were, according to most of them, full of lies, bias and deliberate misconceptions. "Israel," many of them said, "wants to deceive the Arabs and Muslims."

Television, as a medium in the Arab world, is controlled solely by the government and, therefore, television stations are not free to show whatever they please. Their first loyalty is to the government and its policies, whatever they might be. The opinions they express are always the official ones of the country's government and it is not allowed to show anything which contradicts it. This is done mainly in order to convince the audience that what they see is the truth and the only truth. The government is aware of the fact that in order to create a situation in which people believe whatever they see and hear, they must first control the people. The government also knows that in order to do this it must first control the media in all its forms. Lebanese people, for example, have only recently begun publicly speak against their country's brutal occupation by Syria, and whether Syria will fully withdraw its forces is still questionable. Just a few weeks ago a program broadcast on the German news station *Deutsche Welle* (DW) featured an Iranian girl who was telling a Western reporter that people in Iran are not allowed to watch cable television or any station which might contradict the government's policies and that if she were to be caught doing so, she would be severely punished. She also spoke generally about Muslim and Arab regimes, where people are not allowed to expose themselves to a wider variety of television and radio programs coming from the West, or even from more modern Muslim countries such as Turkey.

People might criticize me and say that the same thing can be said about Western media. It is true that this phenomenon can also be found on several channels that exist in Europe and in North America. Like Arab countries, these regions also have several television channels that broadcast the official policies and interests of its governments. This is probably a phenomenon that can be found all over the world, on each and every continent and in each and every country, regardless of its form of government. Every country has at least one channel which represents the official policy of its government and which broadcasts what can be considered by many to be propaganda—every country has either an overt or a covert agenda.

There is one major difference between the Western and Middle Eastern media, however, and this difference is of major importance. In the West, there are private and public television stations that offer an alternative to the official ones, which are controlled by the government.

Persons living in western countries can use their remote control to flip through tens of news channels and other political programs which have no association with a government or a specific political party, without fear. They are thus exposed to many different interpretations of the same event, some of which might contradict their governments' policies. A good example is that of the current situation in the United States. Although it is obvious that the official policies of the government of the United States unequivocally support both the war against Iraq and the global war on terror, politicians, as well as civilians who oppose the war, can freely express their opinions on television and on the radio without fear of their lives. The Raging Grannies,[48] for example, were able to sing songs bashing President Bush and protesting the war in Iraq during a demonstration in Washington D.C (2003), without fearing for their lives. Another good example is what happened in Cuba after the nationwide screening of the anti-Bush movie "Fahrenheit 9/11". Although Castro most definitely succeeded in inciting more hatred towards President Bush and the United States as a whole, he was overwhelmed and disappointed by a completely different outcome of the screening. One Cuban woman who was interviewed after watching the movie said, "I can't believe that in a country like the United States people can make such movies where the president of the United States is being mocked and ridiculed. Here in Cuba, we could never even dream of being able to express our political opinions if they contradict the ideas of the government. People can be imprisoned or even killed. Most of our greatest film directors are unemployed here because the government won't let them create movies which criticize the government of Cuba or the worsening situation of the country. This is amazing."

Although it is true that as a consequence of terror the United States is not willing to exercise the same level of democracy it practiced until the attack on the World Trade Center in New York City, (no country which has known terror has ever remained completely democratic, since the need to implement security may impinge on democratic rights) basic freedoms such as the freedom of expression, are still in place. The fact that a country is democratic does not by any means indicate that it is perfect, or that it does not use its power to abuse those who are not as strong or not as militarily advanced. All throughout history we have seen countries which were considered to be more westernized and democratic abuse weaker states which were at times considered to be "barbarian" or "uncivilized." France, which claims so falsely that it practices full democracy, was and continues to be an abuser of human rights and democratic values. What it does mean, however, is that a democratic country, unlike most if not all the non-democratic countries, has a set of universal laws and rules which must be abided and followed at all times. And, when these rules and laws are abused or manipulated (as is often the case) there is a system which aims at correcting the injustice by thoroughly investigating the incident and punishing those responsible. When American soldiers committed atrocities against Iraqi people, the American and European media was outraged. People all over the world, Muslims and non-Muslims alike, called for much needed justice. The perpetrators were immediately returned to the

United States and tried for the crimes they had committed against humanity. At the same time, the Iraqi militants who were busy beheading people just because they were Jewish or just because they were "infidels" were not only not found and put on trial, but were furthermore promised eternal life in Heaven.

Media can provide either true or false reports, and this can influence the way an entire people behave and act in their daily lives. During the 1967 Six Day War Egyptian radios were broadcasting false news (that Egypt was winning the war and that its army was at the outskirts of Tel Aviv) and calling on Israeli Arabs to revolt against Israel and to join the Egyptian forces. The Israeli Arab population, however, was also listening to Israeli and foreign broadcasts which portrayed the real situation and decided, therefore, to remain passive and not to join the Arab forces. After the war (which was swift and in which all the Arab forces were defeated by the Israeli forces), the Egyptian media continuously claimed that the United Kingdom and the United States had secretly assisted Israel to win the war because the Arab world, which was humiliated by the Israeli forces, needed to hear that Israel alone could not defeat them.

Israeli television has two major channels. Channel One was first broadcast during the Six Day War, when Israel had to counter the Arab propaganda coming from Egyptian president Gamal Abdul Nasser and the Palestinian leader, Ahmad Shuqeiri, who were broadcasting to the Arab world that the Arab forces would "throw the Israelis into the sea." Elihu Katz, the head of the Israeli television's founding team, shaped and guided Channel One between July 1967 and March 1969. Channel Two developed later, in 1993, a couple of years after the First Gulf War, when the demand for alternative broadcasting increased among Israelis. Until recently, there were several programs in Arabic on Channel One, such as a news edition, movies and some programs for children totaling around 20 hours a week. Later, a decision was made to create a new Israeli television station, the Middle East Channel, exclusively in Arabic, which would be separate from Channel One. The hope was that Israeli Arabs as well as people in the neighboring Arab countries would watch this station in order to receive a more accurate picture of the Israeli-Palestinian conflict. Most Israeli Arab people, however, do not subscribe to this channel and choose instead to watch programs coming from Arab countries. It also seems that most Arabs living in Israel's neighboring countries also choose not to subscribe to this channel because of its alleged bias towards Israel. Several Israeli Arabs I spoke to told me that, "The new Israeli channel in Arabic is pure propaganda and does not accurately portray the existing situation." Because of its unpopularity, the Middle East Channel is now transmitted through the Israeli Channel 33 only two hours a day.

Channel One mostly represents the official policies and interests of the Israeli government. For a long time, this was the only channel Israelis could view before Channel Two and cable television appeared in the early and mid 1990's. Even on Channel One, however, one can find those who often harshly criticize the policies of the government, especially those policies implemented within the Occupied Territories. It also deals with domestic issues such as corruption and mismanagement, both which are very prevalent within the Israeli government. Long and complex dialogues (usually turning into boisterous arguments) between people from all political parties who can democratically express themselves can be viewed and listened to each day. Recently I watched a program on Channel One in which religious settlers (both civilians and politicians) supporting the building of more settlements in the Occupied Territories and secular people opposing the settlements faced one another in a public debate. Another time, Israelis working for human rights publicly defended a Palestinian woman who was allegedly abused at a checkpoint by an Israeli female soldier. These politicians and civilians criticize the Israeli government's actions and do not fear to express their opinions publicly, even if they blatantly contradict the policies and interests of the Israeli government. The viewers are, therefore, exposed to a diverse range of opinions from which they can form their own political views and are not limited to the views of the government.

Middle Eastern people, from both Jewish and Muslim countries, are for the most part very politically involved. Wherever you go, whatever you chose to do, you will always find people discussing the political situation. It may surprise people from the West how young children on both the Arab and the Jewish sides are usually very aware of what is going on in the political arena and are often involved in these discussions. A few years ago, someone from my college asked me why young children in Israel are so involved in politics. I immediately thought about how the volume of the radio on Israeli buses is always turned up every half an hour for the news broadcast. It is impossible to escape it. The only thing I could think of telling my friend was, "Because we live it every day and every moment of our lives. We have no choice but to be informed and form an opinion." It is nearly impossible for two or more people to meet without discussing the political situation and how to improve things. While traveling in buses during the two summers in which I undertook the project, I often overheard long and passionate discussions about suicide bombings and what must be done in order to stop them.

Once as I was sitting in a taxi traveling from Tiberias to Tel Aviv, suddenly news of a suicide bombing was announced on the radio. The driver, who was not wearing a *kippa*, a small head cover traditionally worn by religious Jewish men, suddenly pulled out a box filled with such head coverings and small prayer books and insisted on all the male passengers present wearing them and praying for the souls of the murdered. One man who turned out to be a secular *kibbutz* member refused to wear the *kippa*. This was the beginning of a passionate discussion which included yelling and shouting, nearly escalating into physical violence. "The problem is," said the taxi driver, "that people like you who have forgotten God, live in this country." The secular *kibbutznik* replied scathingly, "No, the problem is that people like you want to impose religion on everyone else. What do the religious people here know about what it means to serve in the army and to be in near-death situations? All they do is sit in their *Yeshiva* schools and pray to God. And their so-called God, for years, has decided to do nothing!"

Another time, I attended a huge demonstration in Tel Aviv against the Occupation. Since I was filming the demonstration, I was not taking sides but was simply walking among the people, asking them questions and watching the masses walk down one of the city's central streets. Just before the demonstration ended, I accepted a sticker that was given to me with the words "Land for Peace" written on it. I attached the sticker to the video camera's case and went to a nearby bus station to catch a bus to Hadera. As I was standing in the bus station, a girl in her early twenties approached me and said, "I see that you have a sticker that says 'Land for Peace' on it." I told her that I had picked it up at the demonstration, believing that she wanted one for herself. "You know," she said, "I can't believe that people like you live in this country. People who are willing to give our land to our enemies. What right do you have to walk around with such a sticker?" I froze for a few seconds, not sure what to say to her. I finally said that I believed that at some point, sooner or later, Israel would have to give back some land to the Palestinians. "People like you are exactly what our country does not need," she said, this time much louder. "Because of you we will not have anything left for ourselves." In the bus, she continued to complain about my sticker to two people who were sitting next to her. After about fifteen minutes, a man who was sitting next to me turned to me and said, "You know, I agree with her, but I don't think she should be so rude. People in this country don't know how to argue in a civil way." For the next half an hour Haim and I engaged in an interesting debate and several other people could not resist joining in. And so, people who had never met before and who would probably never meet ever again talked about the last occurrences in the Occupied Territories, the last suicide bombing in Jerusalem or Tel Aviv in which many were killed and the foreign policy of European countries towards Israel. There's always something political to argue about in Israel. It is never boring.

There is no doubt that the Middle East is much more charged with politics and with political debate than the United States, Europe and many other parts of the world. Everyone has a political opinion and most people, no matter what their political orientation, believe that their opinion is the source of absolute truth. It is almost impossible to make someone change their mind when it comes to politics, especially in relation to the Israeli-Palestinian conflict. The media, especially television, on both sides attempts to persuade people to believe that the situation is in fact as the media portrays it. The difference, however, between Israeli and Arab television is that in the Arab media, the absolute truth portrayed is that of the government, whereas in the Israeli media, the absolute truth portrayed is that of the political parties, which are numerous and can freely debate with one another without fear.

The media, as I have already stressed, has an extremely important educational role to play in an individual's upbringing. A person sees things, reads things and above all, observes things that occur around him. When a person is exposed to a more liberal[49] education, they have a greater variety of ideas to choose from and it is up to the person to decide how much this education will affect their life. I feel that at Bates College, for the most part, I received such an education. There was never only one way of looking at things and although professors at times suggested to us to look at something in a certain way, they never forced us to necessarily think like they did. The professors, on their part, believed in us and in our ability to discover new things and learn without restricting ourselves to only one path or solution. The students, using the tools that they were given were not only able, but were actively encouraged to find the way or the answer using their own logic and judgment. This method of education enabled some students to remain more open minded by accepting the fact that there is more than one way of looking at things.

Another kind of education, authoritative education, views the liberty of the students somewhat differently. In this method, students are not encouraged to investigate multiple paths and methods, simply because they are taught to believe that there is only one answer to the questions raised. These restrictions create people with narrow minds, who are not encouraged to develop their own line of thinking and critically investigate a situation. The BBC has aired several programs about North Korean men who were being sent to Russia to become slave laborers. One of the men speaking was a Russian who had studied Qur'anic studies in his university. He was fluent in the Korean language and had visited North Korea numerous times. Although he was also speaking about the poverty in Korea, what struck me the most was what he said about the minds of the Korean people. He said, "I love the Korean people, but I feel so sorry for them. All they know is what their government wants them to know and say. If you ask them anything else, they have no idea what to tell you." Using a metaphor to explain this point and emphasize its importance, I will use a parachute. The first method of education, the liberal one, can be seen as an open parachute which when working well, functions correctly and protects the person from injury and certain death. The second method of education, the authoritative one, is like a parachute that shuts down in mid flight, thus killing the person without leaving any hope for life.

Media in general, but in particular when it is controlled by the state, has many aspects of the authoritative education system. As I have suggested before, the media in the West offers different opinions and interpretations to any given situation. In spite of this fact, even in the West a person who is not educated in a liberal educational system, or who does not bother to look for alternatives or consider other options, will often accept what is being aired as the indisputable truth; not open to interpretation.

The media in most parts of the Arab world is nearly all state controlled and aims at exclusively communicating state policies to the public, without providing people with an alternative. *Al Jazeera*, for example, is a news channel which attempts very much (mostly with success) to keep up a front of being liberal and open minded. In spite of the fact that it does occasionally air people who criticize certain Arab governments and call for change it is still an Arab channel with strong nationalistic views and beliefs. The fact is, most of the Arab world (particularly in countries that strongly oppose Israel) views this channel as portraying the absolute truth which cannot be disputed. Several of the Arab children I interviewed stated that *Al Jazeera* is much more reliable than the Israeli news channels. One girl said to me that according to *Al Jazeera*, hundreds, if not thousands of people were murdered by the Israeli Army in Jenin in the Defensive Shield Mission. She then said, "Then why do the Israeli television stations lie and say that only 50 people died in Jenin?" Even when I said that the claim that hundreds of innocent people had been massacred in Jenin had been proven to be false by the United Nations, she held to her strong belief in *Al Jazeera* and its undisputable coverage of current events.

Is it possible that children in the Middle East will be exposed to more diverse and open-minded ideas and will be able to choose what to believe? Is it possible that children in the Middle East will be encouraged to investigate information they receive in their classrooms and criticize their teachers and, more importantly, their country's policies? Education is something that looks to the future and is not something that can be changed on a whim. When speaking of education and its influence on both children and adults, I am not speaking about something simple which can be changed immediately. It takes a long time for a person to take in new ideas and to change old beliefs which have been engraved in their minds and hearts. An educator is not rewarded as quickly as is a doctor, who almost immediately sees the effects of the medication he had prescribed to a patient. An educator might never see the change within their students, for this is a long process which might take longer than the life span of a human being. In effect, educators invest in the present in order to better the future and they can only hope that they have succeeded in their mission.

If we want any kind of change to happen in the Middle East, we have to immediately find a way of changing the education Jews and Arabs, Israelis and Palestinians receive in their schools and homes. We must provide them with tools so that they can form their own opinions and stay open minded even in the most controversial situations. They must be taught to freely criticize others and also to receive criticism and change themselves when proven wrong. I believe that the Arab side is in much more need of such change because of the fact that most Arab and Muslim countries are non-democratic and their education is mostly authoritative. I also feel very strongly that Israeli Jewish schools should incorporate more classes which teach about the religion, traditions and history of the Arab people. It should encourage Jews to meet with Arabs and listen to their concerns and fears even at a time of political instability. If we begin today, the second and third generations in the future might live a better and more secure life.

Interviews with Adults

Q: How would you assess the relationship between Israeli Jews and Israeli Arabs at the moment, especially following the riots of October 2000?

I will tell you exactly how I feel about the current situation. The relationship at the moment isn't very sympathetic. We have a situation, especially during the last five years, where there's no trust between Jews and Arabs. But I believe that we can all improve the bad relationship, and I will give you an example. In Lod, when you open the door to a house, can you know who is an Arab and who is a Jew? No, you can't distinguish between the two. We all live together. Although the town is surrounded by crime, we live in good neighborly relations. There's no difference between Jew and Arab. Well, I mean, of course the relationship isn't perfect. As a principle things aren't a hundred percent perfect. People do always observe who is a Jew and who is an Arab. In Lod, the population is 60% Jewish and 40% Arab, and people are used to this statistic. If you go to people who are richer, or in simple Hebrew *tzfonim*,[50] or to people who support left wing political parties like Meretz or the Maarach, then they will accept Arabs more. But if you go to Jewish people who support right wing political parties like the Likud, or to the settlers, or generally, to the religious people, then they will not react very nicely to an Arab even if he is a Christian.

I think that especially since the October riots in 2000, the Israeli Jews think that the Arabs all over the world are one people who will never change. They think that all of us think exactly the same about Israel and about the Jewish people. I have heard many Jews say that Arabs will never change their attitude towards the Jews. There is a lot of mistrust on the Jewish side, especially now. But this is not a right and just assumption. I, for example, love and respect some Jewish people very much. So it's not completely true that all of us will not change. If Jews claim this, what they are really saying is that they don't believe in co-existence and I believe that co-existence is a possible thing even if it takes time to establish such a relationship during a time when mistrust dominates everyday life. I know that other Arabs believe this too, and you mustn't forget that on the Jewish side there are also fanatics who might never change their attitude towards Arabs.

We joined the October 2000 riots because we identify with the Palestinian people in the Occupied Territories and because of what the Israeli soldiers are doing there every day. They murder and abuse the people there. Israeli Arabs didn't join the riots because they hate the Jews. Until the thirteen Israeli Arab men were killed by the Israeli police the relationship between Jews and Arabs was okay. But when we saw what was done to our brothers and sisters in the Occupied Territories, we felt their pain and knew we had some kind of a responsibility towards them.

I have to say that in many ways I feel that since October 2000 my friendship with some Jews has become stronger. Maybe it's because we are women and we always have some kind of a connection, but since then, we identify and sympathize with one another and with the pain we are experiencing. Women from both sides are going through a hard time at the moment. Women from both sides have lost their sons, daughters and husbands. We try to look at one another as women, and not as Muslim or Jewish, although it's very hard to do so at times.

Unfortunately, the relationship is very bad at the moment and what I notice the most is that each side is afraid of the other. There is no trust between the two sides. Jews and Arabs refrain from meeting one another and spending time together. It's not like it used to be in the past. In the past, Jews would go to Arab villages to visit their friends or to eat in our restaurants. Arabs used to travel to Jewish towns to shop or even to visit their friends on a *kibbutz*. I am in favor of co-existence, but at the moment it's very hard to believe in such a possibility, maybe even impossible.

A few weeks ago I attended a Sulha. For several days Jews and Arabs met and did all sorts of things together. There were also some Palestinians from the West Bank there. There were all sorts of workshops and sport activities. It was great and people who came there were full of love for each other. People really wanted to get to know the other. From time to time either the Imam or the Rabbi started to pray and everyone, regardless of what religion they were, started to pray as well. No one cared who was leading the prayer and everyone was praying at the same time. It was such a wonderful experience.

Q: Did you discuss any political issues during the Sulha?

No, not at all. No one wanted to speak about politics. People were full of love for each other, not hate.

Q: Do you think that had politics been discussed people would still be full of love for each other?

No, I don't think so. Look, let's say you and I talk about politics. What will we gain? You will continue saying that this is your land and I will continue saying that this is Palestinian land. We will never reach an agreement about these points, right?

Q: Not necessarily. I have been to several conferences where Palestinians, who had never before met Jews and accepted Israel's right to exist, understood that they had to compromise and give up some of their dreams, if they genuinely want peace.

I am very skeptical about these conferences. I can't believe that a Palestinian would compromise on the most important issues such as the Right of Return, for example.

Q: I have seen Palestinians from Gaza give up this right and I have also seen religious Jews compromise. I have seen people from both sides compromise on very important issues, for the sake of peace.

That's interesting. I don't think I have ever seen such a thing happen.

Look, I have to admit that I have tried to detach myself as much as possible from what's going on in Israel and Palestine at the moment. It hurts to hear about suicide bombings and incidents of violence committed by the Israeli Defense Forces in the Occupied Territories. Sometimes I feel like I want to escape from this place and live somewhere else where listening to the news and following the political discourse is not as important. Still, I am a part of the society here, so I can't completely detach myself from everything even if I really want to. I think that if we have peace, we will have a wonderful life here in Israel. We have a wonderful country. It's so beautiful and unique. We have the sea, we have a desert, we have the green Galilee, and we have the *Kinneret*.[51] If things continue like they are now, however, it will be in a way the end of our lives. What will be left for us?

Q: Do you think that each side can forget the hatred and pain with which they have been consumed for the last few decades?

Yes, I think this will eventually be possible, but it might take a very, very long time. I think that even each mother who lost a child to the Israeli-Palestinian conflict can and must say to herself that yes, although she has suffered the most acute pain, she wants to look forward to a hopeful future and not back to a painful past. She will think about saving her remaining sons and daughters from death and suffering and not about losing them in a terrible war.

The situation is not like it used to be a year ago, and this is only because of what is currently happening in the Occupied Territories. We feel that we belong with the Palestinian people because they are our brothers and sisters, and we are really one people that has forcefully been divided into two. The Jews in Israel also view us as Palestinians and not as citizens of Israel. The relationship between Arabs and Jews in Israel is very different than what it used to be in the past. We feel pity for the Palestinians and identify with them. On the other hand, we live in Israel and we have no choice but to respect whatever decisions the Israeli government makes. The conflict will continue for a very long time. I think that it might never end, or at least not in my lifetime.

In the beginning, during the riots, there was a complete separation between the two people, Jews and Arabs. People who used to be a part of groups that wanted to reach a dialogue stopped meeting. Arabs detached themselves from Jews and Jews detached themselves from Arabs. There was a lot of anger and tension felt on both sides because of what happened.

I am a member of a group called "The Open House" which is a part of the Jewish-Arab center in Ramle. My brother is the director of this center. During the riots, it took them a month and a half or even two months to decide to renew the meetings and speak about the situation. People did not feel that they could confront one another and express themselves in an appropriate manner. There was a lot of anger because each side has their reasons and complaints and every side thinks they have it right or that they know it all. Then we finally got together and talked about the social and political situation. People say that meeting one another in such times helps to reduce the tension on both sides. Sometimes I agree with this claim and sometimes I don't. When you meet, you have to open up and communicate with one another and that was extremely hard for Jews and Arabs at that time. It was hard when some of us Arabs were Israelis from Ramle, and others were Israeli Arabs from the Ramallah[52] area. When the Israeli Army bombed Ramallah, one of the women from there conveyed her concern about the occurrence. I was also worried about the people in Ramallah, especially about the children. As I told you, I worked there for several years, and I know many of the Christian people there. I immediately started calling people to see that they were safe. You see, we can't completely separate ourselves from one another. We have to meet and talk and we certainly can't hide things by sweeping them under the carpet. Things happen and the world is a tough place. But I can tell you one thing I noticed about the October events and the Jewish-Arab relationship after them. Israelis weren't very involved in these events. They didn't physically involve themselves by going out and demonstrating against what had happened. They didn't even make a big deal about it in the Israeli news. I didn't see any major interviews with the Arabs about what happened and how they view the events. It is also because of this that the relationship between Jews and Arabs is very cold at the moment. This, however, doesn't mean that hope has been lost on an individual basis. People who believe that things must change and don't lose this hope will never quit their struggle to reach their aim. People who genuinely believe in justice and equality will never give up this fight. Personally, I will never despair of trying to reach peace in this country because the situation is complicated, and it's natural that it is so.

Personally, in practice, I can't feel any significant change in the Jewish-Arab relationship since the riots of October 2000. But you have to remember that I live in a mixed city, so it might be different than in the northern Arab villages. In spite of that, some things have changed. Arabs and Jews don't do things together anymore. Arabs and Jews don't invite one another to their homes anymore. These things are non-existent. The political situation, especially the Israeli-Palestinian conflict, ultimately influences everyone. People aren't generating love towards one another anymore. I think it would be exaggerated to say that they generate hate, but they definitely generate unpleasant feelings. I really mean that people aren't generating love and peace towards one another and there's something dirty and rotten in the middle which ruins everything for everyone.

For me things are still the same. But I have a friend who a month and a half ago told me that she feels afraid for the first time in her life. When I asked her why she was afraid, she said she was afraid that some Jew might throw a stone at her. I told her, "Come on, when did something like this happen here? It won't happen here." Then she apologized to me for thinking such things. I told her that it's her right to think and feel whatever she wants, but that it's important to continue improving the relationship between Jews and Arabs in this country.

I am afraid to go to places where there are a lot of Jews. I am afraid of Jews. And another thing is that it's hard for us to be around Jews when they celebrate their national Independence Day when at the same time the Israeli Defense Force is in Jenin occupying people and killing them. My mother's family is still in Jenin and I don't feel comfortable with all this. It is hard to be sad when I am really so sad and devastated inside me.

The relationship has worsened, there's no doubt. But there's another aspect here, Smadar. For example, you have invited me to come to your house. I know you, and I know that you and your family accept me. But how can I know that your neighbors will accept me if they saw me? How will I know if they want me around the neighborhood? A few years ago, before the Al Aqsa *Intifada* many Jewish people came to the art gallery located in Umm el-Fahem. After October 2000, there was a drastic decrease in the number of Jewish visitors and now hardly any Jews come to visit us. Everyone hears in the news that Umm el-Fahem is a dangerous place, that fanatic religious people dominate the town and that if you go there you might get killed by fanatic Arabs. About a week ago the art gallery, located in the center of Umm el-Fahem, opened and the director of the gallery invited many Jewish people he personally knows to the grand opening ceremony. Many Jews told him that they were too scared to come to Umm el-Fahem at the moment because of the political situation. You know how the media claimed that Umm el-Fahem was harboring terrorists and assisting them in entering Israel and exploding themselves, killing innocent people The gallery's director tried to calm Jews down and explained that there's no danger coming here and that they should not be afraid. At the evening of the gallery's opening, packs of people arrived in organized buses and the entire town of Umm el-Fahem welcomed them. Most of the people were shocked and said that they thought things would be different because of what they see on television, especially on the daily news. So you see, the media does perpetuate some of these feelings of fright and uneasiness which is exactly why Jews and Arabs must meet more. We must see for ourselves that things don't necessarily have to be bad or frightening. The contact, unfortunately, has mostly been broken, but what is left is precious and should be kept. When I speak to you, for example, I think it is your responsibility to tell other Jewish people that not all people in Arara hate Jews and that not all of them are fanatic murderers. You must tell them that you feel safe among us. When you tell me to come to visit you in Jerusalem, I am also afraid. But if I stay here in Arara and don't go anywhere, I am also contributing to the already existing barrier between Jews and Arabs. As an Arab woman, I have a responsibility to go, in spite of the numerous concerns and establish a connection.

To tell you the truth, I don't really feel any change in attitude. Firstly, I speak Hebrew. Maybe my Hebrew isn't perfect, but it sure is good enough. Some people think I am a Jew from Morocco sometimes. I have learned the Jewish mentality and I know it well. Now that I have learned their mentality I know how their head works. I know what's going on. I have a talent when it comes to connecting with people. Even if someone is generating bad feelings towards me, I can eventually change their opinion. This is something God has blessed me with. Secondly, my children attend a mixed school, so they are around Jews all the time. Because they see Jews every day, they know that not all Jews are bad and that not all the Jews hate Arabs. They also know that some Jews help Palestinians and protect their human rights. Let's admit it—some Jews help Palestinians much more than do Arabs and Muslims all over the world.

I am afraid of places where there are orthodox Jews. I felt like this even before the Second *Intifada* started. Do you think I would dare to go to Jerusalem on a Saturday? I won't because I am too scared of what might happen to me. Will I go to Benei Brak[53] on Saturday? No way. It's not even allowed to drive a car on the Sabbath and some orthodox people even throw stones at Jewish people. I can only imagine what they would do to me...

Things changed especially after the Al Aqsa *Intifada* in October. Now when I go to Hadera or to any other place dominated by a Jewish population it's not like it used to be before. Now, people look at me differently, especially because I am wearing a hijjab. People don't treat me well when I walk down the street and sometimes they even yell at me and say horrible things. They publicly yell at me, but when they see that I speak Hebrew and that I am willing to stand up for myself and tell them to shut up, they immediately stop.

I know that many women are afraid to go to Hadera now that the situation between Jews and Arabs has gotten so bad. I am not afraid, but my mother becomes hysterical when I leave the village and go to Jewish towns. She always tells me, "Muna, don't go, there are so many suicide bombings all the time, everywhere. Don't go to Jerusalem. Don't go to Tel Aviv, don't go up North." I think about her a lot when I go, but as for myself, I am not afraid of the Jews.

Q: Do you think that you would be more scared had you been a covered Muslim woman who can easily be detected?

Maybe, but I will never cover, never. In my life I will never do such a thing to myself.

Q: You sound very passionate about this issue. Why is that?

Look, I don't like all this covering thing. Why I hate it so much, I have no idea. Maybe I was born with this hatred. Smadar, you know me, and you know how unconventionally I dress. When I was younger, my mother used to tell me that she didn't like how I dressed. She used to say that I am a woman now and not a small girl like I once used to be. This is why I would like to photograph myself all dressed in black clothes as I am coming out of the sea. And on the black clothes I want to splash red spots which look like and symbolize blood. This is my protest and it symbolizes how I feel about the issue of women's clothes in the Arab society. I don't have a lot of friends who cover because I can't usually connect with such women. I paint on my home's roof and I know that what I paint is considered to be sinful by most of the people living in my village. They always tell me that according to Islam and to our traditions, it's not allowed for one to expose their body in public and here I am drawing pictures of myself nude. I always knew that I was different than most of the Muslim girls in my village and in the Muslim world, but I'm happy the way I am and I am not going to change. I think the society needs to change and not I.

Q: What problem, if at all, do you see in how religion prevails in Israel today? And in some religious people?

I really don't associate with many religious people, no matter what religion they come from. I don't know, I don't like them and I don't want to be like them. The think there is only one way and answer for every given situation in life. It's nearly impossible to argue with religious Muslim people, for example. I just don't want to associate with them if I don't absolutely have to.

Q: Do you think that religion and religious people have had a bad impact on the political situation in Israel and Palestine?

What influence they exactly have I don't know and I can't really say. But it's obvious when you really try to assess the situation that the suicide bombings on the one hand, and the illegal Jewish settlements in the Occupied Territories on the other hand are all encouraged by religious people, or people who call themselves religious. They all think that their religion supports their actions and the ideas they have come from their holy texts and oral traditions. I think that the problem is not in the religion itself, but in the people who mingle with it and change its true meaning. I really don't know a lot about religion, but I am sure that the religions themselves do not call for the doing of these terrible things on both sides. If religions were aimed at doing such terrible things, why would God have even bothered to give us three religions?

Q: Do you think, like most Muslims do, that Islam is the only true religion and that Jewish and Christian texts were manipulated by Jews and Christians?

To say such a thing is arrogant. I don't believe in Islam the way most Muslims do. I told you before that I am not religious and that Islam doesn't mean much to me. But as to your question, no, I don't believe Islam is better or more authentic than any of the other two religions, Judaism and Christianity. People who believe and claim that other people forged their texts are following Islamic teachings blindly and not questioning. How would Muslims feel if a Christian, for example, said to them that Islam is a big lie and that the Qur'an is a fake text which is stupid and unworthy, or that a bunch of men sat one day and wrote the whole thing? I don't think most Muslims would like it, would they? So why do Muslims allow themselves to claim that everything, except their religion, is fake? People should start thinking in a more humane way, which is less judgmental and exclusive. Maybe then the world would really be a better place.

Look, to tell you the truth, for me nothing has changed. The Jewish friends I had before are still my friends. They haven't changed their opinion about me and we've stayed on good terms. I go everywhere and no one harms me or looks at me in a bad or suspicious way. This here is my restaurant [we are sitting in it] and my partners are Jewish. We work together. I don't have any complaints against anyone. If a person is good I love and respect him. And if a person doesn't like me because of who I am, I just keep my distance from him. I am not looking for any trouble whatsoever. Although it is true that the general relationship between Jews and Arabs has changed for the worse, we have to look at the good and not at the bad side of this situation. For example, if a Jew says something nasty to me, I just ignore him, do you understand? Of course there are bad people on both sides, but there are also good people on both sides, and we can't ignore this. Smadar, there are many good people on both sides and the future of this region depends on them. People on both sides who incite hate should not determine how our region looks.

Of course I can see a change in attitude. Wherever we Arabs go in Israel, I can see the extremism Jews have developed against us. A few months ago I went to visit a relative in one of the hospitals in Jerusalem. It happened to be the same night that the *Versaille Tragedy* happened.[54] The hospital said that only people who were injured in this incident would be admitted. However, many Jews who weren't injured and had no connection to the tragedy were admitted. Because we're Arabs, they didn't let us in. We waited and waited for several hours and begged to be let in, but the guards ignored our request. We didn't come to play around there or have a good time. We came to visit a sick person and they wouldn't let us in. In the end he told us to go home and we didn't see our relative.

I feel discriminated against in the bus sometimes. It's there that you feel the attitude Jews have towards you as an Arab. In the bus, I don't like speaking Arabic because if I start speaking Arabic everyone looks at me and I can feel the mistrust and suspicion they feel. They probably start shaking because they think that the entire bus will be blown up in a few seconds. Because I am of fair complexion, many people ask me whether I am Russian. When I say that I am not Russian but Arab they immediately change their attitude towards me and patronize me. They completely change.

Q: You have probably noticed that after suicide bombings some Jews go out to the streets and yell, "Death to the Arabs!" How does this make you feel?

Well, what can I say? I know for sure that this is not a majority. There will always be some people who will hate the Arabs and say such things. These extremists exist everywhere in the world and not only in Israel. Just like there are Palestinian terrorists, there are Jewish terrorists.

Many Israelis, especially right wing people and religious people, see the Arabs this way. A while ago, someone told me, and I am quoting him, "You are guests in this country! You are permanent guests here." I don't know exactly what he meant by "permanent guests," but that's exactly what he said to me. He said, "You are a permanent guest," can you believe this? A permanent guest! Ha! I didn't get too excited by his words. He can say and think whatever he wants. People should not get so excited when other people say such stupid and senseless things. Some people shout, "Death to the Arabs" and it's obvious that people like that are stupid, and that they have no idea what's going on in this country. These people are what I call "certified stupid people."

Q: Do you think that the Israeli left is leaning more towards the right now?

Yes. Look, the fact that Sharon is in power now is enough of an example as to how the right is taking over. And as to the large number of people who identify with these right-wing political groups, it just proves what is going on in Israel at the moment. I agree that this is the situation and I will even say that at the moment the left is nearly non-existent in Israel.

Q: It seems, however, that the more terror Israelis experiences, the more they support Sharon and his tough anti-terrorism policies. Maybe if there were no terror less people would support him and his policies?

No, the Jews never liked the fact that there are Arabs on this land too because when they come here in 1948 they hoped to take all the land for themselves. The fact that they do not like us or that they discriminate against us is not related at all to the fact that Israelis are currently experiencing terror in their cities.

Q: Do you have any criticism of the current Israeli government?

I hate Sharon. His past shows in a very good way who he is. I can't understand how the Jewish people chose him. I mean, if the Jewish people chose Sharon, then obviously they want war. Had they genuinely wanted peace, they wouldn't have chosen him. He hates the Arabs, not only the Arabs here in Palestine, but all the Arabs in the Middle East and in the world. How can Arab countries make peace with Israel while Sharon is in power? Would the Jews have made peace with Germany had Hitler been in the German government after the war was over? I don't think so, right?

Q: Why do you think Sharon was elected?

People thought that he would bring security to this part of the world. You know, there were many suicide bombings at that time. But we can all clearly see that this was a false assumption. Look at all that is happening. Sharon has done the complete opposite. Instead of bringing peace, he started war all over again. And he started this war the moment he entered our Al Aqsa mosque. What, did he think we'd sit quietly while he walks into our mosque and contaminates it?

Q: Do you think that if the Jewish people chose Sharon it says that they think like him and do not want peace?

Yes, but it's not the majority, don't you think? Well yes, I guess the majority did choose him, but many also chose Barak.[55] I think that more than 40% chose Barak. In any case, I would like to believe that there are still many people in Israel who don't support Sharon and his hateful policies.

Q: So you are clearly disappointed that Sharon was elected, aren't you?

In the beginning, I was very disappointed. Now I am a bit less disappointed because I expected him to do much more harm than he actually did. In a way, he wasn't as bad as we thought he would be. But he hates Arabs, and that has never changed and never will. This is why I still think that while Sharon is the Israeli Prime-Minister there will not be peace. Just like the Israelis say that Arafat will not make peace, we believe that Sharon won't.

Q: How would you define yourself? If someone were to come up to you and ask, "Who are you?" what would you reply?

In terms of how I feel, I am a Muslim Arab who is a part of the Arab world. That's the first thing I can tell you about myself. Being a Muslim and an Arab is the most important thing for me and for my family. Then there's the part in me which is Palestinian. The Palestinians are our brothers and sisters and they are really a part of us. Together with this, however, I have Jewish friends here in Israel to whom I am closer than my Arab friends. Whoever treats me with respect, will get respect back from me. I will then love the person.

Q: Do you think that Israeli Arabs, who are mostly Muslim, identify with the Palestinians, who are also mostly Muslim because of their common religion—Islam?

No.

Q: So you don't think that some of the reasons why Israeli Arabs support the Palestinians are because they are Muslim?

Yes, I do agree with that. I thought your question was asking whether Islam calls for these violent actions, to which my answer would be "no." But yes, I think that Israeli Arabs were definitely identifying with the Palestinians and protecting the holy Muslim sites. We are all Muslims and we all believe in Allah. We have to stand together against those who want to harm or destroy our holy places.

Q: What are the main feelings you think that Jews and Arabs have towards one another?

It's a deep feeling of hate for one another. It's terrible. This is all I can say.

I think that if all the Jews were honest, they would all tell you that in their opinion life would be better without us around. Arabs would say the same things about the Jews. You think we want you around us?

You know, it's very sad to live in a place where everyone is afraid of one another. Is this life? I mean, think about it. There is hardly a person in Israel or in Palestine who can safely walk down a street. You walk down the street and you always wonder what is going to happen. You get on a bus and you wonder whether you'll get out alive. And if you're Palestinian, you wonder whether someone will come and wreck your house and whether you will have enough food for your family. So, is this the life we all want to live? Is this what our children will experience? I think that the worse thing is to live in fear. I can't think about something more terrible and sometimes I feel that if this is the way we are doomed to live, then I really don't want to have children and have them go through the same thing.

Q: Do you have Jewish friends?

Yes, and some of them still visit me here. I have one friend whom I see every day. Some friends stopped coming.

Jewish friends? No, not interested to have Jewish friends at the moment. We can't visit one another anyway, so why make an effort?

I have many Jewish women friends whom I live and respect, and I know they feel the same about me. The people I work with treat me very well too. Sometimes I feel that really, if only we didn't have this political situation and these political problems, or the leaders that we have who lead us into war, we could live very well together. We could love one another.

I have Jewish friends, but it's not the same now. Before the suicide bombings began, it was easier to have Jewish friends. But now it's different because after a suicide bombing things change a lot. Although my Jewish friends do not usually talk about a suicide bombing around me, I still know that they think deep inside their heads and hearts. Sometimes they'll talk about a suicide bombing a week after it happens, so that I don't think they are blaming me. But regardless of what they say or don't say, I know very well what they are thinking in their heads and feeling in their hearts. What I can tell you is that it's not the same now. Jews and Arabs just don't mingle freely like they might have done two years ago. That's why I was surprised when I saw you for the first time in the bus station and I heard you speak about your project on the phone. I immediately wanted to offer to help you with it, but I wasn't sure whether you would want me to...with everything that's going on between Jews and Arabs, you know. It's amazing that things like this can still be done even with all the killing and the terror and the fright going on all around us.

No, I don't have any Jewish friends. How can you have friends if you are afraid to visit them, they are afraid to visit you and they are also terrified of inviting you to their home? What, will we just talk on the phone everyday? If we don't trust the Jews and they don't trust us, how do you expect us to maintain a friendship? It's impossible at the moment and look, even my son doesn't want to have Jewish friends now. How will he play with a boy who will soon become a soldier in the Israeli army? That Jewish boy might kill his aunt in Jenin a year or two from now. How will he play with people whose fathers might be in the Israeli Army, killing innocent Palestinian children and women and then laughing about it?

Q: With all the love and respect you have for your Jewish friends and for other Jews, are there moments of tension when you are not sure whether your relationship is true or whether it will survive?

When there's a suicide bombing, I sometimes think about this. I mean, although many people don't say anything to me specifically, I can feel what they think about me. Although we don't speak about the political situation very much, we can see and we can feel. I can see in their eyes that they are afraid of me, even though they know that Abu Ghosh is a friendly Arab village. The Jews see all the Arabs the same when there's a suicide bombing. There is no good Arab and bad Arab, only bad Arabs.

Q: And when the attack comes from the Jewish side, like in the case of Goldstein, what is the atmosphere then? Do you then view all Jews as one unit responsible for the killing of your people?

Yes. And those moments of tension are stronger and more penetrating than the moments of love and respect. This is the tragedy.

Q: So what you are saying is that after a suicide bombing you are the "other side" for most Jews? Thus, you are then seen exclusively as an Arab?

Yes, then I am seen as an Arab and not as an Israeli. This is what's so terrible about the whole thing, Smadar, but it's exactly how I feel.

Q: Is this something that other members of your family or other people you know feel?

Everyone feels like this. I mean I don't want to speak in the name of other people, but I really feel that most of the people in Abu Ghosh feel this way. It is hard for us as Arabs living in Israel to also feel Israeli when Jewish Israelis occupy the West Bank and Gaza. If someone asked me where I was from and I said I was from Israel, they might think that I am one of those people who are committing horrific crimes against the Palestinians.

Q: Can you give me specific examples of how the way some Jews have treated you lately has changed? Can you point at certain instances when you felt discriminated against?

A while ago I was in Tiberias[56] and I was standing in line to buy ice cream for my children. Suddenly a Jewish woman started yelling at me in front of everyone, "Hey you! Go to the end of the line!" Why was she yelling at me even though everyone was pushing? Why did she focus on my when at least ten other women were trying to get to the top of the line? Because I am Arab and because I wear *hijjab*. She could immediately single me out as an Arab and she would rather yell at me than at a Jew. I asked her in Hebrew why she was yelling at me and she calmed down a bit, but it was a really painful experience for me. Not all the Jews are like this, however. There are hundreds of good people everywhere. But unfortunately, many people in Israel are like this at the moment. The relationship has really drastically worsened.

The attitude has definitely changed. Let me give you some examples about this business. I have a cook's certificate. I learned how to cook in a school and I even have a certificate. The teacher in the cooking school had an attendance list and he'd check attendance every day. One day I saw that next to my name Saleh Isa it said "Arab." I thought it said that so that the teacher would know that there's an Arab in class and that he shouldn't say anything bad about Arabs. This exact thing happened to me another time, many years ago. When I was a child I grew up with Jews. I used to go to the Gadna.[57] There they also had an attendance list and again, I saw that after my name, in brackets, it said "Arab." What can I do about these things? Nothing. So I just laugh about the whole thing and continue living.

Personally, no one has said anything offensive to me since the relationship between Jews and Arabs has worsened, but let me tell you something about my mother. My mother used to cover in traditional Palestinian Muslim clothes, so she could easily be detected as an Arab. One day we were returning to our car which was parked in a big parking lot near a highschool. Suddenly, the students who saw my mother started yelling, "Arab! Arab!" and continued to shout and throw stones at us and at our car. My mother was hurt by a stone and injured. Thank God she was only lightly injured and did not have to go to the hospital. The man who owned the parking lot said he would call the police, but he didn't. My mother and father initially wanted to involve the police, but they knew that the police wouldn't take them seriously, so they gave up that idea.

My husband was much older than I am. One day I called for an ambulance because he was having some kind of an attack. I waited and waited for the ambulance to come but I then found out that the hospital didn't send one. When I asked them why they refused to send me an ambulance, they said that it was too dangerous to come to Umm el-Fahem. Can you believe this?

Look, I told you that I am a relaxed person and that I see all these things as something that comes and goes. Why? From generation to generation people's thinking changes. If you look at our society, you'll see that it's composed of three main parts: Arabs, Jews and beginning in the eighties, Russians and Ethiopians. So the way our society looks always changes. These things change with time. Eventually both Arabs and Jews will understand that they have no choice but to live together or at least one next to the other. The way people think will inevitably change will change because they will realize that there isn't any other option. My son and daughter don't think as I do. I think they are more extreme than I am.

I remember when Matan Vilanai came to Ramle. He wanted to be elected for the position of *Keren Ramle LeBituach*, so he summoned me and several other of Ramle's patrons and started listening to us. It was the first time I was able to speak openly with an Israeli representative and tell them exactly what I think Ramle needs. Next to my church, for example, there wasn't any road for over fifty years. At one point it was nearly impossible to even reach the church safely. I still remember saying to Mr. Vilnai, "Come and see this so called road next to my church. Then tell me whether my demand is exaggerated." I really believed that we were entitled to a new and safer road. I remember once even being fined for putting three or four pieces of wood in our cemetery because the city hall believed them to be hazardous. But when you look out the window, what you see is piles of trash and my question is: when will the city come and take it away? I asked Mr. Vilnai when the trash would be finally taken away. So you see how it is? They don't do their job and I had to pay a fine for three pieces of wood laying around. Mr. Vilnai came and looked at the road and today there's a real paved road near our church. For God's sake, it's not so expensive to pave this kind of road and you see how many years it took to pave it? There are many promises given to the Arab sector, even promises of projects which might cost five million dollars. But who knows whether these promises will ever turn into a reality. I think that in Israel, we have to have an affirmative action plan for Arabs and for other minorities. Maybe then Jews and Arabs will really be equal, at least in terms of the opportunities available to them. And in addition to this, people have to confess their mistakes. In our church people confess on a daily basis. This is not an act of weakness, but rather of strength and courage. Unfortunately, however, in politics things are very different. If you confess to making mistakes, it's as though you are weak, or to be blamed for something. On both sides it's this way: if you compromise or make concessions, you are looked at as weak. This is how it is in the Middle East. People cannot show that they are week, even if they are not weak at all. So, this naturally creates a situation where leaders from both sides aren't willing to confess their wrong doings and make necessary changes. Each of us has to go through a process of reconciliation, first within ourselves, and then with our neighbors. Reconciliation and sacrifice mean that you are willing to ignore the political situation and help another person because he or she is a human being. Although there are some people on both sides who are doing this, this important process is generally lacking on both sides and that's a tragedy. Christian Arabs also experience a serious identity crisis. People look at me and say something bad about me being a Christian and an Arab. Then I sometimes feel that I don't want to be an Arab at all. Then there are Jews who view my being an Arab in a bad way and then I want to be an Arab on purpose. So, a Jewish person, for example, would like to ignore my nationality because I am a Christian. On the one hand they are taking away from us our nationality and on the other hand our religion. Can you see how I and other Arab Christians are torn sometimes?

Of course there is discrimination [against Arabs] in Israel. I can see this everywhere. I can see it in the quality of the roads in Arab towns and villages, or in the amount of money Arabs get from the social security system. We are angry, but we keep the anger inside because we don't have the energy to speak out. If we said something they [the Jews] would tell us, "You are always complaining because you are Arabs." So we don't say anything at all and our problem becomes like that of the African American people, where every time a black person complains about social injustice and discrimination, other people say that he's complaining because he is black. So, in the end, people shut up and do not dare to say a thing. We, Israeli Arabs, do not want to misuse our "Arabness" to an extent where people will think we're complaining just because we're Arabs. Some Arabs have good roads, and some Arabs live with the Jews. Where I live, for example, it's very clean. But there are places where only Arabs live and those places are not clean at all. If you an Arab living together with the Jews, you enjoy a higher standard of living, not because you are an Arab or a Christian, but because you are living in a Jewish neighborhood. I have been blessed to have everything, but that doesn't mean that I have to keep quiet and forget those who are not enjoying all the rights they are entitled to as citizens of this country. I base my morals of reconciliation and peace on the New Testament. These are morals of giving something without anyone asking you to. Here the government takes taxes from Arabs, but doesn't provide them with electricity sometimes and I have seen this in my own eyes. Maybe you know this verse, "Give to Caesar what is Caesar's, and to God what to God's." I don't want to get too deeply into politics and religion, but at least if Caesar asks me for something, he should give me something in return. That's all that I ask.

To tell you the truth, according to what I can see, the government wants to give most Israeli Arabs more rights. But as always, when you want to bring a person to drink from a well, things go wrong on the way there. The government changes, the executive director changes, and even if there's a court order to do something, it gets postponed and sometimes forgotten.

There's discrimination everywhere and in everything.

Q: But where exactly? Can you give me a specific example?

Yes, of course. The discrimination can especially be found in the Arab schools and in the amount of money allocated to Arab villages and towns. For example, my village is a part of the Harei Yehuda [Judean Hills] municipality. If I take you to some of our neighboring Jewish villages such as Givaat Yearim, or any other place, you will see the obvious difference in the quality of the roads and the buildings. I used to be a member of a committee which decides how much money to allocate to each and every village. The fact is that my village gets a third of what a Jewish village or town gets, and this happens without any reason. There was a Jewish *Moshav* with about six hundred people living in it. It got a yearly budget of

5,000,000 shekels. Our village is a bit bigger than this *Moshav*, but it only received 700,000 shekels. And notice that we have nearly the same number of people living in both places. We pay all the taxes Jewish people pay, but our villages receive less money from the Israeli government. And what can we do about this? Nothing!

Q: Don't you get angry about this discrimination sometimes?

What can I do? Let's say I got angry, what would that help me? Is there something I can do about the situation? No. Then why get excited?

My son, for example, found a job with the Ministry of Education in Jerusalem. He went there and registered for the job. Next day he went there and they asked for his identification card. When they saw he was Arab they said, "We don't want any Arabs here." At the time, the head of the Ministry of Education was Yossi Sarid. I wanted to call him and complain about this incident, but then decided not to because I am very fond of him, and I didn't want to cause any trouble. My son was very angry and very upset, but what can we do? We can't do anything, so we have to shut up and remain silent. We have to think about the future. But you know what really makes me angry? That I live here, and I don't have any hate towards the state of Israel, but then from time to time I get slapped in the face. I have never done anything bad to the state and I have never even said anything bad about it. But yet from time to time, the state reminds me that I am different, not a regular citizen. They remind you that because you are Arab you are not equal. But then I think, "Hey mister, I live in the same state as you!"

When it comes to getting a job here in Israel, an Arab is definitely second hand material. A few years ago near the entrance to Jerusalem where the Ministry of Foreign Affairs is located they were looking for a cook. I was a hundred percent sure that I would not get that job, but still I went because I wanted to see what would happen. I went there. Shalom, Shalom, they received me very nicely. They asked me where I was from and I said from Ein Rafa.[58] They asked where that was and I said it was near Abu Gosh. When they heard this they immediately told me to leave the premises. They said that they are not even allowed to let me into the building. You see, even if I were killed I would never do anything against Israel. So when you live here and see that people don't trust you, it hurts. Sometimes I get angry, but it passes.

Oh there are many things I could point to. There are many moments when I felt discriminated against, but believe me I have forgotten them all. To tell you the truth, I don't tend to keep anger inside. I was created to laugh, and I just can't hate anyone. And besides, even if I were angry about being discriminated against by Jews, who would listen to me or help me anyway?

Q: How do you deal with the fact that sometimes you do not feel a part of Israeli society, or that sometimes Jews do not treat you as such?

Look, I just shut up and remain silent. What else can I do? I have no option but to remain silent. The Arab leadership isn't doing anything to change things either. Instead of taking care of our village, they spent most of their time and money on feuds and things like that. And you know what? How many Arab parties exist here? Maybe three or four, I am not absolutely sure. I have never voted for them, and I never will. They are not for me and don't represent me at all because all they care about is themselves and the 20,000 Shekels they earn each month. These things don't interest me whatsoever. What does interest me is looking forward into the future. I want my children to live a better life than I did.

Q: Are you satisfied with your son's educational facilities?

The facilities are definitely neglected, but what can I do? My children studied here in the village first and then they went to Abu Ghosh. In Abu Ghosh the education is below any acceptable limit and the students' behavior is too. There was so much violence there that I was really afraid for my kids, especially for my daughter. I wanted my children to go to Beit Tzafafa[59], but I didn't have enough money to pay for their daily transportation there. What can I say? I hope that things will get better for everyone soon. Whatever happens, I laugh, that's the best way.

Q: Do you laugh even when you see on television some Jews shouting, "Kahana[60] was right!"?

I don't pay any attention to those people. It's too bad that so many people pay so much attention to such stupid things. It's just as if someone would say that that old man from Gaza, I can't remember his name, should be released, or that what he says is right. What's his name...that paralyzed man from Gaza?

Q: Do you mean Ahmed Yassin?

Yes, him. It's just like when Palestinians say that he is right. So what? Will I pay attention to people speaking about a senile, stupid, insane prisoner? Of course not. So, what I'm telling you is that we have to make a *sulha*[61] between Jews and Arabs in this country. And if we don't, then we all deserve to be thrown off this land. We have to learn to live together, to respect one another and maybe in the end even love one another. We have no other option. If my son were to fall in love with a Jewish woman and brought her home, I wouldn't object to it because I don't hate Jews. When I see you, my heart is smiling, and don't I love your father too? He was so good to me. One day, late at night when I was working in the Neve Ilan swimming pool, I felt that something wasn't right, and I called your father. He immediately came and helped me. So, what can I say? Only that I hope that things will be okay and that the hate between Jews and Arabs will subside. Maybe the smile will return to people from both sides. But I will tell you one thing—I have never been hurt by a Jew and I will never hurt a Jew.

Q: Especially covered women, but also other people, have told me that after there's a suicide bombing, they are afraid to leave their homes and be seen on the streets. They said that they are afraid to be beaten by Jews. Do you feel the same? Have you had any bad experiences?

I know that after suicide bombings some Arabs are beaten by a raging mob.

Q: Does this scare you?

Look, twelve or thirteen years ago there was a terrorist shooting in King George Street in Jerusalem. I couldn't see the man who was shooting, but I escaped to where *Biqqur Holim*[62] was at that time. People were running and it was quite chaotic—no one knew what to do. I knew that it would take people, who were all in shock, half an hour or so to relax and stop shouting, "Death to the Arabs" and other things. Yes, it's true that in the beginning when there were bombings, some Arabs were beaten because there were no police forces around to protect them. Now things have changed because the police are well prepared for such incidents. But you know what? In these situations, your fate is God's will. I used to work with a man in the Jerusalem Municipality, and one day he was killed in a suicide bombing. That was it, he never returned to his job. It's all fate from God.

Q: Do you think that Israeli Arabs should take to the streets and fight for their rights?

No, I don't want that. The rights I have are enough for me. I will never become a prime minister or someone important in the government. What I have now is enough for me.

Q: Do you believe that equal rights for Arabs in Israel is a feasible thing?

No, no one will get equal rights at the moment. Maybe in the future, after many generations have passed things will get better for Arabs in Israel. Let me tell you, things were very different during Rabin's time. At that time, Ora Namir[63] made many reforms. She increased the social security funds for children. Before that, Jews used to receive more money than Arabs. When Rabin was alive everyone thought that things would get better. But then someone came and killed him and with him killed many other innocent Israelis and Palestinians. Hopefully things will get better again. We have to live with what we have. What can we do? Who can we go against? Here in Israel there are people from everywhere. There are people from Europe, from Morocco and from Yemen. Some people are good and some people are bad. We should hope and pray that the good will overcome the bad.

Q: If you had only one wish, what would you wish for? What kind of country would you want to live in?

I want to live here, and only here. I will never leave this beautiful area. I have always said that this area, from Neve Ilan to Tzoba[64] is the most beautiful part of Israel. Even if someone gave me a lot of money and lands somewhere else, I would never leave. I was born here, I was raised here, and I love this place. I also love our neighbors in Neve Ilan, Kiryat Anavim, and all around. We have a good relationship.

Q: Even though they get more than you do?

Yes, even though. I don't care. Let them have more. What does it matter if one person has a million dollars and another man has only a few shekels? The most important thing is to live because in the end everyone dies and we cannot take things with us then.

Our village was established in 1920. The village was where *Kibbutz Tzoba* is today. As you know, in 1948 there was a war and many people left or escaped to Jordan or to the West Bank. We stayed because we had some lands down the hill and did not want to leave. After the war, we once again returned to our hill and hoped to settle down and start our life once again. At that time we didn't even have a road leading to the village. My parents and grandparents walked down the hill with whatever belongings they had and came to where Ein Rafa is today. Several days later the police came and asked us, "What are you doing here?" We said that we didn't escape but decided to stay on our land. They told us they would decide what to do with us. They said that they would decide whether to let us stay or whether they would throw us across the border.

Q: So you actually lived where there is a Jewish *Kibbutz* now?

Exactly. Where Kibbutz Tzoba is now is where we used to own lands. The Israelis took about 50 dunam from us when they came in 1948.

Q: Why were the lands taken from you?

They [the Jews] took our lands without any reason, just as if someone had decided to take your house from you now, do you understand? We didn't go against the state, we didn't even fight against the state and we certainly didn't cause any harm to it. On the contrary, when my father and grandfather heard that Jewish immigrants were about to come to Palestine, he didn't object at all. During the war, we did not fight against Israel. We just stayed here waiting for the war to end so that we could finally return to no our normal lives.

Q: So when exactly was the land taken from you?

It was either in 1944 or in 1945.

Q: And you did not physically object to the taking of the land by the Jews?

What could we do? We were a small village and they could do whatever they wanted to us. They could have even thrown us across the border had they wanted to. When the Ottomans were here, they let us keep our lands. When the Jews came, they either took the lands from us forcefully, or paid us a small amount like 200 Shekels per dunam [four dunam are approximately one acre]which is much less than the land's worth. It's a ridiculous amount of money, don't you think? So, we refused to sell the lands. Some of the land is still registered under our names and, therefore, belongs to us. We don't have any access to it, however.

Q: Has most of the land been built on?

It's mostly agricultural land at the moment. A lot of land was taken from us, and the village as a whole was given only 600 dunam instead of the 3000 dunam we initially had before being relocated. So, as you can see, our village was drastically reduced in size, even though we have always had peaceful relations with the Israeli government and with the Jews in general. After the war in 1948, we started to work with the Israeli government, received Israeli identification cards and passports and became Israeli citizens. You have to remember that we were here for many generations before the establishment of the State of Israel in 1948. My grandfather and his great grandfather lived here, you see? Look, my great grandfather was born here, so imagine all the generations which lived here before Israel came into existence and before I was born. And you know how it used to be here before, when the land wasn't as developed as it is today. People settled where there was water and they didn't care about anything else. Life was very simple then and people lived on whatever vegetables and other kinds of food they could grow in their gardens. In the summer, people would work very hard, and then in the winter people would sit together in the house and not do too much. If you have time on Shabbat Smadar, I will show you a house which is at least 120 years old. It proves the history of our village and that we were here for many years. There are some houses in Abu Ghosh, the village next to ours, which are 700 years old, did you know?

Q: Have you ever tried to reclaim your lands?

Yes, we tried to do this but in vain. We even agreed to get compensated instead of actually getting our lands back. They offered to give us a miserable amount of money for the lands. For land which was worth at least $50,000 we were offered 200 shekels, so what can we do? They are laughing at us, so the best thing to do is do not do anything about it, because there's nothing we can do.

Q: Do you know of people in your village who are more resentful towards the Jews and feel more strongly about this issue?

I think that most people feel and think like I do. We have all grown up here and have received a sort of *kibbutz*-like upbringing. When there are parties and weddings in the neighboring Jewish villages, you'll see half of our village there too.

Q: So you and your sons have Jewish friends?

Of course we do.

Q: Even now with the political situation being so bad?

Of course. You should see what goes on here on Shabbat when all the Jews come to restaurants in Abu Ghosh. The place is full of Jews because they don't feel that we hate them. And I'll tell you something else. If Jews stop coming here, it's us Arabs who will lose, not the Jews. It's always good to work with Jews and trade with them. It's us Arabs who lose from a frozen relationship, not the Jews. We need them, but they don't need us.

Q: So in a way, you let people step on you all the time, don't you think?

Well, I guess that's kind of right. That's how I am. When I worked in Neve Ilan, one of the Jewish workers always told me that I was too naïve and gullible and that I give too much. What can I do about this? I never wanted to fight. When someone wants something from my shop, let's say it costs five shekels and the person only has four shekels, I will give it to him for four shekels.

Q: Are your sons the same as you?

They are more or less although I have to say that they are not as laid back about the whole thing as I am. Generally, however, they are like me. We don't want to fight. We have many problems in this country. These problems won't go away or disappear in the near future. If we reeducate our children and speak in favor of peace on the radio and on television, maybe things will change for the better. We can't stay like this for a long time. Do you know who does all the hard labor in this country? The Arabs. The Jews don't like to do hard work. So, will we refuse to work together and cooperate? We have to work together.

Q: Doesn't it bother you that some Jews say, "Hey, he's an Arab, let him do the hard work!"?

Look, one has to live, don't you think? What will I say? That I am not willing to do these jobs? Who will pay for my phone bill, for my electricity and food? If I don't work, I won't get all these things for free, will I?

Q: So you just accept the status quo?

Yes, I have accepted how things are a long time ago.

Q: Does your wife feel the same?

Well, you know how women are. They are less politically oriented. They don't care about these things like men do. My wife works here near the mall in Mevasseret[65] and she loves her job. As I have said before some Jews are good and some Jews are bad, like in any other place in the world. What can we do against those who don't like us? We can just earn a living for our children and we have to think about the future, and not about the past.

[The interviewee then saw the *hennah*[66] on my hands. The roles were reversed and now my interviewee started asking me questions]

Q: So, where's the *henna* from?

It's from an engagement party in Arara.

Q: I hate hennah and all these traditional things. Don't you feel like washing it off your hands? So tell me, Smadar, are they angry there in Arara?

Yes, they are very angry, as a matter of fact.

Q: Well, I am not angry at all, believe me. There's nothing to be angry at.

Do you know that during the October riots, some of the local population in Arara blocked several roads?

Q: Yes, I know, and I don't agree with that at all. What, should I go out and demonstrate and get myself killed?

Many of the people in Arara believe that it's at times important to rebel and show that they will not just give up.

Look, in 1948 when the State of Israel was established, the Arabs had their chance to unite and come together with the Jews. They should have realized that things would be better for them this way. It's also the fault of the Jews, because from the very beginning they looked down on the Arabs who were living here. Let me tell you something. Just before 1967, maybe it was in 1965, several 17 year-old boys came to our village. They came in order to learn Arabic and to then become spies in Arab countries. We were told not to speak even one word of Hebrew with them, so that they would learn Arabic as soon as possible. We didn't feel any hate towards them and sometimes even the Shabak[67] came to our village.

[I continued asking the questions now]

Q: How would you define yourself?

I am Israeli. I am Israeli, and nothing can be done about it. I am Israeli, and I am here. I am with the Jews. If suddenly, God forbid, a war will break out between Israel and an Arab country, I am with Israel. I have never done anything against the state, and from the time things became hard, I decided on which side I would be. Even if we had a serious war with Palestine, I would be on Israel's side. I think that many Arabs here in Israel are against Israel because they are unemployed. But with God's help, things will get better. You never know. People in this region can build and destroy. It's hard to build, and it's easy to destroy. Hopefully we'll all chose to build.

Q: Do you have family in either the Gaza Strip or in Jordan?

In the Gaza Strip I don't and we do not have any connection to that place, but in Jordan I have two aunts. You see, beginning in 1945, people here were afraid that the Jews would kill them, so they escaped. My family mostly stayed and today thanks to Allah, the village has about 600 or 700 people in it. With the Help of God, it will grow more. [The same day there was a big demonstration related to the Israeli-Palestinian conflict in East Jerusalem. Israelis, Palestinians and several foreign human rights organizations were about to attend it. The interviewee learned that I was about to go to East Jerusalem to cover this demonstration. He urged me not to go, saying that the Palestinians were still not ready for their own state. He also said that it is a waste of time to attend such a demonstration because until the Palestinians stop their terror there will be no peace anyway. "Why would you danger yourself for something so senseless?" he asked. He repeated this question a few times while we were talking]

Look, a month ago some women police officers asked for my identification card. I gave it to them. Two days later, they asked for it again. I told one of them that I worked here every day and I asked her whether they would ask for my I.D. card every day. She said, "I am doing my job and don't talk too much!" I swear that she said that to me, but I remained silent. I didn't say anything because I was afraid she'd call the police forces and complain about me and maybe even say that I said bad things to her. So, in the case of women, I believe we have to keep a low profile because otherwise they will squash us and we'll pay a high price. It's better to just remain silent. Let me tell you something. One day when I was driving my car on the way to Ramot there was a checkpoint. Next to the checkpoint there was a border patrol jeep. They asked me where I was from and I said I was from Ein Rafa. They told me to pull over and wait. I waited for half an hour. No one came to me or said anything, so after half an hour, I got out of the car and asked them to let me continue if they didn't want to ask me anything. One of them said to me, "Get back in the car immediately before we come and beat you." You see the nerve they have? They have no shame. This is something that hurts me because if it were a Jewish man who had gotten out of the car and faced them, they wouldn't have said anything to him. But what can we do? We have to just let it all pass.

Jews are like the owners of this land. Jews can bring their families from all over the world to live in Israel and we can't. My sister is studying in the University of Haifa and recently got engaged to a member of the family who lives in Jordan. He is a simple and good person and the border to Jordan is open, so we can go and visit him. But why can't he come and visit us? I don't know. My sister asked in the Ministry of the Interior and they told her that he was entitled to a visa every six months. Of course that was a lie and no visa was issued. She asked why it was like this, and they said that it was because of the recent political developments. What, is he bringing a big gun with him to Israel? What is this? Why can't we they meet here? Now every time they want to meet, she has to go with her passport and visa, and he's not allowed to come here. He doesn't even want to live here, he just wants to visit his fiancé. He comes for a week and then goes. He doesn't bring weapons with him. He just wants to see her. So you can see that there are different laws for different people in this country. We all know that Jews can come here whenever they want and even become citizens automatically.

A year or so ago I went to the hospital in Hadera in order to give birth. Most of the nurses were Jewish women of either Moroccan or Yemenite origin. These are the Jews who hate Arabs the most, those Jews coming from Arab countries. The nurses in the hospital humiliated me so much, that the memory is still fresh and painful. When I was lying on the bed and ready to give birth, one of the nurses called me a whore and said, "Yes, you Arabs have sex like animals," and then called me a whore once again. She then told me, "I can imagine your husband climbing on you like a dog in bed."

Look at the law that prohibits Israeli citizenship from Palestinians who marry Israeli citizens. It says it all. Who are the people who mostly marry Palestinians in this country? Israeli Arabs. In the beginning I could not believe this, but now nothing surprises me anymore.

Look, one of the most obvious times I feel discriminated against relates to the mandatory service in the Israeli Army. I remember once asking a very educated man, who is also politically leftist, questions about this issue. You see, there is something in this country called "mandatory army service." The Arabs have a right not to join the Israeli Army and most of them choose to refrain. The Jews, on the other hand, have to join the army. So, whoever serves in the army, in my opinion and according to what I have observed, is a part of society. If you didn't serve in the army, it's as though something is missing. One can't really belong without this factor. When you are interviewed for a job the first thing they ask you is, "Where did you serve in the army?" or "What did you do in the army?" This fact can't be erased or forgotten by anyone, Jew or Arab. Some members of my family decided to actually join the Israeli Army for different reasons. My brother is currently serving the State of Israel.

Discrimination? No, I don't feel any discrimination. This is a country of law and order and if you speak this language then you won't have any problems. Even if this person encounters difficulties, he will eventually get along and be fine.

Of course I feel discrimination. Who cares about the Arabs in this country? We don't get anything from the Israeli government. People here hate the Arabs and if they could, they would kick all of us out. You don't know how it feels to live as a second-class citizen. It's terrible.

The law doesn't know who is an Arab and who is a Jew. If someone knows the law, meaning the laws of society and of the state, he or she can gain equality in everything. The best example is that in 1956 there was a trial involving two Arab villages in the north, Ikrit and Biram[68] and the verdict was in favor of these villages. At the moment, there is a deferment of the verdict on the part of the Israeli side and there is no clear notion when the court's decision will finally be implemented. It might take a very long time but at least there is some kind of legal system people can refer to and work with.

I haven't really experienced discrimination from Jews who have been here for generations. I haven't really felt hatred from them. I have, however, had some very bad experiences with new Jewish immigrants, such as the Ethiopian ones. I used to work in Beer Sheva as a teacher for a few years. One afternoon I went to the shopping mall with my friends. We ran across some Ethiopian girls who heard us speak Arabic and they shouted, "Arabs! Arabs!" I thought to myself, "What do you mean Arabs? What, are we animals?" You see Smadar, I have lived in this country, my parents lived here, my grandparents lived here. These girls are newcomers. They just arrived here. So now I say, "Go back to Ethiopia. Don't come here and curse me." I have not heard such things from Jews who have been here since 1948, only from the ones who were brought here later. This hurts. I started cursing her back in Hebrew, which I could probably speak better than her, and in Arabic because I was so angry. This happened about ten years ago. Another time, my father was in the hospital. In the same room lay an old American Jewish man whose hand was badly broken. His family would come in and out of his room without even greeting us. One day he stayed all alone. No one came to visit him, so my husband and I helped feeding and dressing him. He told his wife and children about this, so they changed their attitude toward us and asked us how we were, and where we were from. They also said, "We didn't know Arabs could be like this. We thought all Arabs were killers and lovers of hate, especially against Jews." So you see how much meeting and talking to one another can reduce the hate and the mistrust? Jews from outside Israel have the worst ideas and thoughts about Arabs.

How Arabs are treated depends very much on the political situation. Now it's different, because people are afraid of terror. Five years ago, I was not religious and I didn't cover. I used to dress like Jewish women. That was when they'd check me. A year ago, I flew with my husband to Istanbul, this time in religious clothing, and they didn't check me at all. So, it depends very much on whether there are suicide bombings and whether people generally feel safe or not.

A few days ago I flew to Marmaris with my husband. In our group there were also Jews and Druze.[69] In the airport, the security guards told my husband and me to wait and stand aside so that they could take all our information. They opened all our suitcases and asked us many questions. I got very angry because I knew that the Druze people were immediately let onto the plane because they serve in the Israeli Army. So for them it's "Yallah, get on the plane. Welcome." My husband told me not to take it so seriously, but it hurt me very much. All the Jews who were there, and none of them knew me, said that I was on the right and were wondering why I was the only one who was checked. Some of them even said, "If they want to check, let them check all of us!" This incident happened before the recent wave of suicide bombings began. I think I was checked because I wear *hijjab* and everyone can see I am Arab and Muslim. When I did not wear *hijjab* people didn't bother me.

A few weeks ago we went to an art exhibition in one of the neighboring Jewish villages. There was security everywhere. One of the security guards saw us, probably me because I am covered and shouted, "No, don't go in there! Who told you to go in? Stop!" They stopped us and questioned us for a long time. You see, they always recognize us because of our clothing. Everyone else was let in freely, but we were even asked who invited us, how we heard about the exhibition, which room we were going to, how we got the invitations. We were very hurt. Once we were inside we were welcomed very nicely by our Jewish friends, but you never forget the feeling of mistrust people exhibit towards you. Sometimes I think that the security is exaggerated. I am always checked and looked at as though I am a potential terrorist or something like that. Not a nice feeling at all.

Q: Does it bother you that most Israeli Jews don't want and are not interested in learning Arabic, and that the Arabic language isn't compulsory in all Israeli Jewish schools, as Arabic in Arab schools?

It doesn't bother me, but I think that it's important for people to learn more languages. A language is a language. And, of course, it would be better if most Israeli Jews could communicate in Arabic because, after all, Jews and Arabs live together. Knowledge of a language is the first step towards learning about someone's culture, traditions and faith. The person has to be interested in learning the language, though. You can't force someone to learn something they don't want.

Yes, it angers me very much. I think that after the October riots even fewer Jews wanted to learn Arabic. I think that Jewish people here are not interested in our language at all. People think that because we're a minority, we have to learn the language of the majority. That's true to an extent, but we're a huge minority, so I think that our language has to be used too. Besides, what if we become a majority one day? That might happen, think about it.

The fact that Jews never learned Arabic shows exactly what they think of us and of the Arab world as a whole. They learn English, they learn French, they even learn Russian and Chinese today. What do they think, that they are a part of Europe? But when I think of it, maybe it's not so bad. If we know your language, and I know yours, don't I have a clear advantage over you? We know you, your language, and how you think, but you don't know anything about us whatsoever.

You might have seen this interview with a Jewish girl in one of the high schools. She was saying how she loves to learn English and Arabic, how interesting it is for her and how good the feeling was to be able to understand people speaking in a different language. This made me feel so happy and hopeful. I felt love for her and warmth. On the other hand, one of the students said, "I don't like Arabs, and I don't like their language." Wouldn't that anger you, to hear such a thing? I started cursing and my husband said to me, "Is this Dalal, my wife speaking?"

Of course it bothers me. It's not enough that we are like 10th class citizens in our country, but the Jews don't even want to learn our language. The Jews always say, "We want peace! We want peace!" but how can you have real peace with people with whom you can't even communicate? Peace is more than just signing papers. It's about trying to understand one another and about making an effort. It's about mutual respect. How can you really respect someone without even being able to tell him Kif Halak [how are you in Arabic]? If Jews aren't forced to learn our language and culture, as we are theirs, then there will never really be peace in this land. I honestly believe this.

Why should my daughter learn Hebrew and a Jewish child does not have to learn how to speak Arabic? And why should my daughter learn English as a third language and a Jewish girl as her second? I mean, why should Jews not learn how to communicate with us in Arabic? And you want to know something? One day when we're a majority here, Jews will have to know Arabic, don't you think?

Q: I would like to turn to another issue now, namely the one of the Arab village in Israel. What do you see when you look at your village? Do you feel that Arab and Jewish villages and towns get equal funding and opportunities?

Well, there are many obvious inequalities I can point to when looking at my village or even at other Arab villages. There are so many inequalities, that I might not even remember them all. The amount of money that is allocated to Arab villages is so insignificant, you can't even believe, especially when comparing it to what Jewish villages and towns receive. Most of the Arab citizens in Israel pay much more taxes than Jews do. There are many expensive projects planned for Arab villages which due to their high costs are never started. I have heard about many projects that are being undertaken in Jewish towns and villages and although we also need these kinds of projects, we can keep dreaming. And of course, there are many other inequalities, but the main one is in the area of work in my opinion. This mainly happens because Israeli Arabs don't serve in the Israeli Army. People who have served in the Israeli Army can find a job more quickly and much more easily. They can also find better jobs than we can. The question everyone is ignoring, however, is why are we not serving in the Israeli Army? How can we serve in the Israeli Army? We don't even feel that we belong here.

Jewish families have everything they need in their villages and towns. They have a sewage system, roads and good schools for their children. In my village even the basic things, such as roads, are not completed. Most of us pay taxes, but we don't get what we deserve.

Arab villages don't get the same amount of investment as do Jewish towns and villages. The main problem is that we refuse to serve in the Israeli Army. Once we don't join the Israeli Army we are automatically given fewer rights, especially in the area of work. The Arab city councils get much less money than the Jewish ones and that's a fact. This is reflected in how our villages and towns look. So, where's the equality everyone's speaking of?

The discrimination isn't only materialistic. It's also something in the mentality of people here. Israeli Arabs lose whatever they choose to do and whatever they choose to think and say. This is what really causes us to feel that we don't belong anywhere. For Jews, I am an Arab, or even a Palestinian and for Palestinians, I am a traitor. Did you know that once a Palestinian called me "Jew"?

A big problem is that Israeli Arabs don't serve in the Israeli Army. That's why we are allocated less money. I have no doubt about it. But it's interesting that Orthodox Jews also don't serve in the army, but they get money from the government every month. They take all their rights and more these religious Jews. And what do they do for the country? Absolutely nothing! So, if you're Jewish, you get money for not going to the Israeli Army, but if you're Arab you're seen as a traitor and live in half developed towns and villages.

It is obvious that there is a neglect [of the Arab village] by the Israeli government. I told you about the long negotiations we had to go through in order to build one road near our church. The same happened when I was in Sahnin.[70] You know, it's a town of twenty five thousand people and two men from there died during the October Riots. The population living there was in negotiations with the Israeli government and they are now waiting to hear from the government. The representatives from Sahnin told the Israeli government at one point that there is an obvious inequality between the Arab and Jewish towns. They then asked that the Israeli government send people to Sahnin in order to assess the inequalities. But you know how it is; the government is always good at making promises and planning things. It is always busy describing its plans to us, but in the end nothing happens and everything stays the same. And there is another important issue connected to the land. I was not allowed to build on my grandfather's land. I was even not allowed by the government to sell it. They said that I couldn't build on it because it's agricultural land. Then they said that if I choose to sell it, I could only do so it for a ridiculously low amount of money because it is agricultural land. But, believe it or not, the government had a plan for this land and they have already begun building the foundations. One day I came back home and I saw that all our olive trees, which belonged to my family for generations, were cut down without our permission, of course. What can I tell you, my tears just came rolling down. I said to one of the city council members, "Michael, you work here, your brother works here and I know both of you. Didn't any of you have control over the fate of my trees?" Can you believe it? Without asking us, they cut down our olive trees. When things like this happen, you learn that you have to use tactics, even manipulative ones and not a kind word. You would think that if you used a kind word, you would receive what you deserve, without taking it forcefully. This kind of discrimination happens everywhere in the world, but here in Israel the financial restrictions against us Arabs are more emphasized because of the political situation. If there's a situation in which there's hardly any budget left, then whoever is in charge of it would rather give it to a Jewish *moshav*, *kibbutz* or town. So, the allocation of money and resources to Arab settlements is postponed and when things get postponed, time flies and people forget. My brother works in construction in our town. Now he is authorized to approve or disapprove construction in certain areas of the town. People in our town told him, "Now let's see if you're an Arab. If you approve the construction in Arab neighborhoods, you're an Arab, but if you're a Jew, you will continue postponing everything for us." My brother told them that it doesn't work like that and that a lot of the discrimination is in their heads.

O: But in Abu Ghosh, for example, a Jewish head of council was given the position because the conflicts between the different families were so bad. Can it be that Arab villages are experiencing some kind of inner turmoil as well?

Yes, we have internal problems as well.

Q: So does everything get postponed for everyone, or can you see this more on the Arab side?

Oh, things are postponed much more on the Arab side. A good example is what happened with Barak's government. His government allocated 3 billion dollars to develop the Arab municipality. In spite of this, it has never really been implemented, and nothing happened. I don't think the same would have happened has these funds been allocated to a Jewish community.

Q: Why do you think nothing happened?

I don't know. I am not the one who decides the government's policies. The discrimination is more evident in the infrastructure, both the schools and the housing that people receive. Some Arabs have nice houses. These houses, however, were randomly and sometimes illegally built by citizens and many problems are being uncovered now. Governments plan such things much better than if families randomly decide to build their own houses. On the other hand, when you have to build a house and the government does not allow you to do so, you eventually build it illegally.

Q: In your opinion, have things always been so tense between Arab and Jews in Israel?

When Oslo began and the treaty was signed, people everywhere were raising olive branches, Jews and Arabs alike. When Sadat[71] came to Israel for a visit, Jews and Arabs in Ramle ran out into the streets to see his car passing by. People want peace more than anything else, the question is what's the price to be paid for it? Everyone wants peace, but no one is willing to sacrifice anything. Peace inevitably means sacrifice, especially when it comes to the Middle East. People can't just say, "We are here and they are there." We are all here. We have to live here. What's all this about here and there? We are here and you are here. It's us. What's happening? What's going on?

Q: Do all Arab citizens of Israel pay taxes nowadays?

Today I think about 50% of the Arab population actually pays taxes. But it's natural. Where do people pay taxes? In places where the city council gives the people full services. In places like Holon, which is a part of Tel Aviv, people receive all the services they pay for. So of course they pay what is demanded of them by the state. Why should we pay if we don't receive all our rights and if we know that the Jews don't really want us here anyway?

Q: So what started first; the fact that people didn't pay, or that the services were bad or even at times not provided?

Well, I think the main problem was that the Arab population has greatly increased in the last few years. It's like in every situation where a family is getting bigger, but the income remains the same. Then the kid wants to go to school, he wants new clothes and other things other people all over the world have and need. The same thing happens everywhere when there's not enough money. But people have to get along somehow, even if it's hard.

Smadar, if you lived here, you would see the inequalities and understand. You should see the poor infrastructure, the roads, or the fact that our children don't have a *Matnas*.[72] After school, our children go out to the streets to play because they don't have anywhere to go to.

Q: Why do you think this inequality exists? Where does it come from and why?

It's out of racism.

Q: What kind of racism? Racism from whom?

From the people who distribute the money to the different sects.

I think that many of the people who claim that they don't receive equal rights just sit at home and whine all day, "They don't give me! They don't give me!" What good is it to always complain but not do anything about it? I think that many Israeli Arabs do not want to make an effort and make change happen. I hate it when people complain but do not do anything about it. They just want people to feel sorry about them. I also think that some Arabs want things to stay the same so that they can continue complaining about Israel. If these problems were solves and the Occupation were terminated, what would they complain about?

You know, there's another issue here. When I go to a Jewish school or *Matnas*, I see that the money for building it was donated by people from abroad mostly. There are many donors among the Jews living in Europe and the United States. One Jew donates a laboratory to a school, another donates a new ward to a hospital. The Jews around the world take care of one another. Here we don't have rich Arabs who could donate money to our schools and institutions. Jews hardly donate money to the Arabs. Naturally, their priority is to their own people.

Q: Please tell me a bit about yourself.

I work as a priest in a small Christian community in Jaffa.[73] I used to come here twice a week, but now since the death of my wife, I only come once a week, on Tuesdays. The rest of the time I spend in Lod where I live with my children. I am currently the spiritual director of the community and I also do counseling sessions, especially for parents. I help to mediate between children and parents who are having familial problems. I was born in Israel in 1953 and I admit that I have an identity crisis because of the political situation here at the moment. When I was in 7th grade, I spoke better Hebrew than Arabic. I then attended a Jewish high school and in many ways became more Jewish than Arab. In university my concentration was Middle Eastern studies, because I felt that I didn't know anything about my own history and culture. I later became a pastor and served in Jerusalem, in Ramallah.

Q: Do you think that the Israeli Arab society has started to give up demanding their rights?

The way things are now, with all the tensions and questions about the future, I would have to say that yes, there is a general feeling that things will not change and that it is better to just give up. In spite of this, after the events of October 2000, one can just hope that people will bond and get closer to one another. Sometimes things get better when they are actually worse. If there's a person I have never spoken to, there is not communication between us. If I communicate with a person and I am honest with him, then our friendship will become stronger over time, even if we don't always agree with one another. Only in this way will Jews and Arabs solve their problems and only in this way will Israelis and Palestinians get to know one another. When you really think about it, Israelis and Palestinians are bonded forever. They have one another whether they like it or not. At this moment, it seems that there is more consideration for the other on the Israeli side and as I have said, this has to come from both sides. You see how it is? There are so many questions to answer and yes, the Israeli Arabs get ignored and pushed aside in a way.

Q: Do you think that Israeli Arabs have not really been able to decide on whose side they are?

I think that we Israeli Arabs can't completely decide on whose side we are. We are confused and don't know what to decide. We are stuck between living here in Israel, but also wanting to belong to the larger Arab community which really hates us. Personally, I choose the way of speaking out and I feel that it's strengthening me and making me more aware of the situation and of the difficulties people on both sides are going through. I am not afraid. If I get to the point where I am afraid to say the truth, I am in a really bad state. Sometimes I feel that I am passive and that I can't do anything about what's going on in Israel and Palestine at the moment. I was glad when you asked to interview me, but I know that not many people want to hear what I have to say. I do not support the Israeli right wing political parties but I also do not like the right wing ones. In our religion, we are not allowed to be anti anything. I am pro everything. I am pro Jewish, pro Arab, and above all, pro humanity. I look at the human suffering as a whole, and then I ask myself what I can do to change things for the better. This is why I work with Neve Shalom[74] and in several other communities that are striving for peace and understanding between Jews and Arabs in Israel. You asked me before on whose side I am. At the moment I feel that we are living in a society in which opinions are constantly changing. When I see that a church is broken down somewhere in the world, I become more

Christian. When I see an Arab child being killed, I feel more Arab and when I see my town, Ramle, where Jews and Arabs live together, become more dirty and polluted, then my Israeli identity becomes stronger because I know that as an Israeli I can make a change if I decide to do so. It changes all the time.

Q: But when you see that for years Israeli Arabs remain second-class citizens, don't you feel anything?

Yes, of course I feel something, but it's the other side, the Jews, who have to realize that this is the situation. At the moment, many of them don't realize, or chose not to realize that this is the situation. It's something we all have to work on together. This is our suffering, but if we persist in trying to change things for the better, maybe we will succeed. If we don't have patience, then nothing will change for the better, only for the worse. It's very hard living with all these pressures and that's why many people on both sides just give up and run away. This is what happens when you are not a Jew, but when you are also not what many would consider an Arab.

Q: What do you think that Jewish Israelis think about Israeli Arabs?

Most Jews only think about the individual. When I was in a Jewish school, people thought of me mostly as a Christian. And if there was a Muslim in a predominantly Jewish class, no one really cared. If this person was studying to be a doctor and he was good, people would tell him, "You are a good doctor." When people judge a whole group, it's bad, but when they look at the individual they can see the person as a human being. There must be a separation between a whole group and the individual within it. If there were not a separation between the two then I would probably feel that I have to hide my identity.

Q: Do you feel that you have to hide your identity at times?

Personally, no, I don't feel that I have to hide my identity. I have stopped hiding my true identity a long time ago. I am proud of who I am now. Because of the political situation in Israel, however, I have learned how to hide my identity and who I am when necessary, especially because of my name. People always ask about my name because they are not sure whether it is an Arab name. As you know, Arabs have a bad reputation all over the world. The Arab reputation is considered to be bad and will be considered bad until there is peace here. Most Jews and Christians in the West feel this way about Arabs at the moment and I say this with much sorrow. I remember how it was when I was in the United States. When I used to say I was Israeli, people were really impressed. When I said that I was Arab, no one would pay any attention to me. So, isn't that anti-Semitism? I can definitely detect anti-Semitism in the United States. And I can definitely tell you that although I am not a Muslim, people in the United States also don't like Muslims or Islam.

Q: Do you have Muslim friends?

Yes, I grew up with Muslims. I also have Jewish friends from school. When we speak about politics, we don't agree about many things, but we still remain friends because we respect and love each other. You don't have to think the same in order to love each other. On the contrary, you can disagree strongly with a person but still love them if you feel that they still respect you as a human being, as a creation of God. It's the same everywhere. If you have a family with five people in it, will everyone agree with one another? Of course not, it is impossible. For you, Smadar, it's different in the United States, or in other places in the world. There, people don't always ask you who you are or what your religion is. And if you say you are a Jew, people are used to me and will mostly not think it is a bad thing. Here in Israel, with the current atmosphere and political ambience, these things are very important for people. People care who you are, where you come from, what your religion is and what your political opinions are. It's when you are afraid to say who you are that you understand the importance of all this. I know that also Jews feel that they are not loved and accepted outside of Israel. We all know what happened to the Jews in Europe during the Second World War. Here, this identity question is a very heavy and aggravating burden on me and on other Israeli Arabs. If the bad reputation most Arabs have does not change and people cannot see me first as a human being and only then as an Arab, then I will always have this burden on my heart. I will always be looked at suspiciously and people will always ask me, "Who are you?" and "What are you?" when leaving the airport or entering a building. These things discriminate between people, but they have become a routine because of the political situation. When I was in the United States, I didn't want to come back to Israel. All the people who live in the United States assimilate and become American. Once they step on American soil for the first time, they immediately want to be American and not what they were before. Or, if they want to maintain their tradition, it does not get in their way of being American. And in spite of the fact that they have many problems there, you are not always confronted with the question, "What's your religion?" Here in Israel you always have to say who you are, where you are from, what religion you believe in, and whether you have served in the Israeli Army You always have to belong to a distinct group and that's very hard at times especially when you do not feel you belong anywhere. Today, at my age, I have stopped being afraid to be who I am. I used to be afraid when I was younger. I have many identities. But still, when I tell someone that I am a Christian, I don't always have the courage to tell them that I am also an Arab. Usually people think that because I am a Christian, I am automatically from Europe or from the United States. As you know, my religion, Christianity, is not my nationality as Judaism is to the Jews. I don't know where the situation is heading, but it sure doesn't look good.

Q: Do you think it is okay that the Jews don't donate their money to Arab institutions?

Yes, of course it's okay. If I could donate money, I wouldn't donate it to the Jews, but first and foremost to the Arabs, my people. The government should distribute money equally between Jews and Arabs. But as to donations, it's a different issue. Look around you and you'll see that it is very rare to find someone who donates money to people who are not from his or her country or religion. When you donate money, you want to take care of your own people first. Then, after you have done that you might think about someone else.

I think the donations should be distributed among all Israelis equally.

We Arabs have also received some donations. We are about to build a new kindergarten in Arara. The Green Party from Germany has supported us for several years now.

Yes, the Green Party has given us some money, but that's because they feel sorry for the Palestinians. They know that rich Palestinians don't donate money to poor ones, that they don't even look at them and that's why they give us money.

Q: How do you support your village?

I prefer to buy from shops in the village than from Jews. For example, let's say there was a Coca Cola factory in Arara and one in Tel Aviv. They both produce exactly the same thing, so why would I buy from Tel Aviv instead of buying from Arara and supporting local businesses? Of course I will buy from Arara. But, if there isn't a Coca Cola factory in Arara, what should I do? Can I go to the Occupied Territories and get what I need? Should I risk my life? In Jordan, Syria and Saudi Arabia people are able to boycott American products. Instead they buy European products. But here, what can we do? We have to buy either from Israel or from America.

Q: Many think that the USA=Israel. What do you think about this?

England and other European countries are just as bad as the United States. These countries will all decide what the future of the world will be. They are the ones who are causing all the problems between Jews and Arabs. Economically, socially and politically they dominate the world and dictate everyone's lives. They could put more pressure on Sharon and Arafat to stop the fighting and the bloodshed. But, it's obvious that they want to continue the conflict.

Q: What do the United States and Europe gain, if at all, from the existence of the conflict between Israelis and Palestinians?

Oh, they all gain a lot from this conflict. If there is peace between the Arab countries and Israel, the United States will lose power. Why, for example, do we have to buy gas from the United States and South America? Why should we bring things from afar? If there were peace, we could buy these things from our neighbors and the United States and Europe would lose a lot of money. Bush and his country would die if we had peace here.

Q: Many say that the USA = Israel in their level of evil and desire to rule the world. This belief is held by many Palestinians and other Arabs all over the world. Do you agree that this is true?

No, Bush helps Israelis like he helps Americans? No. And do Israelis help Americans like they help their own people? I am Palestinian, right? I want to help the Palestinians. The Americans are living on the expense of the Israelis too, believe me. The Americans are probably the worse.

Q: Do you think that Israel and the United States have the right to decide who is and who isn't the right leader for the Palestinians?

I think that only the Palestinian people who experience the life in the Occupied Territories have the right to decide who their ruler will be and whether Arafat is a good and suitable leader.

Q: What do you think that the Palestinians think about Arafat?

Whoever gets to eat from the cake is satisfied with Arafat and those who don't are not. I think they all know that Arafat is bad, but what can they do? In Palestine, can people go out to the streets and protest against Arafat's government? Do they have the freedom to express their political opinions? If they try to do something, they'll be killed.

Q: Do you see yourself as Palestinian?

I am from Arara Village, first and foremost. I would first help people here in Arara, and then other people. And yes, I definitely see myself as Palestinian. What else could I be?

Q: Do you see your prime responsibility towards Israel or towards Palestine?

I am Palestinian, but I live in Israel. I care about my people, the Palestinians and the Arabs first, before anyone else.

Interviews with Children

Q: Do you have Jewish friends?

No

Q: Have you ever had Jewish friends?

No, never had any.

Q: Would you like to have Jewish friends?

No, I am not interested at all.

Q: Why not?

We are different from one another in all aspects. Different language, different religion, different traditions. They believe in the Bible, but we believe in the Holy Qur'an. We know that our book is the only truthful one.

Q: But isn't it a good thing to meet with someone who is different?

No, it's not a good thing. It's not good to change how we are for someone else. The Jews want to change us, so that we're like them. But we are Muslim, and we will not change our faith.

Q: Do you think you'd have to change if you met a Jewish person?

Yes. And besides, I don't trust the Jews. They lie, like they have always done since the days of the Prophet Muhammad, peace and prayers be upon him.

Q: If you were to meet a Jewish boy or girl your age, what would be the first question you would ask him or her?

What's your name? And then, where are you from?

Q: And about the political situation?

I would ask: Do you want to kill all the Arabs and take Al-Quds?

Q: Do you have Jewish friends at the moment?

No, I don't have any Jewish friends at the moment.

Q: Have you ever had Jewish friends?

No, I have never had any Jewish friends.

Q: Would you like to have Jewish friends now, or to meet with Jewish children your age?

No, I have no interest in this. I don't like the Jews, and I don't want to be their friend.

Q: Do you have Jewish friends?

No, I don't have any Jewish friends. I used to have some Jewish friends in the past, a long time ago. My father still has many Jewish friends, but he hasn't visited them for a long time. We don't have time to visit one another. And also, with the political situation, we just don't want to go there, and they don't want to come here.

Q: Why?

Because there are a lot of problems all over the country now. We prefer to stay where we are. I think that everyone is afraid now, on both sides. There's only a small number of people who are willing to visit one another these days.

Q: Would you be interested to meet Jewish kids your age?

Hmmm, I don't know. Actually, no, I am not interested. The political situation is very hard and no one knows what to do. So, people just prefer to stay home. Also, meeting Jews is a problem. I am sure that if we meet Jewish children, we will verbally fight with them. So why meet them at all?

Q: If you met a Jewish child now, what would be the first question you would ask him or her?

I would ask him what his name is, and what he likes to do.

Q: And what would you ask him about the political situation?

I would ask him what he thinks can be done in order to solve the political problem.

Q: Would you like to keep in touch with a Jewish-Israeli boy?

Yes.

Q: But you just said that you are not interested in meeting with Jewish children.

Yes, but that's because of the current political situation. At the moment, we can't go and visit them and they don't want to come here. They think that if they come to an Arab village someone will kill them. That's why I said I don't want to meet with them, because we can't. I would like to speak to Jewish kids and to see what they are studying, or what their interests are. I would like to know what they do during the summer, after school is finished. But at the moment, I don't think it's possible. You see, I would like to meet with them, but what can I do? It's just not possible at the moment.

Q: Do you have Jewish friends?

No, I don't really have any Jewish friends, but I have met many Jews. In one of the courses I have taken, we were six Jews and six Arabs in the group. It was like this all throughout the year. We learned a lot about one another that year. We spoke a lot about politics.

Q: What are some of the things you did in this group?

Look, the group started to meet very shortly after the Al Aqsa *Intifada* started. I think it started on October 29th, or something like that and we started meeting in mid- November. So, in the first meeting not all the people showed up. Many of the Jews didn't come and many of the Arabs didn't come. Most of the Arab teachers in our school were against this meeting, but my friends and I, we felt that it was important for us all to meet. We put some pressure on our teachers, and made it happen. We mainly wanted to communicate to the Jewish students our opinions about the Israeli-Palestinian conflict. We wanted them to know what we thought about it. These meetings were supposed to take place in a *Matnas* in a Jewish town, but you know, we didn't want to go there and they didn't want to come to an Arab village. At the end, we all agreed to meet in *Givat Haviva*.[75] The first meeting was, unfortunately, not very good. Let's just say that it turned into one big fight. I also got into a very passionate and serious argument with one of the Jewish students. I'll tell you something. At the beginning of the *Intifada*, everything was on the table. It was obvious who started it, and all of that. These students didn't understand at all what was going on. They just wanted to fight with us. Another problem was that they were completely secular and don't believe in anything. You know that here we are religious and we understand our religion, because we're Arabs. So, most of them don't believe in God and they didn't understand our claims. It was a disaster. The instructor tried to pull us away from this issue, but he was completely unsuccessful, because both sides wanted to talk about it. But as I said, I realized that they didn't know what they were talking about. They just wanted to pick a fight.

Q: What were some of the things that were said, for example?

One of the boys asked me whether I was in favor of a Palestinian state. I said that yes, of course I was. He said, "Well, if there's ever a Palestinian state, go and live there!" I said to him that I will never leave my village because this is where I was born. I said that I will never leave this land which is Palestine. All this land is Palestine. I will not go and live in the Occupied Territories, even though they are also Palestine, of course. I was born here, and not there. He then asked me why I was in favor of a Palestinian state. I said that it was for the people who were born in the Occupied Territories. They need it. I will not move from my village.

Q: In your view, was this purely a political debate, or did you detect any feelings of dislike towards you because you were Arab?

Throughout all our meetings I felt that they [the Jews] didn't like us. I could feel the feelings of animosity in the air. One of them said something that I didn't agree with at all. He said a very good Arab friend broke contact with him after the *Intifada*. I told him I didn't believe this was the truth. An Arab wouldn't do such a thing.

Q: So you don't think that the breaking of contact can come from the Arab side?

I will tell you why. He told me that his Arab friend was his neighbor. Then I found out later that he [the Jewish boy] lives on a *Kibbutz*. There are NO Arabs living in a *Kibbutz*.

Q: These things happened in the past. But how about now—do you have any Jewish friends?

I study with Jews. You know, we don't go to the same schools, but there are after school courses that we attend together. None of the Jews are my friends. I am currently taking a Biology course. We are doing research and there are three Jewish girls also in the class. Some of the Jewish professors were good to us and others were downright evil. One of the professors told us not to utter a word of Arabic in class. If I said a word in Arabic, he would yell at me in front of everyone in class. She just didn't want to hear this language at all.

Q: Would you like to have Jewish friends?

Let me tell you why I don't want to have Jewish friends. I have tried. But I can't stand those three girls who are with me in this Biology class. They dress like prostitutes. We do a lot of research on the beach. They dress as though they are about to go to a beach party and they think they're the best. Even our professor who is Jewish can't stand these girls. She also thinks that we Arabs are better than these girls. But the girls think they are better. I have also tried to be friends with Jewish people in Tzafit. One time, we all got together for a BBQ. I asked one of the guys what his plans for the future were. He said he wanted to be a soldier. I said I know he was planning to be a soldier, because all of the men and women in Israel go to the army after they finish high school and before they go to university. He then said that his plan was to stay in the army as an officer. That evening, after the BBQ, the guys were playing with a big plastic gun. I took the gun from the Jewish guy and said to him "Look at this gun!" He said, "Yes, in two years I'll have a gun like this." You see Smadar, he's dying to have a gun like that. So I told him, "Let's say you're a soldier and you're confronting me in a demonstration, will you kill me?" He laughed and said, "No, of course not." So I said sarcastically, "Oh, so you'll confront me in a demonstration and simply smile to me and say hi and ask me if I want a cup of coffee won't you? Isn't that what you're going to tell me when you're a soldier?" He couldn't answer this question. Do you understand? All he wants is to have a gun in his hand!

Q: Do you have Jewish friends?

I am completely not interested in having Jewish friends.

Q: Why?

I don't want them coming to our villages. They don't belong here.

Q: Do you have Jewish friends?

No. I used to have Jewish friends, but now I don't.

Q: Why not?

Because I am ashamed of them and of what they have done and continue to do to the Palestinians. I am Palestinian too, you see? I am Palestinian, and that is it! And you know what? The Jewish children are even worse than their parents. The Jewish mothers and fathers give their children a terrorist upbringing. They tell their children, "These are Arabs, so kill them and take their land!"

Q: So, let's say you met a Jewish person your age, what would be the first thing you would say to him or her?

I would ask him or her whether they like to kill. This is exactly what I would ask them. And I also have another question for them: Do you like peace? Do you want peace to come?

Q: Do you trust the Jews enough to make peace with them?

Not at all. How can you trust a people who are murdering children and women in Palestine? Muslims could never trust the Jews.

Q: Do you have Jewish friends?

No.

Q: Why not?

Because of what the Jews are doing to Palestinians. There's a war here and we can't meet one another.

Q: Who is to blame for the war?

The Jews.

Q: Why?

Sharon started everything, but all the Jews think like him, that's why we have a big war here now.

Q: Are you afraid to visit Israeli Jews today?

No, not at all.

Q: Do you think that Jews are afraid to visit Arabs today?

Yes, they are afraid to come here, but we're not afraid at all.

Q: Why do you think that Jews are afraid to come and visit you?

They are afraid because they know that we don't like them. They also know that they took our land and that they are not good people. That's why they are afraid to come here.

Q: What do you think about how the Israeli government treats the Israeli Arabs?

Not good at all. I see that a Jew who kills an Arab sits in jail for a year or two, if at all. An Arab who kills a Jew, however, can even be killed for it.

Q: What did you feel when two years ago thirteen Israeli Arabs were killed by Israeli police?

I thought that now the Jews, who are already killing the Palestinians, want to kill us too. They see us as Palestinians and not belonging to this place. They don't want us here among them.

Q: Do you see yourself as Palestinian?

Yes, I do.

Q: Do you think that the Israeli police forces would have killed these people had they been Jews?

They were killed because they were Arabs. If they were Jews they would have never been shot.

Q: Do you have any anger in your heart because of this treatment?

Of course. I feel that the Arabs are not getting the right treatment in this country. It's our country, our land and still, we don't get any rights in it. The Jews didn't just take the land from us, they also deprive us from our rights in it.

Q: Who would you blame for this inequality?

Sharon, Barak, and all the Jews who were prime ministers.

Q: Do you think that these injustices can be eliminated?

I don't think so. Rabin was good, but now I don't think that things can change for the better.

Q: So you have no solutions whatsoever for these injustices.

I have one solution.

Q: What would it be?

The Jews must leave.

Q: Where should they go?

I don't care.

Q: Can you point to any inequalities between Jews and Arabs in Israel?

I can point to many inequalities. I know, for example, that Jews have everything they need in their schools. We only have classes, and nothing else. They also have the best teachers and the best equipment in all their schools.

Q: Why do you think it's this way?

I think they don't want to let us advance so that they can control us and the Palestinians. Also, maybe they want to keep us doing all the dirty jobs because they don't like doing them.

Q: Does your father have a job now?

He had a job, but now it's very difficult. I think a lot of Jews don't want to employ Arabs now because of the political situation. I saw on television that they bring many workers from China, instead of the Palestinians and the other Arabs.

Q: Why are the Jews doing this?

They say that they are afraid of Arabs, because of what's going on at the moment.

Q: What do you think about this claim?

I think it's stupid.

Q: Why is that?

It's stupid because we are the ones who have to be afraid of the Jews, and not them from us.

Q: Why?

Who are the ones who barge into Jenin? The Jews. Who are the ones who kill Palestinians? The Jews. And who are the ones who wreck houses? The Jews.

Q: And who are the ones who commit suicide bombings and kill tens of innocent civilians?

The Palestinians sometimes do that, but only when they have no other choice. In Islam it is not allowed to kill unless there is no other option.

Q: Have you ever felt afraid living in Israel?

I feel afraid when I see news about a suicide bombing. If my mother or father are in town I feel very anxious and call them immediately. But I am also afraid of other tings like growing up in a place where I might never be accepted. Sometimes I think to myself that maybe it would be better to leave this country and go somewhere else. Maybe in another place people will treat us better and it will be easier to get a job. But then I look at what is going ion in the world and it doesn't seem that people like Arabs more elsewhere.

Q: Do you feel that in a way life in Israel is not so bad for Arabs?

Sometimes I feel that. But then I remember what the Jews did and how they stole our lands. When I remember this, I feel very strong resentment to them and all I want is for them to immediately leave the land and give us what belongs to us—our lands.

Q: Do you think that there is a way for Jews and Arabs to live together in spite of the history of the region and of the events of 1948?

I don't know, but I don't think so. Most Arabs will never forget what happened in 1948. They will never forget that the land belonged to them before the Jews came. If someone took something from you would you be able to forget it and change your attitude towards them?

Q: When and if you ever have children, what will you teach them about Israel and about the Jews?

That all this land once belonged to us and was stolen by the Jews. That they should never forget what happened here in 1948. I will tell them to continue to hope that one day the land will return to us.

Q: Is there an event that changed who you are or your attitude towards Israel?

When the Israeli police forces killed the Israeli Arab men I was very angry. I never liked the Jews or Israel before this event, but after it I even hated them more.

Q: Why? What did you feel?

I was angry because I felt like people from my own family were being killed. We are Arabs, one people, and we are all discriminated against in this country. I never imagined, however, that things would get so worse and that Arab citizens would be shot. The Jews always use force. Against the Palestinians they also use force. They confront children with tanks and guns. Now they did the same to Arabs living in Israel. What's the difference? Maybe all they know is force and violence, but we also know how to defend ourselves and our rights!

Q: Which tights are you talking about?

Our rights to receive equal rights. Our rights to own the lands we owned before the Jews came in 1948.

Media: Interviews with Adults

Q: How do you view the Israeli media in general, and in particular during the October 2000 riots? Do you believe it was objective?

Ah ha! Now we have entered a red zone which has many marshes in it. In my opinion, the media in Israel is very free. The journalists say whatever they think and feel without thinking about it twice. Whoever tries to resist the media can't survive. Azmi Bshara expressed his political opinion. I saw on television that he was interrogated, although he didn't express a personal opinion, but a political one. And in politics there is a wide variety of opinions.

The Israeli newspapers are very different from one another. In *Yediot Ahronot* and *Maariv* all you can see is columnists attacking whatever situation they choose to. They twist the story, make it bigger than it really is and don't understand anything, whether it's related to Jews or Arabs. It's like with the Nimrodi Case where most of the media made a big battle out of it. These two newspapers are only interested in money and not in journalism and media communication. In the 24 Hours Section, they have a few good columns, but all the rest is just about money, nothing else. If you look into these newspapers, you'll see that eighty percent of the content is advertisements. This is an economic battle and today the world is completely dependent on economics. In *Ha'aretz*, on the other hand, people are speaking straight and to the point. If you want to know what's going on, buy this newspaper. Even Tommy Lapid, who is very much a left wing person, although I think he's really a right wing person, speaks to the point. If you know Tommy Lapid now, you probably know that he has changed a lot throughout the years. These days even he speaks to the point.

When the October 2000 events started, the Israeli news didn't give it proper attention. Do you think that if Jews had been killed the media would have forgotten about it so quickly? The Israeli media hid many things during that time because they did not want people to know the truth. I regularly watch a Palestinian channel, and there I can see very well what's going on between Israeli Arabs and Israeli Jews. I think it was in Taybe...I saw what was going on there during the October 2000 riots and the Israeli media was not showing that. Also, the Israeli media rushed through the events without paying real attention to what happened. It was very insulting.

The media here hides many things and I will give you an obvious example. Look at me. I never wanted to sell my lands to the Israeli government. They took it away from me and have never paid me for it. Isn't it enough that our land was taken from us? Isn't enough that Jews can come and live here whenever they want? The media never shows these things to the public and never deals with the real problems Israeli Arabs are currently facing. But, I will tell you one thing. I live here now, and I am not moving anywhere. I would rather die than move. I will die first.

The media was cooperating with the Israeli government during the October riots. The Israeli government wanted to hide everything that really happened during the riots. They wanted to hide the crimes they had committed against the Israeli Arab population. Had this happened to the Jews, everyone all over the world would know about the killing. The media would make sure of that.

When the suicide bombing in the *Dolfinarium* [76] happened, the Israeli media kept this issue in the headlines for many days. All you could see when opening the television was what happened in that night club and how the families were dealing with the situation. But when the thirteen Israeli Arabs were murdered, no one remembered them after a day or two. You could not find more information about the people who were killed by the Israeli police forces. The Israeli media only concentrates on suicide bombings and what happens to the Palestinians or to the Israeli Arabs is forgotten very fast.

I have many complaints against the media, especially because of the development of extremism in Israel. It is true that also the Arabs are getting more and more extreme in their views, but this extremism comes from both sides. I have heard some ridiculous things said by Israeli representatives on television and in the radio. I think it was Nahman Shay[77] who compared Arafat's actions to those of Milosevic. Of course this is false and there is no comparison whatsoever. Milosevic was much worse and killed much more people. We don't have a situation of Palestinian occupation of Israeli lands, but the contrary is true. So sometimes I am surprised by what Israeli representatives say or by how the media portrays some situations. How can someone educated say something like this? Obviously some people want to create a situation where citizens shift to the right and support the right wing political parties. I feel that in order to be successful in Israel today you have to be an extremist. Groups like Peace Now, which have worked for peace for many years, are in complete despair. They are helpless. When one sees what is happening to the Palestinians, it really hurts. To every one Israeli who is killed there are approximately ten Palestinians killed. So the thousands of Palestinians who have been injured, aren't they suffering? Don't they have feelings? Aren't they also human beings? I, as a person living in Israel, don't know even one name of a person who died there. I don't know who is even in charge of publicizing this issue. The media doesn't tell us a lot about what is happening there because of the Israeli occupation. I, as a pastor, had to learn how not to be biased towards one side. Although I am Arab, I have a lot of criticisms against Arabs. Arabs almost never criticize themselves. They never point the finger at themselves. On the Jewish side there are at least some people who, even with all the difficulties today, can rise and criticize the Jewish society in Israel. Some of the media is part of this. This is why the Arab states are in the state they are today. The leaders blame everyone else, especially Israel, when they are really the ones who are suppressing the masses and stealing from them. There must be a shift in Arab public opinion.

The Israeli media, like any other media hides certain things. But in a volatile situation like in the Middle East it's important for people to know what's happening. You have to remember, however, that the Arab countries are also hiding a lot, probably even more than Israel. Israel allows foreign journalists to go into the Palestinian Territories and take photos. Arab countries would never let this happen. When you look at the degree of freedom of the media in Israel and in the Arab states, it is obvious that Israel wins.

The Israeli media didn't cover the October 2000 riots because no one cares about the Arabs in this country. The media definitely cares more about the Jews than about the Arabs and this was evident during that time. There's definitely discrimination between the two people.

Q: What do you think about the words spoken by Israeli member of parliament [MP] Azmi Bshara in Damascus during the summer of 2000? As you might remember Bshara insinuated that the Arab world unite to put pressure on Israel and even oppose it. Why do you think Bshara said what he did?

I watched what Bshara said on television. What he said was fine. Why not? Why should Israeli Arabs not side with the Palestinians and help them? The Israelis are the ones who want to violently suppress the Palestinians living in the Occupied Territories, so why should the Arab nations and the Israeli Arabs not help the Palestinians defend themselves? Even if Arab people and Arab countries can't declare war against Israel, why shouldn't they speak against it? Besides, I don't think that his words would cause a war against Israel. It was more of a verbal identification with the Palestinian people. Politicians talk a lot.

Bshara meant exactly what he said—that the Arab countries must get more involved in the fate of the Palestinian people. But I don't believe that the Arab countries will ever fight against Israel because they want peace. I want peace too.

No, I don't think that was a very wise step by Bshara. What he did just provoked people and caused more hate between Arabs and Jews. He is a doctor of psychology and I think he knew exactly what he was doing. Maybe he became complacent; I think he did. But Israel is a kingdom of brains and they know how to catch the fire at its beginning. I think he just became complacent. What he said didn't contribute anything to the already hard and painful situation, but just made things much worse. Had he said something nice or more constructive, it would have been better and he would have been treated better by the media and by the people of Israel as a whole.

Azmi Bshara expressed his political opinion. I saw on television that he was interrogated by the Israeli authorities, even though he didn't express a personal opinion, but a political one. And in politics there is a wide variety of opinions which must be allowed to be voiced.

I am not for what Bshara said in Damascus. Azmi Bshara doesn't represent me in any way whatsoever. Excuse me for speaking this way, but all the Arab leadership, in Israel and elsewhere, is problematic. My problem with the Arab leadership is that they don't accept criticism and don't speak out. For example, when there's a suicide bombing, they are afraid to respond to it and speak against it, even though most of them don't want this violence. They are afraid to openly condemn these acts of terror and this is mostly evident in the Palestinian Authority's leadership where the leaders are always silent. Israeli Arabs can say more and express themselves more openly than the Palestinian people because of the fact that Israel is a democratic country. My wish is that all Arabs, and especially their leaders, get to the point where they can safely publicly condemn acts of terror.

He should have said what he did a long time ago. Finally an Israeli-Arab says the truth, and says it publicly without being ashamed. What do Jewish people here expect? That we'll be repressed by them and shut up forever?

The Jews should stop complaining about Bshara and what he said in Damascus. What are you so paranoid about? You think the Arab world will actually reach a consensus and fight against Israel? In the past, they never reached a consensus and when they did, they lost the war. And besides, if you really think about what he said, it's natural that he, an Arab, will think this way. Especially when considering how Arabs are treated in this country.

We have a hard situation here, a situation in which the Israeli Arab population is being oppressed. When you are oppressed, you should be able to speak out against the oppressor. That's exactly what Bshara said in Damascus. We are part of the Arab world, do you understand? We are a part of this community even if we live in Israel, so Bshara was calling the Arab world to unite against Israel—a state that for the last 30 years has been abusing our brothers and sisters in the Occupied Territories. If you were abused, wouldn't you be calling other Jews to help you? It's exactly the same thing.

Q: So do you feel more Arab than Israeli?

Yes.

Q: Whose side, if at all, are you in this conflict?

Of the Palestinians, Arabs and Muslims.

Q: As you know, thirteen Israeli Arabs were killed by Israeli forces in the October 2000 riots. How do you feel about this?

This was an unjust act. The police should have acted differently. They could have arrested the people and interrogated them instead of shooting them. They could have even put them in jail if necessary. But to kill them? That was a disaster to kill these people like this, even if they threw a stone at the police forces. I think that God is the only one who has the right to deprive a person of his life. It's the same when there's a suicide bombing. Both these things are wrong because only God has the right to decide when it's a person's time to go.

The Israeli Arabs didn't demonstrate in favor of giving land to the Palestinians. They demonstrated because of Al Aqsa. It's a holy place, the third holiest after Mecca for Muslims all around the world. They started the demonstrations after the Palestinians began the Second *Intifada* in Nablus[78] and Jenin. Although we are angry that Palestinian houses are broken down, we've never gone and violently demonstrated against it. But Al Aqsa is a holy place for Muslims all around the world, not only for Palestinians. You have to remember that tourists were allowed into the Al Aqsa Mosque in order to enjoy its beauty. They were respectful and wanted to feel the wonderful atmosphere. But Sharon, on principle, wanted to go in there just in order to create a big mess. That is exactly what he did and look where we are all toady.

American Jews take care of Israeli Jews because they feel a strong connection to each other. I don't know why people were so surprised when we, Muslims, took the side of the Palestinians when Sharon entered Al Aqsa. So you see? Even in these things there is a law for Jews and a law for Arabs. A Jewish life counts and an Arab life doesn't. When a Jew helps a Jew, everyone understands, but when an Arab helps an Arab, everyone is shocked.

I am not exactly sure why the Israeli Arab men joined the riots. As you know, here in Abu Ghosh we haven't had many violent incidents. We prefer to keep things quiet so that Jews continue to come to our restaurants. But it sounds rational that some Israeli Arabs wanted to identify with the Palestinians and their struggle. Again, here in Abu Ghosh things were quiet, so I can't really answer your question.

I think that it was a huge mistake. But when a friend of mine from Karkur asked me about this incident, I told her that it wasn't entirely the Jew's fault, but rather of the Arab leaders, the members of parliament who sent them to confront the police forces. If I oppose the existence of the Occupied Territories the way they are today, then I can express it in other ways, not by putting myself, or sending my son to confront the Israeli Army or the Israeli police forces and become a *shaheed*. There is a fundamental problem within the Arab society today. We send our children to death too fast. But the problem also came from the Israeli police forces. I don't think I would kill a person who threw a stone at me. It just doesn't seem logical.

Q: But don't you think this makes Arabs ask themselves whether it's even worth being a citizen of this country if they can be killed in it when demonstrating?

On the contrary. I think that we have to try as much as we can to be a part of Israel, so that something like this doesn't happen again. We have to find ways to be with the country and not against it, so that the state doesn't go against us as it has before. We have to think how we can help the state and although this might not happen with Sharon as the prime minister, it can happen with another leader. The fact is that we must live together even if we don't like the idea. We, as Israeli Arabs, have to find a way to live together with the Israeli Jews. I don't have anything against the Jews and my sister even tells me that I am more Jewish than the Jews themselves and that I care more about the Jews than about the Arabs. But I don't care more about Jews specifically, I care about people, about human beings, period. Look, I am not afraid to walk down the streets of Tel Aviv even after suicide bombings. But my mother calls me on my cellular phone because she's worried. When I think of her, I also think about a Jewish mother who is calling her daughter because she's worried. And then I also think about the Palestinian mother. I think about everyone and I don't care who they are. There are Jews, Arabs, Israelis and Palestinians whom I don't like, but I love human beings.

How do I feel? What do you think? It was terrible. Think about yourself, if the Israeli forces murdered your son. It would hurt, wouldn't it? Even if this happened to a Jewish mother, I can feel her pain. A few weeks ago there was a suicide bombing and I cried when I saw the families who had lost their loved ones. Even when something painful happens to Jews, I hurt. So imagine when something so terrible happens to someone from my same religion and culture. I can still remember the pain and frustration I felt at the time.

Q: Do you think the Israeli forces had to shoot, or did they have other alternatives?

No! What's this? Shots against a stone? This was totally unnecessary and it was plain violence for the sole aim of killing. The Israeli forces wanted to kill these people in order to shut them up. This was pure violence aimed at Arab and Muslim people. During the October 2000 riots, the police forces shot Arabs all over Israel. One of my relatives got a bullet right in his back, can you believe?

Q: Had the demonstrators been Jews, do you think they would have been shot too?

The demonstrators were shot because they were Arab. The police would never shoot Jews here. About ten years ago in Rishon le Zion an Israeli Jew shot several Arabs. And after he did that, what did the police tell him? That he's crazy, that he's mentally sick, that he didn't intend to do what he did. When Jews go out and demonstrate are they killed? Never.

The Israeli police shooting at Jewish citizens? What a crazy idea! I will probably never live to see this.

Of course they wouldn't have shot Jews. There was one main thing that bothered me during these riots. In Nazareth, the Israeli police beat and even stepped on some Arab women who were just passing by. The police did this without any reason. We all saw it on television and it made me very angry. These girls were not even from my family and even if they were Jewish girls I would get angry if something like this happened to them. How do men dare to do such things to women? Aren't they ashamed of themselves? The other things that happened...I don't know what to think. Look, when the riots started, I was very close to the village of Arara. I could see some Arab men burning a gas station, and also a bank. I am against things like this and I don't care who does it. Personally, I can't hate anyone and I definitely can't kill anyone.

Q: So you weren't upset when you saw Israeli Arabs being shot?

I don't know. And you know, even if I were angry, what could I have done? We were very far from where the riots happened and we were very detached. And besides, we could never participate in such rioting. I don't feel that I can go and riot against a country in which I live, you understand? Even though I am Arab, this is still my country because I live here. What, will I go and throw a stone at Davor [the author's father]? He is Jewish, but he is a person whom I love and respect very much, so how can I even think of throwing a stone on him? I am not exactly sure what happened during the October 2000 riots because I live in a very small village and we work together with the Jews, and make a living together. What I saw about the riots was mostly through the television screen. I only spent a few hours in the north when the riots began and then returned to my village. How could

I then get up one morning and go against people who have always been my friends and helped me? And especially since most of them haven't done anything against me...how could I go and hurt them? I'll tell you another thing about this issue. Even during the riots, which I think lasted about four days, Jews continued coming to our village, especially on the weekend, on *Shabbat*. We didn't feel hatred from them towards us, seriously. Even today, Jews come to our village. Only a few weeks ago a young Jewish couple came to our village and sat together with us. I love the Jews and don't have anything against them. Of course, there are some bad Jews, but that doesn't mean that all of them are bad. If one Jew, let's say from the Israeli Border Patrol, did something bad to me, does this automatically mean that all Jews are bad? Of course not.

Q: Many Arabs I have spoken to told me that they aren't equal citizens in this country.

Well, maybe they feel that way, it's their right. But to tell you the truth, I don't really share their feeling. As I have said, our lands were taken away from us and that is not right. I don't feel, however, that I am really being discriminated against in Israel today.

Q: I have spoken to many Arabs, especially those living in Arara and the surrounding villages. Many of them said that the solution for the problem of their inequality in Israel is to join the Palestinians in the Occupied Territories and resist Israel. What do you think about this? Do you share their feeling and course of action?

No, I don't agree with them. I will never betray this country. I live here. I have been here during all the wars. I worked from the early morning to very late at night during the wars here. Believe me that people who saw what I did in the war would never even think of joining a war. At times I didn't even remember that I am an Arab. I felt that I was Jewish. I swear to you that I cried when I saw what I saw. I have a conscience. I am a good man. In places like Neve Ilan I feel at home, believe me. I have never felt any discrimination when working in Neve Ilan's swimming pool. I was always in charge of the opening and closing shifts, and if I needed help, I would always call Davor. I really loved the place, but I was fired, what can I do?

Q: Do you have any criticism towards the Israeli forces that reacted to the riots?

As I have said, the forces would have never shot Jews. You know that the Orthodox Jews used to demonstrate and block the road leading to

Ramot, or the road next to the central bus station. I have never heard that the police forces shot, not even in the air, against them. In October, the forces shot at people to frighten them, or maybe they were shot by mistake...how many were shot?

Q: Thirteen people were killed.

Thirteen, you see? Now they have an investigating Commission, but I am not sure what will come of it.

Q: Do you trust that the *Orr Commission* will bring justice to the people who were killed in the riots?

Yes, of course. Look, when a judge sits up there, it's not something simple, you know? If this were a committee composed of policemen, then it would be something different because they would probably lie and cover for one another. But a judge, in this case, even if he is a Jew, will say the truth and find the truth. I highly respect the judges in Israel and the court system in this country, because these judges weren't just people who were brought from the streets. These are wise people who understand the general situation and who know the law. I hope that things will get better and that the relationship between Jews and Arabs will go back to how it used to be before all these problems began about a year ago.

Look, this Commission, although it listens to the evidences and the reasons for what happened, will never condemn the Israeli police forces. It won't do anything. They should blame Sharon for going to Al Aqsa, because all of the problems started when he entered this place. But they won't condemn him either. But instead of doing that they will probably blame the Arab demonstrators for going out to the streets and defending their fundamental rights. Just wait and see.

I will tell you one thing about these riots. Barak is also responsible for the current situation. Sharon first, then Barak. Barak was prime minister at the time Sharon entered Al Aqsa and all these demonstrations started in the Palestinian Territories. Had Barak given orders not to kill the Arabs who demonstrated, none of this would have happened and everything would be okay. Instead of that the elections were cancelled. Barak also killed peace, not only Sharon.

I think that if the demonstrators were Jewish, they might have been interrogated. But killed? Of course not! That would never happen. Besides, I don't want anyone to die.

Of course Jews wouldn't have been shot. Are you joking? Where did you get this idea from? Even if Jews went out and cursed Arafat, or all of the Arabs in the world, the Israeli forces wouldn't harm or even touch them. You know that some Jews go out and yell, "Death to the Arabs" and no one touches them. That's because everyone agrees with them. When I say everyone here I mean the police forces. They, too, agree with these exclamations, so they protect Jews instead of Arabs.

You're kidding me, right?

Jews might have been shot. During the fighting in Jenin, Jews demonstrated and the police treated them like the Arabs.

Q: But were these Jews actually killed?

No.

Q: How did you feel after the October 2000 riots?

I have this feeling that I never really felt ever before. I am afraid for my life now. Who knows? Maybe some Jew will want to kill me?

A year and a half ago I went to see an art exhibition in Tel Aviv. We passed by a group of Jewish people who also came to the museum. At that time, the exhibition showed was a politically oriented one and it dealt with contemporary problems in Israel and Palestine such as the checkpoints and women's status in Arab society, especially in the Occupied Territories. Our director asked their director to sit down and talk about these issues and we all sat outside together. The conversation immediately turned to the thirteen *shaheeds*, the Israeli Arabs who were killed by the Israeli police after Sharon entered Al Aqsa and all the riots began. One woman looked at us and said, "You are Israeli Arabs and enjoy all the rights in this country. How can you suddenly decide to go against us?" And then, you know, our group of Israeli Arabs started speaking about the Jews and they argued with us until suddenly someone who was standing by and listening said to everyone, both Jews and Arabs, "All of you people, if you're arguing like this with one another, then go and live with Arafat. We don't need more people like you in this country, we have enough of them as it is."

Q: I spoke to many Arabs about the October 2000 riots. Many of them said that the riots were a response to years of silenced frustration. Do you agree with this claim?

Let me tell you something. Had I seen my children participate in these riots, I would have grabbed them and dragged them back home, do you understand? Why would I let them stay there? I think that most of the demonstrators in the October 2000 riots were probably unemployed and they didn't think that the police would come and that things would end so badly.

Q: Why do you think the police shot the demonstrators?

I don't know. They [the police forces] say that their lives were in danger, but I don't really believe this. If the policemen were in danger, they could have shot the men's legs and injured them. But instead, these men were shot right in the head. Something seems very strange here, don't you think?

Q: So, do you think that a Jew's life is worth more than an Arab's life?

Look, the police would never have shot Jews and had they shot Jews, there would have been an uprising here. People would go out into the street to riot and the media would be talking about it for months, maybe even for years. But what can I tell you? People have to ask the top officials who gave the order to shoot these people why they did so.

Q: **Many Arabs told me that the media mostly ignored the incident of the killing of the thirteen Israeli Arab men. They said that there was hardly any coverage of it. Do you think that this is true?**

To tell you the truth, I am not completely sure. I read the newspaper maybe once a month nowadays. I only scan the headlines and do you want to know something? I haven't even watched television in a month now because I am so fed up with the situation. Every day all we hear is that someone was killed. It is so depressing. I have lost interest in the news and in the media as a whole. When I am at work, I sometimes listen to the radio because it's almost impossible to avoid it in Israel. But then, you know that any moment you might hear about a suicide bombing somewhere. I used to have a television in my shop and when something like a suicide bombing happened, everyone came running in to see what was going on. In the end I decided to get rid of the television, because it was just too depressing.

Q: **You might have heard in the media about the *Orr Commission* whose job it is to investigate the Israeli Arab involvement during the October events. It is supposed to determine whether the men participating in the riots were unjustly killed. Do you believe that the *Orr Commission* can bring justice to Israeli Arabs?**

No, I don't believe in the *Orr Commission* whatsoever. This Commission is just a cover for the Israeli media in Israel, in the Arab countries, and the world as a whole. They will never arrest any of the people who shot the Arab men. It's all one big joke this Commission.

Wait, is this *Orr Commission* an international one?

Q: **No, it's a national one.**

Then no, it will not bring justice to Arabs in Israel.

Q: **Why not?**

Because even if they get to the root of the problem, I am sure the Commission will hide many things it doesn't want people to know about.

Q: **So, would you say that the life of a Jew and an Arab are not viewed as being equally important?**

Yes, the life of a Jew and that of an Arab is not viewed as being equal in this country. Listen, even in everyday life here in Israel it's evident. For example, I am a religious woman, and I want to cover, as my religion tells me to do. You know, in Qur'an women are commanded to cover themselves in order to maintain their modesty. But, at the moment I can't do this because if I cover, I will always be stopped in the street and questioned by the police. Because of this, I have decided not to cover. As a student, I can't be detained all the time because I might be late for classes. I observe all the other Muslim laws and obligations, especially the fasting during *Ramadan*.[79] I also pray five times every day when I can. It's just easier not to cover in Israel at the moment because of the political situation. This way I will also be able to find a job more easily. I used to work as a cashier in a store for a while. Have you ever seen a covered woman working as a cashier? If I stay uncovered, life will be easier for me and it's also easier for the Jews. Every day I feel the difficulties my mother, my cousins and my aunts who are covered encounter.

Q: Do you feel that not being able to cover takes away from who you are?

Yes.

Q: Can you imagine a time when you'll be able to walk around covered without feeling intimidated?

Only when there's co-existence between Jews and Arabs living in Israel. Only when people respect one another and one another's religion. Only when we reach the point where there's no difference between Jews and Arabs.

Q: The October riots allegedly began as a response to Sharon entering the Al Aqsa Mosque. Jews believe that the Western Wall is their holy site. Do you accept this claim?

Of course. I accept every person who is religious.

Q: The Jews believe it is their holy site and the Muslims believe it is theirs. How can this be solved?

Every person should believe in their own religion and pray in their own unique manner.

Q: The Jews believe that they have a holy site in Hebron, and in several other places. What do you think about this claim?

I know you Jews claim this in your Bible. But we follow Qur'an, and our Book says something completely different.

Q: For example?

Well, the Jews say that their forefather is Abraham and that he was buried in Hebron. You say that his son Isaac was nearly sacrificed. Our Qur'an says that his name was Ibrahim and that he nearly sacrificed Ishmael. We know that the Qur'an is the right one and that the Jews don't have any claim to these holy places, or to the land. The Qur'an is the only holy text that was never edited by human beings and has remained in its original form. This is why we know that it is the *only* truthful text.

Q: Do you think that there is a chance that the Qur'an was edited at some point in time?

I cannot believe you said this. Of course it was never edited or changed by human beings. This is why the Qur'an is different from the Jewish and Christian texts. The Jews and the Christians changed the text and added or subtracted whatever they wanted. We accept that the Torah and the New Testament were also given to humans by God, but we also know for a fact that the texts Jews and Christians read today are very different from the original ones. This is why God sent human beings the Qur'an—because there was a need for a pure text which contains the direct words of God to mankind. We Muslims know, therefore, that the Qur'an is the only text which would be followed today and this is why we are glad when people become Muslim and adopt Islam as their religion. It means that they understand the supremacy of the Qur'an. It means that they will look good in the eyes of God on the Day of Judgment.

Q: Do you think that there is a way for Jews and Muslims to coexist when Muslims claim that the Jews changed their holy texts and manipulated the word of God?

It is not a matter of whether Jews and Muslims can coexist. Whether they can or can't has nothing to do with my belief that Islam is the right way and that the Qur'an was never edited by human beings. We *know* that we are right and we *know* that the way of Islam will ultimately triumph. It will triumph because it is the *only* pure way of reaching God.

Q: Do you think that Jews and Christians can peacefully share the holy sites, those they both believe are holy to them?

These places are not holy to the Jews. Jerusalem, Hebron and all the other places are Muslim places and we have the right to them. When this is a Palestinian state the Jews have no right to come there and worship.

Q: Why do you think that many Israeli Arabs, who according to you can openly condemn acts of terror, don't?

Because they want to be like Bshara who has become more extreme. Look, if there's no reconciliation and no love between people on both sides, there will always be hatred and suspicion between the two groups. This also applies to the leadership which I don't trust at all.

Why condemn the death of Jews? Did any Jew genuinely condemn the killing of the thirteen Israeli Arabs? Of course not, and I am sure most of them were even happy about it. So, we treat them like they treat us.

Smadar, if you lived in a place where you weren't seen as an equal citizen, would you feel any sympathy for it and for its people? I don't think you would.

Q: Please tell me a bit about the Arab communities you know, in terms of their daily life during these hard times.

Look, I want to emphasize that everyone has work if they want it. Look we have over 400,000 foreign workers in Israel. That means that there's work, doesn't it? The Jews don't want to work hard, the Arabs don't want to work hard, so that's it. Yes, there's work for everyone. Isn't there work in agriculture? Isn't there work in construction? Don't we need more teachers in our schools? Aren't there enough odd jobs to be done? Everything's available. But you know what the problem is? The problem is that the minimum wage isn't really worth working for. An unemployed person gets the same amount a working person gets, so why work? All of this is connected to the education people receive. And it's no secret that people in Arab villages in Israel aren't receiving a great education. In every society, education must be good and effective. But it's more than that. Education is something that begins at home, in the family. If a family strives to educate their children, then the children will be educated. I feel that many Arabs don't put an emphasis on their children's education. I can't always blame the Ministry of Education for all the faults in our education, or the Ministry of Health for all the diseases, or the Ministry of Transportation for all the car accidents. These things are also a matter of culture. Something which begins in one's home, with the education one gets from one's parents. What I am trying to say is that within the Arab village, within the Arab family unit, there are also fundamental problems. Not everything comes from the outside, although some definitely does. Look, it's just like with car accidents in this country. There's an accident because people don't care and don't pay attention. It's the same with education for some people here. Many Arab people don't care. The Arab mentality has a part in the backwardness of the people, but it's not everything, of course. The family and one's culture is a big part of a person's life and upbringing.

There is a problem for women within the Arab society. An Arab woman can't usually say "No" to her parents. If we say "No" it's as though the end of the world has come. In our society, there are many things which are taboo. These things are kept in secret and not talked about. The best example is the one about a girl living with her boyfriend before getting married. If an Arab woman from Arara has a boyfriend, she must keep it as a deep secret or she might be killed. If a woman is married to a man whom she doesn't love, it's still very hard for her and sometimes even impossible, to get a divorce. She might have to walk to the end of the world and even beyond in order to get it and better her life. I have a friend who is a teacher. She got married and divorced, but her family and the society in which she was living, didn't accept the divorce. The thing is that no one even tried to think or figure out why she asked for the divorce in the first place. No one thought, or maybe people just chose to ignore, that for twenty-five years she was suffering physical and emotional abuse. Here they think that if you are a woman and you suffered for twenty-five years, you can suffer for twenty-five more until you die.

Q: But do you think that Arab society has more problems and restrictions concerning women that the Jewish society in Israel, for example?

How do you generally view Arab Israeli society? Is it becoming more open, or more restricted and closed?

Let me tell you something. The Israeli Arab society in not open in all respects. I think that to an extent we have advanced in the field of education. We have more people, both men and women, who have at least a high school level of education. Arabs have to put more emphasis on their education. I will give you another example of an area which has not advanced whatsoever. Of course, it's connected to women, as it usually is. I love to belly dance. I don't want to do this as a profession, but it's definitely a hobby of mine. Here, there's no way I can belly dance. If I start learning how to belly dance, my culture will define me as a whore. I have another example. When I started painting, I was very much drawn to the symbol of the Cross. I incorporated crosses into all of my paintings. I was immediately confronted by many covered women who asked me, "Why do you draw such things?" And truthfully, I have no idea why I did it. I just did. Here people always ask, "Why?" "Why?" They always want answers to everything. If you try to be different, or make a change, people think the end of the world has come. They will turn an intimate and personal thing into a public crime so that everyone knows your business. When I paint, I paint whatever comes into my mind and hand. It's a personal thing that just comes into being. I never plan what I am going to paint, things just happen. Last year, for example, I created a piece of art about the human egg and sperm. This idea came to me very suddenly, even though I knew it was taboo in our society. At the same time, I got a phone call saying that my uncle who was living in the West Bank was shot by the Israeli Army. I was working and crying at the time. I worked like a mad woman in order to finish this final work. I love to create things about erotica and sexual relations even though it is against Islam. I also created a piece of art made out of bread rolls and without planning, it also turned out into sexually-oriented work. So, as you can see, I create things about issues most Muslim Israeli Arab women would not dare to publicly touch and speak about. I think it is a pity they do not want or cannot speak about these things because these are some of the most serious problems our society is facing. If we want to change our society we have to listen to women and see what their needs are. The problem is that in our society the emphasis is usually not necessarily on what is good for the women.

Q: How do you use art to express your feelings about the Israeli Arab society you call restrictive? I saw your art piece in which you put images of naked women into tightly sealed glass jugs filled with oil. Who are these women?

Smadar, these are Arab women. It's me, it's her [pointing at her sister] and almost every Arab woman. There is a kind of restriction in our society which isn't changing for the better. There are hardly any Arab women here who cross the line and take a chance. There are hardly any Arab women who do what *they* want to do. There are so many Arab women who still can't leave their homes and who are living in continuous fear from their husbands and brothers. I am not like that and maybe I have a friend or two who is not like that. I am not like that because I will not allow myself to be like that. But the woman we spoke to yesterday who said that the Arab woman is still restricted by her society, religion and tradition was right. It's as though Arab women are stuck fifty years ago.

Q: Do you create any political art such as the art exhibited in the Umm el-Fahem art gallery?

No, in my art I don't primarily convey political ideas. I first and foremost concentrate on women and their status in the Arab society. In a way, I am trying to liberate myself from who I am, from myself as a woman. In my art I try to express what I, as Muna, who is a woman wants. I think that one day, if there's time, I will start to create political art as well. Now I am thinking about myself as a woman and I am thinking about mothers and sisters.

Q: Have you had any negative experiences within the Arab society because of your openness?

Yes, I had some negative experiences in the Umm el-Fahem art gallery. One of the women working in the gallery told our director that many parents won't send their children to the gallery because of how I dress. She told the director that my clothing does not fit the standard of the Umm el-Fahem population. The director told me this and I looked at him and said, "Today you'll tell me how to dress, tomorrow how to talk, the day after it will be where I can go and not go and after all that you'll control each and every move I make. I don't want this job, I am leaving." He started muttering and saying that he personally didn't care how I dressed and that it was the other people who had a problem with it. I just repeated that I didn't want the job and then resigned and left. What matters to me about all this is who I am. That's much more important to me that both money and fame. I stopped working there and I didn't even work in their summer camp. They hired two other women, one of whom is covered and the other wearing long and modest clothes. I just said goodbye.

Q: Do you see this as a global problem within Arab society?

I think that there are different degrees of oppression within Arab society. Some women suffer more, some less and some not at all. But yes, generally I view this as a problem the world's Arab Muslim society is dealing with, more than any other society. It is enough to look at Muslim and Arab women in the Middle East and even in other regions of the world. Why are most of them the poorest, most uneducated and least advanced women in the world? Why have they not been able to advance? Why are they still stuck? There must be a reason because it can't only be by chance that hundreds of millions of women from the same religion are in the same sad and even tragic situation.

Q: If you could choose what to do with your life, what would you do?

I would really like to leave the village, rent an apartment in Tel Aviv and work in an art gallery. Also, I would really like to have a boyfriend and maybe even get married. In the village a woman can wait all her life and not get married. Here, a woman has to wait for a man to propose marriage and she is not allowed to initiate any contact. I know people don't speak about this often, but I know for a fact that some women are murdered here by their husbands and brothers in the name of the family's honor. Can you even believe that this is still happening? I know that no one will marry me here. I am too different, too independent, too free.

Q: Do you think you will be able to leave the village and do what you want?

No.

I think that sometimes we have really big problems in our family. No, it's not specifically in the family, but in our society as a whole. For example, some people have religious weddings, so men and women are separated. Some people, however, prefer to have a secular wedding where men and women can dance together if they want. In Islam it is not allowed for men and women to dance together in public, especially if they are not married. The thing is that one has to admit that a secular wedding is much more fun than a religious one. It's freer, people dress how they wish and families are not torn apart. Tonight, as you know, there's a wedding. The groom's mother is Palestinian and she's very religious. His father isn't that religious but he wanted to have a religious wedding to satisfy his wife. The groom didn't agree. He wanted a secular wedding where everyone can mingle. His mother attended the Henna party and the Hamam celebration, where the groom takes a shower in a friend's home and then is shaved and prepared for the wedding, but she did not go to the wedding. My husband is much more religious than I am. So he stayed home tonight while I went to the wedding together with my daughter. What's the point of this? It's much more fun to have everyone sit together and enjoy the wedding.

I am about to finish high school. I will try to get into an Israeli university, but if I can't I will go to Irbid. When I was in high-school here, I had to write an extensive paper which is something like a thesis. I wrote about the British Mandate in Israel. I got a very high grade and I was even called for an interview because the teachers thought I had copied it from somewhere. It was such a great paper and everyone was reading it.

Q: Why do you want to go to university?

I think we have a problem with women in our society. Many women still marry at a very early age and are not able to go to university and become educated. Because of this, they are always dependent on a man to provide for them. They get pregnant and don't have tome to study or do whatever she likes. I want to study now. I am young. I still have many years to find a husband and marry. If I marry now, I will have to either stay in my village or go to my husband's village. I will not able to complete my degree. And even if he will let me complete my degree, I will still not be completely independent. I don't want to be like so many other Arab and Muslim women. I want a career and to know that I an independent. I mean, you never know if something will happen to your husband. What if, God forbid, something bad happens to him and I am all alone? I have to be able to be in charge of my life. Then I can marry and have children.

Q: Last year when I was here you were not wearing the *hijjab* right?

No, I was not. You have a great memory. I started wearing it about a year ago, during Ramadan.

Q: Why did you decide to wear it?

I felt that I had to, that God wanted me to do this. No one forced this on me. It was my own decision and I think it's my responsibility. You know, in Islam this is something women must do, according to the Holy Qur'an. I feel that I can make my decisions now and this was one of the most important decisions I have ever made.

I have worn a *hijjab* for years now. It's a wonderful thing. No wonder God wanted women to wear it. The problem is that many Muslim women start neglecting themselves once they wear it. They stop going to the hairdresser and taking care of their hair. They stop taking care of their face—they neglect their eye brows and skin. I think that even when a woman starts wearing a *hijjab* she should take care of how she looks and not neglect her body. Look at the women who were in the wedding. Many of them wore a *hijjab* but they also wore nice clothes and put on some make up. One must not exaggerate, of course, but some light make up and a nice long dress makes me feel that yes, I am religious and modest, but I am also a woman who wants to look elegant. Many Muslim women forget this and look terribly neglected. A *hijjab* is supposed to help us stay modest, but I don't think it's supposed to make up look ugly and neglected. I still go to the hairdresser and still take care of myself.

Islam is the only true and perfect religion and the Qur'an is the only true manifestation of God on this earth. Let me tell you why. It is not only because it's the only holy text which was not edited and was not forged by people. Think about this. Everything is written in the Qur'an. Everything which happened and everything which is about to happen in the future. All you need to do is read the Qur'an and you'll see that this is true. The people who are converting to Islam today are not only simple people who might not be educated. Even scientists are converting to Islam. Do you know why? Because they find out that everything they know, everything they conducted experiments in order to prove is written in the Qur'an. The best example is about the human body. For years scientists were debating what was created first; the flesh or the bones. After many experiments it was determined that the bones were created before the flesh. Do you know how many years they had to work in order to figure this opt? All they should have done is read the Qur'an and they would have found this answer. Today many educated people are realizing that everything they need is in the Qur'an. This book has answers for everything human beings need and want to know. This is why so many scientists and educated people are converting to Islam. If you really want to know the truth, many Jews even believe in the Qur'an but they don't want to admit it. Ever Rabbis believe in it, and many Christians as well. They see that it's a perfect text which predicts the future and are too embarrassed to speak out and say that they believe in it.

I am from South American origin, from Argentina. I met my husband many years ago and moved to live in Israel. He is Israeli-Arab. I have been here for nearly twenty one years. I speak Arabic very well, but I have not had a chance to perfect my Hebrew. I would like to speak Hebrew as well so that I can communicate more freely with Jewish Israelis. When I decided to move here, I converted to Islam.

Q: Why did you choose to do this? Do you believe in Islam?

No, I don't believe in it at all, but I converted so that I can marry my husband. It's hard to live in an Arab village if you're not a Muslim. For me, the religion is not important. Had a met a Jewish man and fallen in love with him, I would have probably converted to Judaism. For me, it was important to find a good husband. Then I could decide what religion I wanted to be. I chose Islam because it makes my life better. But I don't believe in it as a religion. Sometimes you have to do what makes your life easier.

In order to come and live in this Arab village, I converted to Islam.

Q: How did you do this? Did you go to an Imam? Did you have to study something?

Not really. It was very easy. I went with my husband to someone in Jerusalem, who is authorized to convert people to Islam. I then had to recite the Fatiha.

Q: Did you know it by heart?

Not at all. I didn't know Arabic there. I was holding a page in my hand which had the Fatiha written in English letters. I said it and then I was Muslim. It took about two seconds.

Q: Did you know what you were saying?

Well, not exactly. As I said, it took only a few seconds. I didn't have to prepare for it or anything. I just knew that it would make my life easier in terms of being accepted by the family and by the community.

Many people, especially women, are moving to our village. They convert to Islam, learn Arabic and stay. Some of them are even more religious that women who were born Muslim. Many of the converts wear the *hijjab* and observe Ramadan. They also read the Qur'an everyday.

Q: Could a woman who is not Muslim comfortably live in your village?

No, I don't think so. It's important for us that people are Muslim. If a Jewish or Christian woman, for example, converts to Islam then everything's fine and there is no problem. Several Jewish and Christian women have already converted to Islam and moved to my village. But if they don't convert it's a problem. According to Jews, if the mother is Jewish, the child is Jewish. According to us, if the father is Muslim, the child is Muslim. If the woman doesn't convert, it'll just cause the child, as well as the parents, many unnecessary problems. Their life could become quite miserable. It's best for the woman to convert and to agree to raise the child Muslim. Then it's fine and the marriage is accepted. We have a German woman here who was a Christian but who converted to Islam and came here.

Q: Was she accepted?

In the beginning it was a bit hard because she and her husband lived together in Europe before they got married. I think they lived together for seven or eight years. The family didn't accept this and told their son that he couldn't bring her back to the village with him. He was very stubborn, however. He said, "I am building a house in the village and I am bringing my wife back with me!" He did exactly that. She came here and as a first stage converted to Islam. Then she started dressing more conservatively. Her husband's family still did not accept her and didn't invite her to their house. After a year or so she gave birth to a son. That was when the family started to accept her. First they invited their son, her husband, and the child to the house. Then they started inviting her to the house too. They saw that she was a good woman and that she respected Islam. Now they love her and invite her to their house all the time. She has several sons now and they are raised, thank God, Muslim. So, as you can see, it's a process. And converting to Islam solves a lot of the problems.

Q: In the United States there are more and more intermarriages happening. Jews marry Muslims, Christians marry Jews and Muslims. Many times the couple decides to raise the child with both religions or with no religion at all. What do you think about this?

This is very bad. Firstly, a child must have a religion. It can be Jewish and it can be Muslim or Christian. But it must be one of these religions. Secondly, it's not wise to raise a child with more than one religion. How will he know which one is right? How will he grow according to two sets or laws and rules which at times contradict one another? It's an impossible thing and I think it would result in the torture of the child. The parents must decide; either the child is Jewish, or he's Muslim. The two can't go together, naturally.

Media: Interviews with Children

Q: Are you generally interested in politics?

Yes, I am, but I hate hearing the news because it makes me very angry.

Q: Why?

I was watching the news one evening and I saw an Israeli soldier kill Palestinian children. The Palestinian children don't know how to defend themselves and the Israeli Army comes with their tanks and guns and fights against them. Did you see how the soldiers killed Muhammad al-Durrah?[80] What chance did he have against their guns? He was hiding behind his father and then the soldiers killed him. I saw all of that on television, on *Al Jazeera*.

Q: What do people in your house say after they watch the news?

They say that the Jews are killing the Palestinians and that *Inshallah* [God willing] the land will return to the Palestinians and will be called Palestine once again. My father listens to the news every day and he usually tells me what happened that day in Palestine. So I know for a fact that every day Palestinian women and children are killed there, especially in Jenin.

Q: Do you think that everything that is said in the news is true?

Yes.

Q: Why?

I don't know why, but I don't see any reason why they wouldn't tell us the truth.

Q: Generally speaking, are you interested in politics?

Yes, very much.

Q: Where do you usually hear the news?

I mostly hear it on *Al Jazeera* and also on a Syrian channel from time to time.

Q: Do you hear the news on Israeli channels as well?

No, not very often. I don't like hearing the news anymore.

Q: You don't like hearing the news at all, or on Israeli channels?

Generally, but especially on Israeli channels.

Q: Why?

It's terrible how they lie and how they pretend that Palestinians aren't getting killed in the Occupied Territories. I can't watch it anymore.

Q: When you watch the news, do you think that everything that is said is true?

Yes, I think so.

Q: Do you see any differences between the Israeli and Arab news channels at all?

Yes, of course, there are many I could point to.

Q: Can you provide me with an example?

The news in *Al Jazeera* is very different from the Israeli news. Israeli news channels don't bring the news in a good and truthful way. *Al Jazeera* brings all the news without hiding anything. *Al Jazeera* is bringing the truth to the people while the Jews are hiding a lot of what they are doing. If I want to know what is going on, I can't trust the Jewish channels at all.

Q: How do you know this?

When there was a suicide bombing, the Jews said that fifty people were injured and killed, but in actuality it was only twenty three people. So why did they say in the news that it was fifty?

Q: But on *Al Jazeera* and on other Arab stations they said that over hundreds of people were killed by the Israelis in Jenin. In the end, it was proven that about fifty were killed, mostly terrorists.

No, no, that was a mistake. There were more than fifty people killed in Jenin. The Jews killed much more and then lied about the whole thing.

Q: Do you think that everything that is said in the news is the truth?

There are some things which are complete lies. There are news programs and individuals who lie on the Israeli side and some who lie on the Palestinian side. Those who are on the Palestinian side say things which will turn all the Arabs and Muslims in the world against Israel and those on the Israeli side say things to turn all the Jews in the world to the Israeli side. Not everything in the news is a lie, but I think that there are a lot of lies on both sides.

Q: When you watch the news, are there some things you can't understand from time to time?

Yes, sometimes there are words I can't understand, so I ask my parents, and they explain things to me.

Q: Do you think that there are differences between the Hebrew and Arabic news programs?

I think that usually the news programs are the same, but sometimes I feel that the news programs in Hebrew take the news in Arabic and translate it into Hebrew. Then they make some changes and present it to the public.

Q: Do you thing that there are negative effects to the news?

I think that sometimes there are negative effects because there are a lot of lies in the news and people argue with one another using these lies. Then in the end one really doesn't know what is the truth and what is a lie.

Q: Where do you usually watch the news?

I watch it on *Al Jazeera* and sometimes also in a channel coming from Saudi Arabia. I watch a few more Arab channels, but I can't remember their names at the moment.

Q: Do you watch the news every day?

I watch the news nearly every day. I watch it especially when something bad happens in Palestine.

Q: When you watch the news, what are some of the things that stick in your mind?

I can remember well when I saw Muhammad al-Durrah.

Q: What did you see?

Well, he was there with his father and there were shots everywhere.

Q: Who was shooting?

The Israeli Army was shooting because they wanted to kill Muhammad.

Q: What happened in the end?

The soldiers shot him in the head.

Q: Some people say that it is possible that Muhammad was killed by the Palestinians and not by the Israelis.

This is nonsense. It is not possible. Everyone knows it was the Israelis because it was shown on television.

Q: What do you think of Muhammad al-Durrah?

I think he is a hero and he was lucky to die this way. He is an example for all Palestinians.

Q: When there's a suicide bombing, what television channel do you turn to?

Sometimes the Israeli channel, but usually a channel from one of the Arab countries, I can't remember exactly which one.

Q: Why do you prefer the Arab channels?

I know that on the Israeli channel the reporters always lie about the true situation.

Q: Can you give me a specific example?

On the Israeli channel, they call the person who exploded himself a terrorist who committed suicide. On the Arab channels they call him a *shaheed*. It's obvious that the person who blew himself up is a *shaheed* and not just someone who died for nothing. The Israeli news channels will never admit that that is what he is. They will say that he has killed innocent people and that he is a murderer. That's why I go to the Arab channels where they respect the *shaheed*.

Q: Is it possible that a *shaheed* is really someone who murdered innocent civilians?

No.

Q: Why not?

People who took our land are not innocent people.

Q: Where do you usually see the news?

On Al Jazeera.

Q: Why on that one in particular?

Because it's the most reliable one. It comes from an Arab state.

Q: Do you think that every piece of news that comes from an Arab state is the truth?

Yes, they know what they are talking about.

Q: And the Israeli news channels? Do you watch them?

No, never. It's all lies anyway, so why watch?

Q: Who told you this?

My family and my friends. We never watch the Israeli news channels because what they broadcast is fake and full of lies.

Q: Are you generally interested in politics?

No, I am not interested at all. People in this part of the world only think about politics. Everything is politics, politics, politics. People get together and can't talk about anything else. They even talk about politics in weddings and in happy occasions. It gets boring and annoying. I like to watch movies and not think about how bad things are now.

Q: Which movies do you like?

I like movies with Rambo, and also movies with cowboys.

Q: Are you generally interested in politics?

Sometimes I am and sometimes I am not.

Q: What do you mean?

I hate the political situation here now and the news depresses me. Sometimes I also get bored—things are always the same and always bad. When I feel like this I don't care about anything I don't watch the news. Other times when something really important happens, I open the television and watch the news.

Q: What do you mean by "something important?"

When there is a suicide bombing, for example, or when something happens in the Occupied Territories.

Q: Do you understand everything that is said in the news?

Yes. I always watch the news on Arabic news channels, so I can understand almost everything they are saying.

Q: Why do you watch Arab channels and not Israeli ones?

I don't trust what the Jews say about the situation.

Q: Why is that?

The Jews want all the land to themselves so in the news they show only what they want people to see. They want people to think that they are the victims and that they are the ones who are being attacked.

Q: Aren't they also being attacked sometimes?

If they are being attacked, it is their own fault. They get what they deserve.

Q: What do you mean?

If they didn't take the lands from the Palestinians, then from the very beginning all this mess wouldn't have happened. And if they left the Occupied Territories, then maybe the situation would change.

Q: There are Israeli Jews who support a withdrawal from the West Bank and Gaza. Many of them are afraid, however, that once the Israeli Army withdraws from these areas, fundamental Muslim terror will continue. What do you think?

The Muslims will never like the Jews.

Q: Why?

The Jews were never good to the Muslims. They always rejected Islam and did not accept is and convert.

Q: Let us assume that what you just said is true. Don't you think that enough time has passed since this happened? Do you not think that the situation is now different and that people should look to the future?

Even if we have to look to the future it does not mean that the Jews change. They are who they are. Who they always were. They will not change their ways.

Education: Interviews with Adults

Q: Do you believe that there is a difference between the education Jews and Arabs receive?

Of course. There's even a difference in the quality of education different groups of Jews receive. Tel Aviv is the most classic example. Look at northern Tel Aviv versus southern Tel Aviv. There's a huge difference between the two. In the northern part you'll see clean and organized children and in the southern part you will see dirty and disorganized ones. In the southern part you'll find uncontrollable youth inclined to participate in crime. The Arabs are a part of all these groups. So you can see that the divisions are not only between Arabs and Jews, but also among the Jews. And I know that the same thing happens among the Arabs. Some are richer and some are poorer. Isn't it like that all over the world?

The field of education is one in which Arabs have always been discriminated against. I suspect that the Jews have always wanted to keep us uneducated so that we would not take over. But, as you might know, we will take over. We will have more babies than you will. Wait and see.

Some of the problems in terms of the education Arabs receive are caused by the mentality of our culture. Finally we are starting to join fields of study in which we were never interested before. Us Arabs, we don't want to learn everything, only the selective professions that are considered to be good, such as being a doctor. I don't think that all the problems come from the state. Many Arab students aren't encouraged by their high schools to go and further their education. They don't receive any advice from their teachers. Some students start majoring in one thing and then, after two or three years decide to suddenly change it. I think, therefore, that a lot of the inequality in the field of education comes from the Israeli Arab society itself. Then there are things, like the security issue, which come from above. I do feel that Arabs are not allowed to be involved in all aspects of society, especially security, and that they can't be promoted beyond a certain point. In spite of this, I don't object. If I were living in an Arab country such as Syria, I probably wouldn't let a member of the minority, especially if we were at war, participate in all aspects of the security sector.

Look Smadar, there are definitely differences between Jewish and Arab schools. We still have many children learning in pre-fabricated houses, not in regular buildings. We also have small classrooms, which never have air conditioning. And we don't usually have laboratories in our schools. What I am telling you is that we don't have anything in our schools. Nothing. Go to a Jewish school and you'll see that most of them have all these things. They have basketball courts and football fields, playgrounds. They have all the things that our school in Arara doesn't have, for example.

I think that if a school's principal asked for funds he would get it. If he doesn't ask, he will not get anything. I have seen Arab schools which are identical to Jewish schools. I don't think that this problem comes necessarily only from the state. I can't just sit around and complain. I have to make sure the state knows I exist and want something. Sometimes I feel that we complain too much without doing anything. For example, *Mifal Hapayis*[81] gave us many things, and a lot of money. Many things were done in our village with this money at the time when people in the village were fighting about who would be the next mayor.

That there is no real discrimination is correct, but when you dig into things, you'll find some cases. I will give you an example. Most Arab people don't go to university to learn how to be a doctor or a lawyer. And you know, today many Israelis, or let's say most Israelis who have the ability to study, go to Europe to study, even though it's much better to stay here. Most Arabs can't choose what kind of an education they want. Now, whoever served in the Israeli military will find it much easier to study in Israel or abroad. For them it's very easy. The media, of course, says it's all about finances. They say that whoever has the money can go and study, or do anything else they might want. He can start a fight and no one will stop him. As I have said before, everything's about money.

There is a serious economic inequality here. I visit many Israeli Jewish schools. I see their computer facilities, their libraries which are full of books, their laboratories. In all of Arara and in all of Arara's schools we don't have any of these things, only empty classrooms. We don't even have air conditioning here.

As an Arab, if I want to study something like being a pilot or even a doctor, I can't do so. We can't get promoted in certain fields of education. And there's another issue here. There are also some educational restrictions such as being allowed to begin studying some fields only at the age of twenty one. Why? The Arab student goes to university at the age of eighteen, and the Jew goes to the Israeli Army. Here, they don't allow Arabs to study immediately after high school.

Q: I spoke to a Jewish Israeli person and he told me about an idea which has begun surfacing in Israel lately. He said that maybe there should be a total separation between Israeli Jews and Israeli Arabs. What do you think about such an idea? Do you think it's feasible?

Whoever has such an opinion is not only stupid, but worse than that, a complete idiot. A total separation is not possible. It just isn't possible at all. Maybe when you have a specific isolated settlement far away, or in a *Moshav* in the south it's possible to just build a fence and segregate people. But when you have an every day life like in Israel where people live together, it's impossible. No, it would be too hard to do such a thing. There are more than a million Arabs in Israel, how can segregation be possible? When looking for work, Jews and Arabs meet. When standing in the social security lines, Jews and Arabs meet. People meet. Whoever said that a separation is possible is an idiot. We are speaking about millions of people on both sides, not about one person.

It can't be, and it's not possible to separate Jews and Arabs here. You tell me: do you think that such a ridiculous thing is possible?

Look, I have relatives in Jordan and also in Ramallah. So what? People have no right to speak about such a separation, or to say such things. People like that harm me, because I have decided to make my future in Israel. I think it's good for a person to criticize his own country. I criticize Israel many times, just like some Jews who love Israel do. I criticize the state in order to make things better, and not worse, God forbid. The problem I have here is that if I criticize Israel or the Jews, I am automatically viewed as anti-Semitic or a Jew hater. I have to be able to reach a point where I can, as an Israeli citizen living in Israel, criticize my country and call for justice and equality without being viewed as an Arab who hates the Jews. As I have said before, the Arab leadership in the world is failing. They are fractured, and they care only about themselves. On the other hand, we Arabs also want the Jewish leadership to recognize that we are currently suffering, and that we have gone through a lot of pain. So all those people who speak of complete separation between the two forget that we have also been here for a long time, and that we have no where to go. We have no where to go, and the Jews have no where to go. What does that mean? That we better learn how to live together, so that at least we have one safe haven. If we kill one another here, what will we achieve?

Q: How do you feel when hearing that some Jews don't see Arabs as citizens of Israel and call for separation?

I am not surprised to hear such claims by Jews. I told you already that what I see when I look at the Jews is extremism, and not a will for coexistence. It's something they learn in their schools and homes. I am not surprised. The people in the Israeli government, and other people here don't even have a right to say such a thing.

I have never even thought about a possibility of separation between Jews and Arabs in Israel. I don't know what to tell you. But now that I hear that some Jews are hoping for such a thing, I feel very hurt.

The future depends on the children. If they are raised to be tolerant, the future might be good. If not, then we are all doomed. Schools, as well as the home, have an important role here, and it's obvious that some children, on both sides, are not being educated to respect the other side.

Yes, I know that some people in Israel feel this way, but I really don't think it's the majority of the population. And those who say these things, let them say what they want. In every country there are people like that, what can you do? Because someone thinks this way will I stop my life and get all depressed? No. I will continue living my life just the way it is at the moment. I will continue to follow Jesus Christ and His words when he said that we should love everyone, and that even sinners should not be hated. I must be tolerant towards these people even if I don't like them, and even if I strongly disagree with what they think. Maybe if I don't go down to the level of these people, they will change their behavior. If I go down to their level, I am certain that they will never change. My aim is to remain tolerant because I am the one who wants to live in peace with myself. Even if I am alone in my belief, like Jesus Christ was when only a dozen people followed him in the beginning, I can still succeed in what I believe.

Q: Do you think there's democracy in Israel?

Democracy? There's democracy everywhere in the world, also in Israel, but only for those who are strong and in control. Those who are not strong lose. What's democracy? It's for people who are strong and can do whatever they want to. If someone came and asked me to enter the Mahsom Carney now, I would tell him he can't because he doesn't have a permit. But if he has connections, he can call a few people and get permission to enter. So people chose their leader, is this democracy? Then in the every day life, democracy disappears. It's the strong ones who decide what will happen. I will give you an example from life in Israel. The radio is controlled by specific families. If I want to go and work in a radio station, I can't because I am not a part of that family. So is this democracy? Democracy is about who is strong and about who has connections. And in economics, is there democracy? No, it's all about making money. And even in a democracy there are stupid rules and regulations. Is the law that allows women to rent their wombs in order to carry the fetus of another man and woman a democratic law? This is stupidity. So you see, democracy also does things like this. But in a rational society, in my opinion, and I am a Muslim, or in the opinion of a religious Jew, such things aren't acceptable. A religious Jew will say this is not an acceptable or allowed thing, and a person living on a *Kibbutz* will say that it's a perfectly normal thing.

Maybe there's democracy for Jews in Israel, but not for the Arab citizens. For Arabs there is no democracy here. Look, in this country, a Jew can speak up and say whatever he or she wants. An Arab, even if he says something of no importance can be taken to the Shabak for an interrogation. There they would ask him why he said what he said, and what his intentions might have been. And you know, there are people who secretly work with the Shabak and the Mossad everywhere. A few years ago, I was sitting with some friends of mine in our village, and we were talking about politics, as usual. Everyone was saying how Israel was stronger than all the Arab countries. And I agreed, because I do believe that Israel is the strongest country in the Middle East at the moment. One of the men then said, "You never know what the Arabs have. You sure don't know what they have." After a few days he was summoned to be interrogated as to what he said, and why he might have said it. He said that he was just joking, but you see how it is? If he were a Jew, he would never have been summoned and interrogated. If you are an Arab in Israel, you have to be extremely careful with what you say, and even what you think. Even if you live here, and even if you have never done anything against the state, you have to be very careful when talking. So, when it comes to democracy, there is a very big difference between Jew and Arab. Democracy should mean that everyone has the same opportunities in everything, right? In Israel it is obvious that it is better to be Jewish, and that the more Jewish you are, the more democracy you receive. The best example relates to the military service. All the work places know that most Arabs did not serve in the Israeli Army. In spite of this, they still consider to the Army as a prerequisite for getting a job. So, of course a Jew will get the Job before an Arab, and that is not fair.

Q: Some Jews I have spoken to believe that Jews and Arabs should not live together. This belief is taught in some Jewish households where people believe that the Arabs are only guests on this land. What do you feel when you hear such things?

Look, there is no choice but for Israeli Jews and Israeli Arabs to live together. There's not enough room for separation, and we have always lived together. This is a small country, one can cross it with a car in a few hours all the way from Eilat in the south, to Kiryan Shemona and the Golan in the north. I think it's a huge mistake to say such things. Where would the Arabs go? People think that the Arabs here in Israel have many places to go to. But if they knew about politics, they would know that the Arabs in the Arab countries around us don't like us at all. They even don't like the Palestinians, so how would they like us? But you know what? Let the Jews who think and speak this way say whatever they want. It will never happen. We can't be separated. What, will they cut the state into two? Don't they have enough problems with separating the Israelis and the Palestinians already? Or will the state take more than a million Arabs and just throw them aside? The politicians in the government, those chosen by the people, they will never agree to doing such a ridiculous thing, even if there are some Jews who want this to happen. And I am sure that only a minority of Jews want this to happen. If it happened, do you know what would happen? The other countries around the world would say, "Israel is an anti-Semitic country!" And then how will Israel be viewed by the world? It's already viewed by the world in a negative way, don't you think? Do you know what I personally think should be done? I think that a new page between Jews and Arabs should be opened. We don't have to look at Gaza and at what's happening there. We live together here, and that's what we have to concentrate on. What do I care about what happens there?

Q: Do you celebrate the "Land Day[82]"?

I have never participated in these things.

Q: Even though your lands were taken from you?

Even though.

Q: Why?

What would it help me if I did? And will I go against my neighbor from Kiryat Anavim or Tzoba? We are good neighbors, how could I go against them? No, I have never participated in any of these days, and I am not thinking of doing so. We, as a family, have never participated in these things. And you want to know something? I am not ashamed to say this. You think we'd have a better life here if this were a Palestinian state? Let me tell you something, no, things would be much worse here at the moment.

Q: So in a way you would like to maintain the status-quo and live like you do now, with the discrimination and the suspicion?

Yes, yes, that's correct.

Q: And your sons, do they feel the same?

What can they do? Give me another alternative? We can't do anything against the state, and at the same time, we have to continue living here. But I have to say, that they are a bit less tolerant than myself. *Inshallah*, God willing, things will get better.

Q: Do you celebrate the Land Day?

The Land Day is very important to me, and I celebrate it. I think every Israeli Arab should celebrate this day, because we are also Palestinians, and after all, the land was taken from us too. People shouldn't necessarily get violent, but this is sort of a memorial day, a grieving day.

Q: What do you grieve for?

We grieve that the Jews ever came here, and took our lands.

Q: When did you last celebrate this day?

I think it was a year ago. In my village, we rioted against Jews taking away 40,000 dunams of my ancestral land. The Israeli forces came into our village, took our children from their school, and smashed the school's windows. Had we not physically resisted, they would have taken our land away without any effort at all. Would this be done to land owned by Jews? They want to take everything from us. That's why I celebrate the Land Day, and I always will.

Q: Do you feel in a way that democracy applies more to Jews than to Arabs in Israel?

Of course. The Jews are the owners of this state, no? They can do anything they want, they are all powerful. That's obvious. Jews have more freedom than Arabs. Everywhere. Wherever a Jew steps he has more rights than we do.

Q: For example?

For example here in Carney. The Jewish workers have more freedom to walk around and mind their own business. The same applies to airports. Arabs are told, "Stand and wait for inspection." I am Arab and several times they opened up my suitcases and turned everything over. This happened even when I had a small bag with a shirt or two and a pair of pants. But a Jew, especially one who has served in the army, it's easy, and no one bothers them. This is only a small example. Let me give you another example. Whoever didn't go to the army, can't get employed for many jobs here in Israel. This is the simplest example. I think that even an Arab who went to the army, and not many go, would be privileged over an Arab who didn't go.

Democracy? Not for everyone. As an Arab like me, if I raise my voice and ask for my rights, people will view me as an extremist. Among the Jews there are people who are surprised when I say what I told you today. Some Jews are more liberal and open, and some are more closed-minded. In some circles, these closed-minded people are a majority, and then there isn't openness to such conversations. Today I feel that the majority of people on both sides aren't open to conversation.

There's democracy to a certain extent. It's for Jews, and not for Arabs.

Q: What do you mean?

Not everyone can say what they think in this country. If I were to publicly say that Sharon is a bad leader, or that Jews are really extremists, I would probably be reported to the police because I am Arab. I am very afraid to say such things to other people. And these are not the only things I am afraid to say. There are more things, much simpler, that I am afraid to say in this country today.

Q: Such as?

Like what? Let's see. It's like the case in the hospital where the security guard wouldn't let us in because we're Arabs. I am not like a Jewish girl who can yell and scream at him, or curse him and shut him up. If an Arab girl yelled at him, and Smadar I am telling you what I genuinely feel, if I were to scream at him, he would probably bring the police and arrest me.

Q: Do you feel like a second class citizen sometimes?

I feel that I am a third and even fourth class citizen.

I don't really feel that I am a second-class citizen, but I have many friends who do feel like this, and even worse.

I think that the events of October 2000 emphasized the question of whether the Arabs are second third or even fourth-class citizens. Personally, it's true that I don't suffer from the situation because I don't work directly with many Jews or Arabs. I did, however, listen to my community and there were some people who were fired from their jobs during the riots. I also heard some Arabs say that Jews didn't want to work side by side with them anymore. There was so much tension in the air. That's when I got annoyed. We live together, and I know that people used to go out and demonstrate on many occasions. The police could have controlled them without shooting them. I remember that this thought frightened me. I am an Israeli, I am here, and I have decided that my future, and my children's future will be in Israel. I was born here, and I speak Hebrew. Even my culture is Israeli, and if someone asked me to choose between being here or there [in Palestine] I would choose to stay Israel. Psychologically, I feel much better here in Israel, but here we have suffered differently from the Palestinians. We have suffered by hearing what the Jews think about us, and by being discriminated against because of the fact that the Palestinians carry out suicide bombings. Of course, they [the Palestinians] have a reason for what they are doing, but in any case, we would not have any way to control the decisions they make. And I can't say that I condone their behavior. I can't condone any act of violence against a human being. I am for non-violence, but I also think that the Israeli Arabs shouldn't suffer because of the Palestinians' behavior.

Q: Has this ever happened to you?

Yes. I applied for a job, and a Jewish girl applied for it too. I was clearly more qualified, but she got it. This is only one example, but it goes beyond this. I am generally very disappointed with the State of Israel.

Q: Is it hard for you to live here when you feel this way?

Yes, it's very hard, but what can we do? We have no choice.

Q: Do you sometimes think that it would have been better had the Jews never come here?

I think about this a lot, actually. On the one hand I feel that if I were living under an Arab government, life would be better for me and my family. I could study and learn, and I wouldn't feel that because I am an Arab I am less worthy. On the other hand, I see the Arab countries around Israel, and I can see how their governments function, and how they treat people. They have no democracy, and people's opinions don't count and can't be safely voiced. So, at the end of the day, I would rather stay under Jewish rule. Still, I want to have all my rights here, like other citizens. We're legally considered citizens, aren't we? Therefore, we're entitled to our rights.

I feel like a tenth class citizen. We Arabs don't get our rights like the Jews do. We don't have the same rights to a job, for example. If I were to apply for a job at the same time that a Jewish girl applied for it, they would definitely choose her over me. Even if I am more educated than her and even if she has less experience, she would still get the job before me.

I don't feel like a citizen at all. I feel like a foreigner that no one likes or respects, and everyone tries to get rid of.

Q: What are some of the main obstacles you can point to on the way to peace?

One of the main problems is that of the settlers. These people are the most horrible people in the world. They sit there in Hebron and Gaza, only a handful of them surrounded by Arabs, and everyone has to stop their lives for them. Because of them, Arabs can't go and worship in holy places whenever they want. What nerve these people have! My simple answer would be: co-existence. If there's co-existence then people will eventually trust one another and visit one another once again. But Smadar, at this moment, if a settler were to come here, I wouldn't even look at him, and I wouldn't even talk to him. I hate those people because I know, and I can see that they hate Arabs. These people have to be forced to leave the settlements, and the sooner this happens, the better for everyone. These people have so much blood on their hands, you can't even imagine.

Q: So in your opinion, until they leave there's no chance for peace?

No chance. Well, it's actually two things: the settlers and Al Aqsa. These are two things the Arabs will never compromise on. Once the settlers are gone and Al Aqsa is under Arab control, then we can talk. We've been in war for many years because of all this. The main thing, in my opinion, is Al Aqsa. The other things are less important. Al Aqsa is for the Muslims.

Q: Do you think that Israeli Arabs should join the Israeli Army?

They should not. It makes no sense. How could they go and fight Palestinian people?

Look, there's something I thought of. If the Israeli Arabs were sent to the Territories in order to help the Palestinian people there, then I wouldn't object to it so much. But they shouldn't go if they are sent there with a gun in order to shoot and kill Muslim Arabs who are just like us. *Haram*,[83] do you understand?

Of course Arabs shouldn't join the Israeli Army. We can't fight our own people, and definitely not for Israel. And you have to remember that orthodox Jews don't have to serve in the army either, but they receive money from the Israeli government. The Jews know very well why the Arabs don't serve in the army, and they should understand. And don't ask me about the Druze...

This is ridiculous. I mean, how can Israeli Arabs fight against their Palestinian brothers and sisters? We're not like the Druze people who are willing to fight one another, and don't have any ethics whatsoever. They fight against the Palestinians, and they are the worse. The Druze abuse the Palestinians more than the Jews, believe me. We are not like that. We have families in the Occupied Territories. So what will I do? Send my son to fight his cousin who lives in Jenin? And let me ask you something. Would you like to have an American Jew fight against you? It doesn't make any sense, does it? So why are people so surprised that we don't want to fight the Palestinians who are Muslim like us? We identify with them, how can we kill them?

Q: As a woman, what do you think is your role in educating the next generation and advocating for peace?

I, as a mother, have the responsibility to tell my kids that the suicide bombings are fundamentally bad. I have to teach my children that we have to live together with the Jews, respect them, and even visit them. We have to send our children to neighboring Jewish villages in order to meet and dialogue with Jewish children. Only if we do this will Arabs and Jews get closer to one another.

Q: And in a more political way, what do you believe is your role?

When I see a Jewish soldier killing a Palestinian child, I must tell my children that just like there are bad Arabs, there are also bad Jews. I have to tell them that just like there are Arabs who do not like Jews, there are Jews who do not like Arabs. I will also tell my child that if a Jew kills an Arab in Israel, the Jew will be tried and get punished according to the law, just like the soldier who killed Muhammad al-Durrah, or the policemen who killed Arabs during the Al Aqsa *Intifada*.

Q: Do you think that there is propaganda on the Israeli and Palestinian sides?

There is propaganda on both sides. When I go to Hadera, I can see the faces of the new immigrants when they look at me, and I know that they hate Arabs. Do you know why they hate Arabs? When they come to Israel, they go through orientation sessions, and that's where they are taught to hate Arabs. That's where Zionism is instilled in them.

Q: Do you think that Zionism is a bad thing?

Zionism as a concept is not a bad thing, but if it turns into hatred against Arabs, then yes, it turns into something bad. Then Zionism turns into something bad and ugly. Many people in Israel today think, "This is our country, our land, and only we should be able to live and work here!" This is wrong.

There is a conspiracy against Islam in the world. It is lead by the United States and by the evil Zionist enemy. Together, they want to kill all the Muslims in the world. The first step is to take away their political power. After that everything is possible because the Unites States and Israeli are strong. The Zionist enemy is very dangerous because it pretends to be weak when it is really very strong.

Q: But there are Muslim entities in the world who use terror against innocent civilians as a way to make changes. Do you think this is a legitimate and acceptable way in which to operate?

Why terror? This is not terror but self-defense against the United States and the Zionist enemy.

Q: But terror takes place in other places too, not only in Israel and the United States. Look what happened in Istanbul or even in Saudi Arabia.

Everyone knows that the United States and Israel control everything in the world. Without the United States and Israel world politics would be completely different.

Q: But do you think that terror can be justified?

It is not terror. Of course it would be better if the change could happen in a different way, but it can't.

Why do people call Usama bin Laden a bad man? Is he any worse that Bush or Sharon? He is doing good things in order to liberate Muslims all over the world.

Q: You mean by killing innocent people all over the world?

And Bush is not killing people all over the world?

Q: I am talking to you about Bin Laden now, not about Bush.

Look, the United States has declared a war against Muslims a ling time ago. So why should people like Bin Laden not do something to counter this war? Sometimes it is allowed to kill, especially if Muslims are in danger.

Q: But the people who were killed in Istanbul, for example, were mostly Muslim, and many of the people who were killed in the World Trade Center had nothing to do with the oppression of the Palestinian people or with the oppression of Muslims in the world, don't you think?

The Turks also support the United States and Israel. We want to live in peace with other people, but we also need to protect ourselves.

Education: Interviews with Children

Q: How important is it, in your opinion to go to school and gain an education?

It's very important. The Jews want to keep us uneducated so that we don't take over their country. If we go to school, we can learn and advance ourselves. If we don't go to school, then the Jews will always have the best jobs, the best of everything, and we will have nothing.

It is very important to go to school and become an educated person. If a person today doesn't have a certificate, they can't live a good life. Learning is for the future. If a person wants to have a house and a family, they must go to school and gain an education.

It's very important for children to go to school and gain an education. We have to learn how to read and write because our future depends on it. I would like to be a doctor once I'm older.

It's very important for us to learn how to read and write.

I have a horse at home. I want to become a veterinarian. But here in Israel, I can't go to university to learn how to become a veterinarian. In class, we hardly even learn English, so how will I get into university and continue my studies? If I want to learn how to be a doctor, I will have to go to another country where they treat Arabs better and give them more opportunities.

I like reading books for children. One day I will be able to read books for grown ups.

I don't know. My dad can read and write, but he can't find a job. So even if I can read and write, I might not get a job in this country.

Q: How important is it in your opinion to go to school?

It's very important for children to go to school. A person who does not go to school will not have a future. If we don't learn how to speak English and Hebrew, we won't be able to advance ourselves.

Q: Why is it important for you to learn Hebrew in school?

It's important because most of the people in Israel speak Hebrew and they don't want to learn Arabic. If someone asks me a question in Hebrew, I must be able to understand what they are saying and respond.

Q: Do you think Jews should learn Arabic in their schools?

Yes, of course. Some learn Arabic but only for a year and then they stop. Most of them can't speak in Arabic and they always expect us to speak Hebrew.

Q: What are your favorite classes in school?

I love my Hebrew class. The teacher is really good and he makes the lessons very interesting.

Q: When you listen to your teachers in school, do you think that everything they say is the truth?

Yes, I think that everything the teachers tell us is the truth.

Q: Do you think that all Israeli citizens receive the same opportunities to go to school and gain an education?

No, they don't get the same opportunity to go to school. Jews are much more educated than we are. They get more opportunities to go to school or to university.

Q: Do you speak about the political situation in class?

Not really. Sometimes something happens and we hear about it in the news. Then people talk about the situation in class or during the break.

Q: What do children and teachers say?

They talk about how the Jews are killing our brothers and sisters in the Occupied Territories.

Q: Do they also talk about the suicide bombers?

Yes.

Q: What do they usually say about them?

That they are brave.

Q: Are you generally interested in politics?

Yes, I am very interested. I watch the news every day.

Q: Where do you usually get the news?

I watch it on television. I don't really like to listen to the radio because they sometimes speak to fast and I can't understand everything they are saying.

Q: What channels do you usually watch?

I watch the news on *Al Jazeera* and also on the Dubai news channel.

Q: Do you listen to the news on the Israeli channels as well?

Yes, I watch channel 1 and 2 and I usually listen to the news in Arabic.

Q: When you listen to the news, do you understand what is being spoken of?

Well, I understand most of what they are saying. Sometimes when I don't understand something in Hebrew, I'll ask my dad and he will explain it to me. He understands a lot about politics and is fluent in Hebrew.

Q: What do people at your home speak about after they watch the news? What do they say?

They always speak about Israel and Palestine and about the war. After there's a suicide bombing we talk about that and about how the people in Jenin have no other choice but to blow themselves up and become *shaheeds*. And we always talk about how the Israeli Army invades the West Bank and Gaza and kills innocent people there. So it's always either about the suicide bombings, or about how people died in Palestine because of the Jews.

Q: Generally speaking, are you interested in politics?

Yes, it's something that is very important to me. I feel that I have no choice but to stay involved in what's going on.

Q: Where do you usually hear the news?

In all the channels, both Israeli and Arab, both in Hebrew and in Arabic.

Q: Do you believe that everything said in the news is the truth?

No. See, I compare the different channels and the different news programs.

Q: What are some of the differences, if at all, that you can spot?

Every channel is different and every channel presents the news according to how they believe things should be. There are different kinds of news. There's news where the reporter gives his or her own personal views about the event being reported. This can particularly be seen on Channel Two, the Israeli channel. It can also be seen, but to a lesser extent, on Channel One. On both of these channels, the reporters give their own opinions instead of objectively telling us exactly what is going on. The viewers can detect what the reporter thinks about the situation, and this is bad. In other channels, you can see exactly what's going on. This is most evident in *Al Jazeera* which comes from Qatar. Here you can hear the truth about what's going on between the Israelis and Palestinians. Walid el Omri, the reporter for Israeli and Palestinian affairs, reports from Ramallah, Jerusalem and Jenin. He photographs everything, and passes on a true picture of the situation without incorporating his own ideas into his report.

Q: So what you are saying is that the Arab channels are generally more reliable in the portrayal of the Israeli-Palestinian conflict?

Not all of them. Some of them are not interested at all in what's going on in the Occupied Territories. There is a problem with the reliability of the Egyptian channels, for example. You see, the problem is that Mubarak[84] and Bush are more or less friends, so the Egyptian channels can't say everything about the Occupied Territories, about Israel, or about who George Bush exactly is. So, some channels can't give all the news. But generally speaking, the Arab channels are much more reliable than the Israeli or American ones.

Q: Do you think that the news, the way we hear it today, has any negative influence on people?

No, not usually. But I think that maybe the news has a small negative influence on us today. The news, naturally, wants the viewer to think in a specific way. If, for example, we're six people in the house, then each person might see things in a different way. This causes a lot of tension between the members of the family, and this is a bad thing. In my family, for example, people don't always think the same about the political situation. Some are more extreme and some are less. Sometimes we verbally fight around the dinner table, especially after a suicide bombing.

Q: What are some of the things said in your house after you all watch the news together?

When it comes to suicide bombings, some condemn it and some condone it. Most people understand why the Palestinians are doing this. They have no other way to fight the Israeli soldiers who come with their guns and tanks. When it comes to what Israel is doing in the Occupied Territories, everyone condemns Israel and sides with the Palestinians.

Q: How important is it, in your opinion, for children to go to school and gain an education?

I think that it's a hundred percent important for all children to go to school.

Q: Why?

Because we have a war here and people are closing their shops because there is no business. Maybe if we study, we'll have a better future. There's not work here at the moment, do you understand?

Q: What do you like the most about your school?

I like the computers the most. All the kids in our school like our computer classes.

Q: Who is your favorite teacher?

Usama is my favorite teacher. He's our Hebrew/Arabic teacher. He's very patient and gives all his time to the students.

Q: Do you like studying Hebrew?

Not really.

Q: Why not?

When I speak this language I feel that I am not who I am supposed to be. I am an Arab and a Muslim. I feel that it is not normal for me to be able to speak Hebrew, the language of the Jews. Look at Arabs in other countries. Do they speak Hebrew? Of course they don't because there is no reason for them to know it.

Q: Do you speak about the political situation in class?

In the past we used to speak about it much more than now. Now so many bad things happen that we can't spend too much time discussing it.

Q: Who starts the conversation in class and what is usually said?

The teacher usually starts the conversation by speaking about the political situation in class. He would say that we are currently at war and that the situation is very bad. He also used to say that we have to study as hard as we can.

Q: Do you think that everything the teacher says in class is the truth?

What the teacher says in class is not a hundred percent true, but maybe fifty percent true.

Q: What do you mean?

I don't know where the teacher gets the information from. Maybe not all of it is true?

Q: What do children in your class say about the political situation?

In class people don't say much about the political situation anymore. It's like we have gotten used to what's happening every day. It's boring to speak about it. Every day something bad happens. Every day the Jews kill more people.

Q: Do you think that Jewish and Arab children get the same opportunities to have an education in Israel?

I think that yes, more or less, children get the same opportunities.

Q: How do you think the Israeli government treats Israeli Arabs?

Exactly the same as Jews.

Q: So everything's equal for everyone?

Well, I think that when it comes to education, there's more or less equality. But there's other things that are not equal at all, such as the work force. There are many Arabs who have worked for Jews for years and are now being fired. I think that Jews are afraid of having Arabs work for them. That's why it's much harder for Arabs to find a job in Israel today. You see, Arabs don't have a lot of money and Jews do. Jews control everything, not only here, but in the whole world, so they can do whatever they want.

Q: Do you think that the education Palestinian children receive in the Occupied Territories is better than in Israel?

How do you expect them to study there? They have a war going on, they can't concentrate on studying. They also don't have money to put into education, so they can't study at all. When there's war, there's no education.

Q: But here in Israel we also have a war going on, but still, we have schools.

The situation in the Occupied Territories is much worse than here. I saw on television that children in Jenin don't have food to eat. They really have a war there, a much more serious one than we have here.

Q: What do you think that Palestinian children in the Occupied Territories learn about Jews?

Nothing.

Q: Are you generally interested in politics?

Not really.

Q: Where do you usually hear the news?

I usually listen to the news on Channel One, I watch *Mabat*.[85] I also listen to the news in Arabic at 7:30 p.m.

Q: When you watch the news with your family do you speak about it?

Yes, sometimes. People always comment on how hard the situation is with the war and all and how everyone wants to leave Israel and go somewhere else. It's a very hard situation for everyone at the moment.

Q: What are people's responses when they see in the news what's going on between the Israelis and the Palestinians?

Two days ago, for example, there was a terrorist attack in Umm el-Fahem and then there was one in Kfar Saba, so everyone was speaking about how hard the situation is but also about how they understand why the Palestinians would do such a thing.

Q: Why would they do such a thing?

To protect themselves against the Israeli tanks and to end the occupation and live in freedom from the Jews.

It is very important for Arab children all over the world to go to school and learn how to read and write. But when I think about this, I get very angry with the United States.

Q: What do you mean?

I know exactly what the United States is trying to do, we all know here, even if people there don't think we know.

Q: What is the United States trying to do?

Are you sure you want me to tell you the whole thing?

Q: Yes, of course. Tell me what's on your mind. I am interested to learn.

Well, it's very easy. The United States steals all the best minds in the world. The United States pays for people from Muslim and Arab countries to come to American universities and study. In these universities, these Muslim people learn really sophisticated things like developing weapons and other things. So, the United States is teaching them to make these things, but what happens then after they have learned all of these things?

Q: What happens?

The United States uses these weapons against Muslims and Arabs. Do you see?

Q: Tell me more please.

What happens in the end is that Muslim and Arab people are killed by weapons that they helped develop. The United States knows very well what its aim is: destroying the Muslim world. I hate the United States.

Q: Where did you get all this information from?

Everyone here says this and I saw it on television as well.

Q: But don't you think that Muslims who go to the United States know that this is what is happening?

Some do and some don't. The United States is lying to many of them, I am sure. And also, people need money, you know?

Q: Why don't they have money in their countries?

The United States takes everything.

2
Israeli Arabs and the Palestinians

Living in the Middle: an Identity Crisis

Recently, Ha'aretz, the leading left-wing Israeli newspaper, has started publishing articles dealing with the Israeli Arab population and their relationship with the Jewish State of Israel. Gideon Levi, in his article "Humiliation is the Message" asks, "What should we expect? That Israel's Arabs will turn their backs on their brethren who are suffering under the Israeli occupation?... That Israel's actions in the territories will not affect their attitude toward the state?" Zvi Bar'el, when writing about the Israeli Arabs wrote in his article "The Jewish Islamic Complex," "This is evident first and foremost in the term Jews use to define this community. They are not 'the Arabs of Israel,' because this would connote Israeli mastery; they are not 'Israeli Palestinians,' because this would indicate a national identity that could, heaven forbid, conflict with their loyalty to the state; nor are they just plain 'Arabs' because 'Arab' also presumably constitutes some form of identity." He then stresses the complexity of the issue when he says, "The problem is that Israel's Arabs - all of them - have come to be viewed as 'suspicious objects' with respect to their relationship with the state." And indeed, The International Jerusalem Post has, on a number of occasions, allowed the advertising of an "Advertorial" which says, "Have you not learned over the past two years that even an Israeli Arab community, such as Umm el-Fahem, urges the continued slaying of Jews. No protest will ever arise from Arabs with regard to the inhumane behavior of many of its members."

There is no doubt that Jewish Israelis are waking up to reality maybe for the first time and facing something bigger than they can imagine. When I went home in the summer of 2001, many Jews I spoke to mentioned Azmi Bshara and his speech in Damascus. "Look at this sly [one]," they would say, "an Israeli citizen who is also a member of the Israeli Knesset dares to go to an Arab country, speak against Israel and even call the Arab world to oppose it. Who would have expected such a thing to happen?" One of my interviewees, an Arab woman in her thirties, pointed out the sentiment some Jews exhibited towards her when, after Bshara's words, they questioned her loyalty [and the loyalty of other Israeli Arabs] to Israel. Many Jewish Israelis even publicly supported the idea of opening a criminal investigation against Bshara and even having him serve time in jail for betraying Israel.[86] When some of my friends and acquaintances heard that I was going to go into Israeli Arab villages and interview people there, they found it hard to believe and told me, "Why do you want to go in there and talk to traitors? Don't you have anything better to do? Look at the Arabs, they publicly admit that they hate the Jews and want them annihilated and no Israeli Arab member of the Knesset publicly condemns their words." Now, over three years after the beginning of my project, many more Israeli Jews are getting concerned about the existence of a large Arab minority within Israel which is becoming increasingly supportive of the Palestinians and their struggle against Israel.

In 1947, most Arabs living on the land later to be called Israel had the chance to stay within the borders of the future Jewish state and become Israeli citizens and receive, at least in theory, equal rights.[87] Since their response to this offer was not uniform and since most Israelis feared them, they were subjected to Israeli military rule until 1956. After the Sinai War the military rule ended and Arabs who accepted Israeli citizenship came under the Israeli government, as did the Jews. There was a feeling, especially among Israeli intellectuals, that the Arabs had learned to live peacefully with the Jews. The intellectuals pointed out the fact that the Arabs living in Israel did not revolt against Israel in the 1967 Six Day War and that Israeli Arabs remained passive while the Israeli Army forces ruled over the West Bank. Many believed that the Arabs genuinely accepted Israeli rule and that they were Israelis in every way, only distinguished by their religion, whether Christianity or Islam. Among the general Israeli Jewish public, however, the situation was somewhat different and there was deep mistrust exhibited towards the Arab population. Although it was not necessarily evident in every day Israeli life, most Jewish Israelis were suspicious of the Arabs and did not trust them or their loyalty to the state. Many Jews viewed the Arabs as a Fifth Column which would one day turn against Israel, the Jewish state and join the Arab states in a call for its annihilation. There were apparently minor things that the Israeli intellectuals ignored when assessing the Arabs' identification with the Israeli state. They failed to notice that most, if not all, Arabs failed to celebrate Israeli Independence Day and instead sometimes even celebrated *Yaum al Nakba*.[88] They failed to see that Arabs living in Israel rarely, and maybe even never, held up an Israeli flag or sang the Israeli national anthem. And they failed, above all, to realize that many Arabs felt so detached from the Israeli state that, although they wanted to receive equal rights, they were unwilling to contribute to the state.

When we speak about citizenship and about the concept of equal rights, we must consider the responsibilities of the citizen to the state and not only those given by the state to the citizen. There is no state in the world that is based solely on giving services to its citizens and that does not expect anything in return. This reciprocation usually comes in the form of taxes, or military service, especially if the country is in a state of war.[89] Citizens sing the national anthem and fly the flag that represents the country in which they live. They also agree to defend their country, especially in hard times, even if they reject some of the politics their government follows at that specific time. The questions remain, however: What happens when a group of people does not feel that it is a part of a certain country or political entity? What happens when an entire group of people does not feel that it should contribute to the state? If a group does not contribute to the state, should its member receive full rights as citizens? What should the group's responsibilities, if any, be towards the state? In Israel, left wing people and the political left in general, clung to their super liberal ideology, wanting to show that Israel was more enlightened than any other country and ignored all these warning signs. It was the right wing people who asked questions and as they asked these questions, a stronger opposition among Jewish Israeli society towards the "Arab problem" developed.

The main problem among the Israeli Jewish intellectual circles at that time was that they ignored what was happening within the Arab sector. Instead of looking into the Arab sector and trying to identify some root problems in order to find solutions for them, they were still clung to their liberal ideologies. Jewish Israeli liberal writers, for example, were genuinely happy that the Arabs living in Israel accepted the peace treaty that was signed between Israel and Egypt in 1979. They failed, however, to look deeper into the Arab sector and into the undercurrents existing in it. They failed to do so mainly because of the fact that most of them could not speak the Arabic language and were unable, therefore, to closely assess Arab opinion. This miscommunication was the main obstacle that prevented Jewish Israeli intellectuals and writers from truly understanding the Arab sector and its frustration and noticing the resentment many within it felt towards Israel. In short, their naïveté and the fact that they ignored the discrimination that existed (and this discrimination was often inflicted by these liberal Israelis) caused them to hear whatever they wanted to hear—that the Arabs were with them and had become integral part of Israeli society.

When I was talking to Israeli Arab adults and children, I could see some of the complexities they were forced to deal with. They wanted to make it clear that they were Israeli citizens who were deprived of many of their rights. There is no doubt that Israeli Arabs are not lying when they say that they do not receive all the rights they are entitled to as Israeli citizens, as guaranteed by the Israeli Declaration of Independence. Although they are seen as equal citizens under Israeli law, in actuality they do not receive all the rights they due to them as citizens of a democratic state. This discrimination was at times systematically encouraged by the Israeli government which wanted to reach a situation where Arabs did not feel a part of Israeli society and thus distanced themselves from the Israeli state. However, it was very important for many of my interviewees to maintain their Arab Muslim identity and distinguish themselves as a separate group that has different priorities than those of the Israeli government, or of many Jewish Israeli citizens. They call themselves Palestinians, or Palestinians living in Israel and adamantly refuse to serve in the Israeli Army.

They are not viewed truly Palestinian, however, by many Israeli Jews mainly because of the fact that the concept of "Palestine" as a political identity is a new one. It is in effect a re-awakening of the name given to the region by the Romans as early as the 2nd Century A.D. It was adopted by the Arabs as a response to Zionism as Theodor Herzel interpreted it, once their dreams of a Greater Syria and an Arab Ummah had been shattered into pieces with the assistance of the French and the English. It is a fact that all peoples in today's world formed their identity and connection to a specific geographical area at a certain point in time. Hence, no matter when the name "Palestine" was first associated with a national group, people who call themselves Palestinians have the right to self-determination. If we assume that this is true, then the Jews' identity, which was formed much earlier and their connection to Zion, should also be respected and acknowledged and not dismissed as it usually is by many Arabs living in Israel and abroad. Israelis, just like Palestinians have the right to self-determination and to their own homeland. Most of the Israeli Muslim Arabs to whom I spoke viewed themselves as Muslim Arab Palestinians, omitting the word "Israeli" from their description. Most children defined themselves simply as Palestinians who "happen to live in Israel and have an Israeli passport."

I could see how this complexity affected Israeli Arabs when I was attending an Israeli-Palestinian conference in Copenhagen about a year and a half ago. One of the members of the Israeli delegation was a Christian Israeli Arab student whose opinions mostly complimented those of the Palestinians from the West Bank and Gaza. A bystander would probably never have guessed that this person came to the conference with an Israeli delegation. He made an effort to stay on good terms with both the Israelis and the Palestinians, even when the two groups were arguing with one another. When the two delegations separately met with their organizers, however, he decided not to join either group. If he had joined the Israeli delegation, he would be betraying his feelings and identification with the Palestinian people to whom he felt a strong connection. If he had joined the Palestinian delegation, he would be betraying his Israeli colleagues with whom he had a good relationship and also identified. Whatever decision he made, he could not have won. There would always be someone who viewed him as an outsider, a traitor, he who does not belong. In effect, he represented the Israeli Arab society as a whole—a society stuck in the middle and which often remains silent.

When I interviewed Israeli Arabs, I could detect two distinct groups, notably different from one another. One group, although it recognized that it was being discriminated against, still identified itself as Israeli. Some of these people write for the website Arabs for Israel (www.arabsforisrael.com) This group accepted the Jews' right to the land and accepted the fact that Jews also have holy sites in Jerusalem and Hebron. People in this group mostly spoke to me as Israeli citizens who wanted to be a part of the Israeli state, but who felt that they were not being treated equally to Jews and that they were being discriminated against by Jews on a daily basis. Their answers mostly focused on the financial and social aspects of their discrimination, although some of them even pointed out the fact that this discrimination is not a government policy in Israel, but rather something which developed after suicide bombings and terrorist attacks began. They spoke to me about the Israeli-Palestinian conflict, but at times somewhat reluctantly and they did not make it a point to go back to 1948 and discuss the events of that year. "It's senseless to go back to the past all the time," said one of my interviewees. "Israeli Arabs and Palestinians have to look to the future if they want to advance and succeed," she concluded. Many people in this group preferred focusing on social problems which had more importance to them and did not always want to get into a political debate, even if they did sympathize, to some extent, with the Palestinian people and their cause. Most of them elaborated on the crisis within the Arab world and to the problems Arab and Muslim states were encountering—they mostly spoke about the corruption within Arab and Muslim regimes and on the need to democratize the Middle East.

The other group of people was quite different, in that it fundamentally did not accept the existence of the State of Israel and the Jews' right to their own country in this specific land. This is something Aharon Lisch, a writer for Ha'aretz, tackled in his article "Damage to the Relationship: The Good Will of Those Fighting for Arab Equality in Israel is used in favor of a two-Nation State."[90] In the article, he speaks mainly about [Israeli Arab] Dr. Gnam, who in one of his lectures claimed that a two-nation state should immediately be enacted because "Israeli Arabs have not yet accepted the results of the war in 1948."[91] According to Lisch and to Professor Mordechai Kremnitzer (who is mentioned in the article) "There is a large group of Israeli Arabs that does not accept the existence of Israel and which is aspiring to change the demographics and current status-quo, both by a high birth rate and by the return of Palestinian refugees to Israel, so that Jews become a minority." I myself heard this view expressed by some Israeli Arabs, especially young children and teenagers I interviewed.

Towards the end of the summer vacation, the Shiva[92] [Return] summer camp, attended by approximately 300 Israeli Arab children in the village of Kabul in Northern Israel, was inspected by the Israeli police force after allegations were made that anti-Israeli propaganda was being taught to the children. The newspaper *Ha'aretz* reported the ideologies taught in summer camp saying, "Studies of nationhood of whose heroes are Palestinian murderers, songs praising the daily suicide bombings, songs promoting the Palestinian Right of Return to Jaffo, Ashdod and Haifa[93] and dreams of a Palestinian state from the [Mediterranean] sea to Jordan are only part of the daily curriculum of this summer camp." At one point and this was seen on Israeli television, children were heard to sing loudly, "We don't want flour and sardines—we want bombs," and when one girl was asked where the Jews should go to, she answered, "Where they came from—Poland and Russia." Different people reacted to the incident in different ways. Some reacted to the event with shock, just like some people reacted with shock to Bshara's speech in Damascus. Other people were not at all surprised, but still expressed great uneasiness and distress when watching the summer camp's activities on television. The discovery of such a summer camp only further intensified the relationship between Israeli Arabs and Jews. Many Israeli Jews believed that this camp proved that Israeli Arabs were not only far from being Israeli, but, furthermore, that they wanted Israel's annihilation, just like many Arab countries surrounding Israel did. One of my Israeli Jewish acquaintances, upon reading the article about the summer camp told me, "I am not surprised about this at all. What surprises me is that this surprises some Jewish Israelis."

Who are Israeli Arabs? There is no doubt that they themselves are not sure who they are or how to define their identity when asked to do so. They prefer calling themselves Palestinians, but are aware of the fact that most Palestinians view Israeli Arabs as traitors who have accepted the existence of the Jewish state. About this issue, Majli writes:

To start the story of Israeli Arabs from Egypt is nearly absurd...However, it was there that I had to answer the question, to which an answer has not yet been found: Who are you, Israeli Arabs, and what are you? People asked if I am an Arab. They did not believe that there were Arabs in Israel. One of the Egyptian men, who was eventually convinced that there were, asked: "Well, then you're a Jewish kind of Arab, no?" I returned from Egypt brokenhearted and hurt. It was not only the Egyptians who reacted like this. We even used to meet with Lebanese and Syrian Arabs or with Libyans living in Eastern Europe and they all turned their backs on us. They didn't want to speak to us and some of them even blatantly told us, "You are agents of Zionism."[94]

In one of my interviews a man in his late fifties told me, "The Palestinians call us Jews. They think we love the Jews and support them." Several children to whom I spoke also mentioned this fact to me and one girl said this makes her "very sad." It was evident to me that Israeli Arabs of all ages are caught between two very distinct groups; a Jewish one and an Arab one. Several of my interviewees told me about how Arabs from other countries could not believe that Arabs lived in Israel and that they had maintained their Muslim identity. In the same breath they told me about how Israeli Jews did not accept them as truly being Israeli because they are Arab and Muslim. It is an extremely complex situation in which each side views the Israeli Arab as cooperating with the other side. Salman Natur[95] in his article, "I am the First Arab Palestinian Hebrew Israeli" testifies about himself:

I belong to two cultures. On the one hand, the Arab-Palestinian and on the other hand, the Hebrew-Israeli. In the political reality we find ourselves in, there has been a clash between these two identities, ever since 1948. This is not an intellectual or verbal clash, but rather a physical one which is violent and results in victims on both sides. In fact, this reality must be reflected in who I am, in my consciousness and in my personality. Theoretically speaking, an Arab in Israel is the embodiment of a person's identity complex, which to the outsider might seem as a type of schizophrenia, a split personality.[96]

Regardless of how Israeli Jews feel towards Israeli Arabs and the fact that an increasing number of Israeli Arabs do not identify themselves as Israeli and do not view themselves as part of the Jewish State, they must receive equal rights and be treated equally. Although I find it at times hard to accept the fact that there is a fairly large group of Israeli citizens which in many ways does not want to contribute to the state and does not want to be Israeli, I also acknowledge that Israel, by the mere fact that it is a democratic state, must provide this group with equal rights. Israel must also face this harsh reality and take responsibility for its part in creating it—people do not just wake up one morning and decide that they do not identify with their country. What is inevitable in this situation in my opinion, however, is the way many Israeli Jews are reacting to their Israeli Arab neighbors: with suspicion, mistrust and dislike. It is not surprising that many Jews do not feel close to and hesitate being in contact with those people who blatantly oppose the existence of their state. It is not surprising that there is a social and ideological gap between Jews and those Israeli Arabs who call for the destruction of Israel and yearn for its downfall. It seems that Israeli society is caught in a vicious circle—but where did this circle start? Were Arabs first discriminated by the state and then hostile towards it, or were they first hostile towards it and then discriminated by it? Where this circle of negative feelings started is hard to tell, but it seems as if it may go on forever, or at least until some kind of change, on both sides, takes place. It seems to me that this harsh reality is unfortunately inevitable in a country where so many people have different interests and priorities and where so many people simply do not feel, for whatever reasons, that they belong.

Interviews with Adults

Q: Please tell me a bit about your family's background, and how that is connected, if at all, to how you feel about the Israeli-Palestinian conflict.

My grandfather, that is my father's father, was originally from Arara, but he lived in Haifa where he married my grandmother. It is said that my grandmother's family originated from Turkey and came here many generations ago. My mother is from Jenin. She was born there and grew up there until she married my father and came to Israel. My mother's mother and my father's mother are sisters and this is how they met one another. In 1967 the borders were opened and that's how they eventually got married. My mother's family still lives in the Occupied Territories and my mother hasn't been able to visit them for a long time now. Last year, in the beginning of July, my uncle was killed in Jenin by the Israeli Army in the Occupied Territories.

Q: What happened to him?

To tell you the truth, I am not sure why he was killed by the Israeli Army. All I know for sure is that he was killed by Israeli soldiers.

Q: How do you feel towards Israel and Palestine? Who are you?

I am an Israeli Arab. My mother never told me that I was half Palestinian when I was a child and growing up here in Arara. [Now the interviewee turned to her mother and asked:] When did you tell me that I am half Palestinian? Did you ever tell me when I was young? You see Smadar, this is my mother. She never told me that I was Palestinian. How do I introduce myself? I am Muna Melhem and I am from Arara. I am from Arara in Dawlat Israil [the State of Israel]. Do I want to say that I am Palestinian now?

Q: Do you want to say that? Do you feel any connection to Palestine?

I don't have any connection to Palestine. The Palestinians are Palestinians and I am Israeli. I am in Arara, my life is in Arara and Arara is a part of Israel. It has never been a part of the Occupied Territories and it will never be. And if it ever becomes a part of what will be Palestine, then I will leave and go somewhere else that is within the Israeli borders.

Q: But many Palestinians claim that all of this was once a part of Palestine.

Let them claim that, it's their problem. You see Smadar, these people are stuck in the past and are not looking towards the future. These people must think realistically before it's too late. Israel as a state has existed for 54 years now. It's not going anywhere. It's a fact. Look at what the Palestinians and the Israelis have done to one another. And look at what the Palestinians have done to themselves. They could have helped one another and done good things to one another, but they didn't. Instead, they are still stuck in 1948. Enough! Their lives are always bad, don't they realize? And what for? Just because they are still stuck in the past? They have to finally accept the fact that Israel exists and that it's staying put. My solution would be to make Jerusalem an international city with access to everyone, not only to Jews, Muslims and Christians. I think it should be supervised in some ways by Israel.

Q: Why specifically by Israel?

Israel will invest in it. If it's under Palestinian supervision, I don't know what will happen to the place. Maybe they won't invest enough money in it.

Q: I think you are the first Israeli Arab I have interviewed who did not say, "I am Palestinian" when I asked them "Who are you?"

The answer is very simple, Smadar. I have already told you that my mother always told me, "You are from Arara in the State of Israel." This has always been clear to me. Every year during Israel's independence day, we used to celebrate with Jewish people. Sometimes we even celebrated more than the Jews themselves. This was before the situation deteriorated and worsened. Now we're afraid to go and celebrate with the Jews.

Q: Do you support the Right of Return for Palestinians?

My father also lost lands to the Israelis, but he's put all of that in the past. Now he lives here, in Israel. My grandmother still has memories from that time, but we don't. We have continued forward into the future. I have no connection to Palestine. Those who want to come back, let them come back. Most of those who would have come back have probably died and the ones who are still alive have their lives elsewhere. But if they want to come, let them come, there's enough room for everyone. And most of them won't return anyway. Many of them verbally express their will to return, but realistically, what will they do here in Israel now? Will these people leave their life of fifty years, or even more, to return to a place which isn't at all what it used to be in the past? I saw a documentary film on television about three years ago. It was about people who left the United States in order to come back to Ramallah. In the United States they were considered to be quite rich, but in Ramallah they were sleeping four people in a room. So, is this a life? Most of the Palestinians will come for visits, but they won't stay. They will come to Jerusalem to pray and then will leave and go back to wherever they live. By the way, I think it is stupid to fight for the right to pray somewhere. But at the same time, I think that people should be allowed to live or visit wherever they want. If I suddenly want to leave Arara, it's my right to do so and I should be able to go anywhere I please without being restricted.

Q: What is to you a holy place? Is it worth fighting for a holy place?

It is not worth fighting for anything considered by humans to be holy. I have always believed that the most important thing is the human being and his or her life. We forget sometimes how hard God worked to create us and we so easily kill one another. I think that a human being is more important than anything else and definitely more important than a stone or a building.

Q: What about the suicide bombings? Do you unconditionally condemn the suicide bombings, or is there a "but" here too?

I cry for a person who dies in a suicide bombing, just like I do for a Palestinian person who dies in Jenin. I see the houses that were ruined by the Israeli Army in Jenin, or the blood everywhere after a suicide bombing and I ask myself again and again, "What is this all for?" When I think about suicide bombings, I condemn them without any "buts" whatsoever. A suicide bombing is an unacceptable act, just like the demolition of a house in Jenin. Both acts are unacceptable in my opinion. I am not saying that a suicide bombing is not okay, while everything that happens in the Occupied Territories is fine. Both are unacceptable and what is not allowed for one side is not allowed for the other.

Q: When you look at the bad situation the Occupied Territories are in? Who do you blame, if at all? Why is the situation like this in your opinion?

There is more than only the Israeli occupation which is contributing to the worsening situation in the Occupied Territories. Some [of it] is definitely caused by the Israeli occupation. Externally, there is no doubt that the Israeli occupation has not allowed the Palestinians to live freely and in adequate conditions. The Palestinian Authority is a place that is always in a state of *Intifada*. And you know what causes the *Intifada*? When Palestinians had jobs, they occupied themselves and had enough money. They forgot about the potential problems they might encounter. They focused on working and creating a life for their children. The problem is that the Palestinian leaders don't want the people to live like this. They changed this by dividing the money among selected individuals and leaving most other people poor and uneducated. That's when people start fighting. So, to tell you the truth, I don't think that the main problem was that Sharon entered Al Aqsa, but that the Palestinians already had a lot of frustration building up inside them. Okay, so Sharon entered Al Aqsa. So what? And if Arafat were to go to your holy place? So what? I don't think the Jews would have started rioting. Ahlan wa Sahlan [in Arabic: welcome] to everyone, I always say.

Q: Do you think that in a way Arafat and his people have an interest in leaving his people poor?

Yes, of course. They want the Palestinians to go through this. You can't imagine what it is to be poor. That's when you don't care to kill other people. But I always say that the Palestinians are not only killing the Jews, but they are killing themselves and one another because of the poverty they are experiencing and living in. I think that a lot has happened in the Palestinian towns and villages because of poverty. It's not only Arafat who is doing this, but his entire family too and also his close friends. In my opinion they are pursuing wrong tactics, because they are leaving their people poor. I mean, for them it's good, but eventually the people will get sick and tired of being poor. People want to live. There is money in the Palestinian Authority, but where is it? All the world gave the Palestinians money to create a state, so where is it? The Palestinian leaders have not done anything for the Palestinian people. Nothing whatsoever. They have taken all the money and put it in their own bank account. Arafat himself has millions of dollars in Swiss banks.

Q: Do you think that Arafat is the right leader for the Palestinians and that he is the right leader for bringing peace to the region?

I don't know whether he's the right leader for the Palestinian people. It seems like they think he is, though. I have hardly heard anyone speak against him. As to a leader for bringing peace, I really don't know. Arafat has signed treaties but as to actually doing something, I don't think he's done anything new. I don't know whether he has the power to do something new and revolutionary.

Q: Why do you think he rejected Barak's offer in which he would have gotten a large part of the Occupied Territories?

I don't know. I really don't know. I have no idea what his considerations might have been at the time, but I think there's a problem with the decisions he has made and with his list of priorities. Why did he reject Barak's offer? He was given many offers that we know of and probably many offers we don't know of. I have realized that he has never said "yes" to anything.

Q: How do you think the Jewish Israeli sector has reacted to the Israeli-Palestinian conflict?

I think that many Jews here see their mission to bring Jews and Arabs together as very important. I can see this in many of my friends who are artists. They disregard Sharon and work using art in order to bring people together. The art exhibition in Umm el-Fahem, in which there is art created by Jews and Arabs alike, is a good example of the cooperation for which some people on both sides are advocating. All the benefits from this art exhibition are donated to the Doctors Association of Palestine. There are people who think about the simple people on both sides, Israelis and Palestinians, and these are the people with whom I associate. I know that many people believe that Jewish Israelis don't care about the Palestinians, but this is completely false. Many Jewish Israelis are very concerned about the Palestinians and do whatever is possible to help them. More Jews help the Palestinians than Arabs, and this is a fact!

A few months ago, I went to Jerusalem. As always, a discussion started among people who were waiting in line. Some of the Arab women who were there expressed their hope for the end of the Israeli occupation in the West bank and Gaza. Just as we were all talking, there was a suicide bombing near Mus Mus[97] village in Wadi Arra. One of the Jewish women who was standing there said to us, "How can you speak about the end of the occupation when there's been a suicide bombing two seconds ago, as we are speaking?" I'm telling you Smadar, it was like a war there. Jews against Arabs. People wanted to eat one another alive with their anger and all of that just because someone said that ending the occupation would be a good thing. One woman then said that she can't sleep at night because her son is serving in the Occupied Territories. Well, you know what? That is her problem, not the problem of the Palestinian people. Maybe her son shouldn't have been there in the first place. Also the Palestinian mother can't sleep at night because she is worried about her children and about the fact that any moment her house might be demolished by an Israeli bulldozer. Mothers feel the same, and why is all this happening? For what? Why do Israeli and Palestinian children have to die and what for exactly? Because of a piece of land? What land? Is the land worth this?

Q: What do you think about Yasser Arafat? Do you think he's the right leader who will bring peace between Israelis and Palestinians?

Arafat wants peace with Israel and he's definitely the right leader for the Palestinian people. It's not true what some people say about him, that he only takes money for himself. He has not taken anything from the Palestinian people. He wants peace and that's the important point. The problem is the Jews, Israel.

Q: Do you think that during the October riots there was a reason for Israeli Arabs to identify with the Palestinian people?

We want the Jews to understand that we demonstrated with the Palestinians not necessarily because we hate the Jews, but because we feel closer to the Palestinians. What I mean is that we want to be more accepted by the Israeli society, but we are being ignored by it. We want to know for sure whether we are a part of this society, or not. There were and still are people in the Israeli government such as Ghandi, who openly suggested to load the Israeli Arabs onto buses and ship them to the neighboring Arab countries. You see? There are a number of parliament members who openly call for such a terrible thing. What right does he, or any Jew who remembers the Holocaust and anti-Semitism, to say such a thing? So, in fact, this Jew is doing what was done to him, so what's the point of the whole thing? If you, as a person who has suffered, do the same thing to another person, you become like him and not better than him. If you, as a Jew, just want to kill an Arab just because he is an Arab, then what makes you better than those who, throughout history, wanted to kill you? It seems that the Jews have forgotten a lot, so why should we not support the Palestinians who are also suffering because of them?

Listen, I was a bit confused about what happened during the [October 2000] riots. Everything happened so fast. Even the *Orr Commission* isn't so sure about how things evolved. I don't condone people who go out, throw stones and block roads. When there's tension and hatred, however, not everyone can resist it. I heard about a soldier who attended a peace program and then applied it to his military job of standing at a checkpoint and treating Palestinian women with respect. But how many righteous people like this do we have on both sides? Of course there are individuals who choose to do whatever they feel is right and behave like Rambo in the movies. And believe me, movies influence us so much today. We want to be heroes and win prizes for our supposedly courageous acts. The violence on television is terrible and leads to despair among many youths all over the world. Here in Israel, the left wing people have shifted more and more to the right, and the Arab side associates itself more and more with extreme groups such as *Hamas*.[98] The drama on television, both in the movies and on the news, has contributed to these feelings on both sides.

Of course. We are Palestinians. They are like us, and we are like them. We are all Muslims. Why should we not identify with them when they are suffering?

The Israelis think, and rightfully so, that we are Palestinians. That's why they shot us. There were other solutions to the riots, but they took the easy way for them. It's like them to do such a horrible thing.

We know whose side we are on. The Palestinian side Our side.

Q: How do you view the Palestinians? Do you identify with them?

These are very hard questions.

Q: You must have some ideas about this issue, don't you?

Well, I will tell you the way I view and understand the situation. When I watch television and see Palestinians being killed, it hurts me very much. When I see this happen, I feel as though my own brother is being killed. We have the same blood. Come on, we're both Muslim. I know people who live in the Occupied Territories and some of them are even distant family members. Yes, I definitely feel that there is a connection between us.

Q: Do you consider them to be one people entitled to their own country?

Definitely. I absolutely believe this to be true. They are one people, the Palestinian people, and they should have gotten their country a long time ago. Actually, their land should have never been taken from them in the first place.

Q: If you so strongly identify with the Palestinians and feel for their pain and suffering, how do you feel about Israel?

Look, on the one hand, I identify with the Palestinians and feel their pain, but on the other hand, Israel is also dealing with a very hard situation. I still understand that Israel is also going through a hard time at the moment.

Q: Can you understand why the Israeli Arabs joined the October 2000 riots?

Yes. They are, after all, brothers fighting for the same thing.

Q: Would you have joined the riots?

No. I have to accept whoever is in power. I can't go out and fight the police or the government. How would that help me at the moment? If I did that, I wouldn't be able to work or study and I would probably spend the rest of my life in jail. So, how would that benefit my life?

Q: So your primary responsibility is to Israel?

Yes, that's true.

Q: Even though you have claimed that the Israeli government isn't treating you well?

Yes, to an extent this is true. It's not that I want to feel like this, it's that I have no choice. I would have chosen different priorities if I could.

Q: Let's assume that there will be a Palestinian state soon. Would you prefer living in Israel, or moving to the new Palestinian state?

Well, I don't know. Wherever I receive my rights, that's where I'll go.

Q: Do you think that a Palestinian state would give you all your rights?

If the Palestinian state were more organized and more democratic like some other Arab countries, then yes. But if it remains the way it is now, then no, I would never go there. Even though I feel discriminated against in Israel, it's still a better place than Palestine would be.

Q: What do you think about Arafat?

I think he is a good leader. As we have seen, he can control the people when he needs to.

Q: Several people, including some 8 year-olds, said that Arafat is neglecting his people while accumulating a huge amount of wealth.

I don't think so. He has the characteristics a head of a state needs. Generally speaking, he is taking care of the Palestinian people. He's not the kind of person who would take money from the Arab countries and use it for his personal needs. No, I don't believe this.

Q: Do you think he can bring peace to the region, especially after he declined Barak's offer in Camp David?

Look, the most important thing Arafat should do is take care of our city, Al Quds. All the concessions Barak was willing to give were not worth anything if we can't have Jerusalem as our capital. Al Aqsa is the most important thing, and that's exactly what Barak neglected.

Q: What does Al Aqsa mean to you? Who do you think it belongs to?

It means everything to me, and of course it belongs to the Muslims. It's the third holiest place for Muslims, after Mecca and Medina.

Q: What about the Western Wall?

Well, Jerusalem should be a city of all religions and Jews and Christians should have the right to come and pray there. It should be under Muslim rule, that's what I meant.

Q: But it seems like many people from both sides don't want to share Jerusalem, especially Jews who remember that before 1967 Jews didn't have access to their holy sites.

I think that Jerusalem and its status is the main problem today and this is what's dividing Jews and Muslims, not only in Israel, but all over the world, especially in the Arab world. This is what everyone's fighting over.

Q: Do you think that Jerusalem is a just cause for fighting?

What do you mean?

Q: Do you think that Jerusalem is worth killing and getting killed for?

God didn't call us or tell us to kill. He wants us to get along together and I am sure he would like Jews, Muslims and Christians to all have access to their holy sites. I don't think that God would like people to kill one another for a building.

Q: So why do some Muslims believe that they are killing themselves in the name of Allah?

I don't know and I have never been in favor of such things. I am in favor of voicing our opinion and saying what we think. I am against terrorists killing people. I am also against the Jews killing Palestinians. They shouldn't do such things either.

Q: How do you feel about the Israeli actions in the Occupied Territories and last year against Israeli Arabs?

After the October 2000 riots I began to fear for my life. Let me ask you a question. The thirteen Israeli Arabs who protested against Israel last October didn't go out to the street with guns, right? And this is supposed to be a democratic country, right? So, the Israeli police committed a crime and meant to commit this crime when they killed the people. Once you kill a person, that's it, this person can't come back to life and speak his or her own opinion.

Q: Why do you think the Israeli Army did this?

They wanted a big mess to happen.

Q: Where do you think most of the problems the Palestinian people are experiencing come from?

Most of the problems come from within the Palestinian people.

Q: For example? Because many Palestinians say, "It's the Occupation!"

No, it's not the occupation alone. The occupation forces are actually more aware of the corruption in Arafat's government than the Palestinians themselves. When the Jews came from all over the world they worked together. They planted trees and worked in a *Kibbutz* and created cooperatives emphasizing togetherness. Why did they do this? Because they wanted to improve the standard of their living. But now, Arafat's friends and relatives from Libya, Algeria and Jordan have come here and taken all the financial resources while the Palestinian people who have been here for generations have remained without anything. The newcomers have not helped the Palestinians who have always been here. There is no equality between Arafat's people who came here later and those who have been living here for generations.

Q: What about the Arab world as a whole? Does it care about the Palestinian people and their struggle?

The Arab leaders all take money from Bush, so why should they care about the Palestinian people? The Arab countries have forgotten about the Palestinian people a long, long time ago. The Arab countries which give money to the Palestinians do it as a bribe, not because they care. Do you know when they remember the Palestinian people? When there's an *Intifada* and when there are disturbances and children are blowing themselves up. Even then they don't really care what happened to the people in Nablus, Ramallah and Jenin. What can the average person in the Occupied Territories do? Look, if we participate in a demonstration for peace here in Israel, then in spite of all the security, which is good for everyone, things mostly go calmly. The police don't kill the people, as long as they are not out of control. If there's a demonstration in Cairo or in Amman, the police will kill people who show support for the Palestinians. The police work for leaders who are scared of losing their power and leadership. And the opposite happens in other Arab countries. There, if you want to show support for anyone but the Palestinians, you will also get killed. Do you see the difference and why people in Palestine can't do a thing against the people who are keeping them poor?

Q: I have spoken to many Palestinians currently living in Turkey and most of them, if not all, viewed the year 1948 as a year in which a catastrophe occurred to the Palestinian people. How do you feel about the year 1948 and about what happened?

I was not here at that time, so it's hard for me to judge. However, I see my mother and how she cries about her brothers and sisters. I don't know any of my mother's or father's siblings. I have never seen them because they all live in Syria. They escaped from Palestine when the Jews came and took the land. My mother hasn't seen her brothers and sisters since 1948. This is my pain. My mother cries every day. One of my uncles died and it was only two years later, through people who came from Jordan to visit us, that we learned of his death. We can't visit our families in Syria because we have Israeli passports and that hurts.

Q: As an Israeli-Arab-Muslim woman, do you identify with the Palestinian people?

Of course. I am Muslim and they are Muslim too. They are Arab and I am Arab too. I identify with all the nations who are suffering, where there aren't any human rights for people. Everyone deserves rights, even black people in Africa. Why can't we all live together? There's enough land, enough work and enough life everywhere. If each and every one of us thinks positively and about each other, many of the problems would be solved.

Q: Do you think that Israeli-Arabs should serve in the Israeli Army?

There's a big problem with this. I would never allow my sons to join the Israeli Army. Firstly, I don't want to lose my son. Secondly, just as I will not let my son fight against the Syrians, I will not let him fight against the Palestinians who are Muslims like us. I always curse the Druze. Druze in Israel are willing to kill Druze in Lebanon. They can't be trusted at all, they have no ethics whatsoever. I am against such things. A Jew against a Jew, a Muslim against a Muslim, a Druze against a Druze, it's all Haram. So, no, I would never let my son go and kill Muslims or get killed for Israel. Israeli Arabs can't serve in the Israeli Army, it just isn't possible. The Arabs already look at us as traitors. Can you imagine what they would think of us if we joined the Israeli Army?

Q: Since most Arabs don't join the Israeli Army, do you think that there's somewhat of a justification for the inequality in the law?

I think that some Arabs engage in other activities that benefit the state. There are many Jews who don't join the Israeli Army and refuse to fight in it. Many of your religious people don't join the Israeli Army but they get monthly stipends from the Israeli government. These people want to read the Bible all day long. Okay, bring me the Bible, I want to read it too. I'll read it and when my son is eighteen, he will read it too. So give me a stipend too! Why does a Jewish orthodox person get all these rights and I don't? Don't you think there's something very unequal here?

Q: What do you think should be done on the Israeli and Palestinian sides in order for peace to come?

Well, no one has to leave, except the settlers. The people must decide that they want peace. The settlers must go. Then everything will be solved.

Q: After all the suicide bombings and acts of the Israeli Army, do you think that the hatred between Israelis and Palestinians can ever disappear?

Yes, if the settlers disappear, there's a Palestinian state controlled by the Palestinians, arrests of Palestinians stop and the checkpoints disappear, then yes, there will be peace. I want to stress to you that I have never hated Jews. I have seen several movies about Hitler and about the Jews in the Holocaust. Believe me when I say that I cried a lot when I saw how they killed the Jews and burnt them in those ovens. When I see a movie about how they brought mothers and children and old people and killed them, I cry. Even when I see a Druze die, I cry, and I hate the Druze. This is about people's lives and I don't hate anyone. I love to live, and other people love to live too. During the *Intifada* there was a program on television where a Palestinian woman was pregnant and every time her husband left the house, even if it was just to go to the toilet which was outside, she didn't know if he would come back alive. The poor woman. Doesn't a pregnant Jewish woman suffer just like a Palestinian woman does? They are the same. A human being is important.

If Sharon and Arafat change their attitude things will change for the best. If they both start thinking about their people and not only about themselves and their power, then and only then will things finally change. They both must think about the children and mothers in Israel and Palestine. We have to forget about the land as a restricting thing. People should be able to live wherever they want. Why should people be restricted? If we all live together, then things will be better.

Q: For many Jewish people living in Israel there is a problem with this idea of living together. There are millions of Palestinians who are dreaming about going back to their lands. Jews see this as a danger to the existence of Israel as a Jewish state, especially since this is the only place in which Jews can feel relatively safe.

Look, many new immigrants come here each year and get a house and lots of help from the Israeli government. So, I think that Palestinians who left their homes in 1948 should have the right to return to this area. I think that a very small minority, if any at all, will come back. You have to remember that these people have been living in another place for a very long time. I don't think that most of them will leave for something so uncertain. Whoever wants to come back should be able to and whoever wants to stay where they are should be able to do so too. I know many Palestinian people who still cry for Haifa and Jaffa every day. Why should they die without ever seeing it again? Why shouldn't they be able to return? This was their land before the Jews came!

Q: Israel, as a Jewish state whose interest it is to maintain a Jewish state, sees this as a risk. Letting Palestinians return is taking a big chance, don't you think? Especially considering the high birth rates among Palestinians and Israeli Arabs...

If you look around you, Smadar, you'll see that most women don't have a lot of children here. It's not like it used to be in the past. This is not the point. And besides, why do people from Ethiopia, whose fathers, mothers and grandparents have never been here, come here? And why can't my uncle, who used to live here, but now lives in Jenin, ever come here again? You Jews always hear about these old people from Russia and you go and get them and bring them to live here. You bring these old people, whose hands are already shaking because they are so old and give them salaries so that they can live in Israel. So, you just waste the country's money. Why?

Q: The Jews claim that the State of Israel was unique, like nothing else. It followed persecution and a very deep religious longing lasting thousands of years. Many Jews believe that these are some of the reasons why Israel should have a Jewish character. Do you accept that there's something in these claims? Or does Israel, in your opinion,

have to forget about Zionism and let everyone who wants to come here come?

Just as Jews should have the right to come here, so should the Palestinians who left their lands in 1948. For the Jews it's better to compensate these people with money, of course. But I think that the Palestinians will think a hundred times at the age of fifty whether to make the move. It's not easy to leave and those who have only a little plot of land waiting for them will never come. I think that many will accept the monetary compensation.

Q: Why do you think the Palestinians left their lands in 1948?

They were terrified and they were also told that the move would only be for two weeks, until the Jews were beaten. My mother told me that they believed that they [the Arabs] would beat the Jews in two or three days. But the Jews came from the sea and the air and shot everyone. Then, of course, people left and those who left never came back. My uncle took money, went to Haifa, got on a boat and left for Lebanon and then to Syria.

My grandmother left everything because she was afraid for the children. She put them on a horse and then ran away without looking back even once. People were panicking and most of them thought that they would only be gone for a few weeks.

Q: Do you think that the United Nations had the right to vote on giving this land to the Jews?

No, I don't think it had the right to do that. Maybe, if the Jews came here with the intention to live in peace, then it would have been okay to make such a decision. But how could people come and live in the same houses and on the same land which all belonged to other people who had to run away? What, would it be okay for someone to come to my house today, or to your house and tell me to leave so that they can move in and live there? I wouldn't allow that, would you? Jews just came here, shot people and then took their property. Is this a just way to behave?

Q: So, do you think peace will ever come?

It depends on us all, not only on the Palestinians. It depends on each and every one of us here. On both sides. Then this will be the land of milk and honey, as the Jews say.

Q: Do you genuinely believe that Israelis and Palestinians will ever be able to trust one another and visit one another?

Yes, I believe it's possible, because it used to be like that before all the problems started. Once, my Jewish-Moroccan friend used to invite me to their *Mimuna*[99]. It was wonderful, but I haven't gone for a few years now. There's no reason to go now. We've gotten to a situation where many Israelis have been hurt by suicide bombings and I am afraid that maybe someone there lost a loved one and doesn't like Arabs. I don't want to go there and not have a good time, or maybe even get into a fight. So I don't go anymore.

I miss the days before the Al Aqsa *Intifada*. Before that, Jews and Israeli Arabs used to go to Jenin, Tulkarem and Nablus. It was also good for the Palestinians because they made money out of both Jews and Arabs. People sat together in restaurants, ate and drank and talked to one another. I have a Jewish friend who is an artist. She lost her husband in a suicide bombing a few months ago. It hurts me to see her now. She's an amazing woman who even after she lost her husband donated one of her pieces of art to a doctor's organization in the Occupied Territories. Her husband died in Haifa. So you see? She lost her husband in a suicide bombing. I am very angry about what she's been through and it hurts me to see her in such grief. And after everything she's been through she donated something to the Palestinians—what a wonderful act of peace and love.

Q: Do you think that the situation between Israelis and Palestinians is being manipulated by someone?

Of course it is. It is manipulated by the governments on both sides and this is not only exclusive to Israel and Palestine. It's the same all over the world. In each and every place today there is hate, so we need people to come together and genuinely try and solve these painful problems. All of us here in Israel and Palestine deserve to rest and relax a bit. I sometimes meet Jewish people and it hurts to see that they no longer trust in us.

It's not a new thing that neighbors fight against one another. The governments want this fighting because they gain from it. If I want peace, then what I have to do is slow down, stop and think for a moment.

Q: What do you think is taught in Palestinian schools?

I don't have friends or family in the Occupied Territories, so I don't think I can really answer your question.

Q: Do you think that Israelis care about the Palestinians?

I have a Jewish friend who told me that sometimes she feels like leaving Israel because of what the Israeli Army is doing to the Palestinian people. I think that many Israelis identify with the Palestinians and don't like what's going on. I have a Jewish Israeli friend who helps the Palestinians all the time. The situation, however, has deteriorated. I am afraid to leave Arara since the year 2000 when things got so much worse.

I have a friend from Tivon who teaches in *Oranim College*.[100] She's a good friend of mine and a very courageous woman. When the *Intifada* began in October 2000 she started criticizing Israel and helping the Palestinians by collecting clothes and food to send to them. Because she was doing this, some Israelis cursed her and treated her unjustly. When she invited us to her house, some of her neighbors told her, "What? You are still letting Arabs into your house?" So, you see, there are always bad people around, on both sides. In spite of this fact, we have to get over these people and their beliefs and try to decrease their number and teach them that we have to work together in order to make things better, not worse.

Q: Do you think that Jerusalem should be the capital of both Israel and Palestine?

Jerusalem should be a city where everyone can come and pray. Not only Palestinians, but Muslims from all over the world. And not only Muslims, but also Christians and Jews.

Jerusalem is a holy place for many people all over the world, so who are you, or I, or your government to say who can go there and who can not? People should come together and believe and pray.

Q: Children are the most straightforward humans, which is exactly why I wanted to devote some of this summer to interviewing them. A child will usually say what's on his or her mind. It's true that a child will also say what he or she hears at home or sees on television, but

they will say it, regardless. Just this morning I spoke to a 9 year-old boy who told me that he would want to become a *shaheed* if he were asked to. When I asked him why he would like to become a *shaheed* he said that he would do it because he would then enter the gates of Heaven. When I asked him where he heard this, he said that he heard it at school and at home.

I don't believe this. I don't believe that a teacher here would say such a thing. The boy was probably telling you that the children in the Occupied Territories were told such things by those who send them to do such things. I think that here a teacher would be afraid to say such a thing in class, especially because some of their fathers know the Israeli police force. I don't think a teacher here would take the chance of saying such things and maybe losing their profession. Maybe the boy didn't completely understand what he was told, but I don't believe that our children here in Arara would say such things. By the way, there was a question I wanted to ask you, may I?

Q: Of course, you may ask me anything on your mind.

How are things in the United States now? Before September 11, I wanted to send my children to study there. Now I hear that life is very hard there for Arabs because the Americans don't like them and are afraid of them and of Islam. Is that true in your opinion? It's ironic because here in Israel we watch American movies and we always identify with the American soldiers who are fighting for freedom. But when you really look into the matter, you see what criminals they really are in real life. The Jews suffered very much in Germany, much more than the Palestinians are suffering today. No other nation suffered like the Jews suffered in Germany. This is why the Jews in the United States are so strong and make all the decisions. They vote together and vote together and take care of one another. Look how many Muslims and Arabs there are in the United States today. There are probably more Muslims than Jews. If all the Muslims worked together and voted for the same political parties and organizations, they would be very powerful.

Q: So why do you think Muslims and Arabs aren't doing this in the United States?

Because they are stupid. All they care about is money. Everyone wants to accumulate personal wealth. They can't work together, unfortunately. This is the same in all the Muslim and Arab countries.

Q: **You have touched the issue of Jewish suffering, an issue that only a few Palestinians speak of with such sensitivity. Many Palestinians actually believe that what the Jews suffered in Europe and what the Palestinians are experiencing now is the same. Do you think this is true? Do you think that the claim many Palestinians voice, that the Jews have become Nazis is true?**

I have never compared one event to the other. It's impossible. And no, I don't think that the Israelis are like the Nazis. Maybe Sharon is a Nazi. He hates Arabs and wants them all dead. What he did in *Sabra and Shatila*[101], only someone like him could do. But believe me, most of the Israeli soldiers who go into the Occupied Territories can't be blamed for everything. There is a lot that is beyond their personal choices and decisions. A month ago there was a program about soldiers who serve in the Occupied Territories. Two of the soldiers even cried when they were speaking. One of the soldiers has a pregnant wife and he said that every time he leaves her he cries. He might die and never see his son or daughter. You can't compare the Jews and the Nazis. Hitler and his people rounded up millions of Jews and threw them into gas chambers. Everyone knows this is not happening in the Occupied Territories at the moment. How could Hitler do this to the Jews? I just don't understand. I saw a documentary about a little boy who escaped from a concentration camp and you should have seen that. There were huge frightening dogs chasing him in the forest. I cried for a week after I watched this terrible thing. I don't think that the events that happened in the Holocaust can be compared to anything else, to anything. In Islam, we accept and respect the Jews as a people. They are also *ahal-al-kitab* [people of the Book]. When we pray, we also have a prayer called *Israiliyyat*.[102] I also know a Jewish boy here who reads the Qur'an. I think that a person who respects another person is serving his country much more than he who hates.

Q: **Why do you think that the world sees Islam as such a threatening religion, even as terrorizing?**

There is a problem with the people who control Islam. Bin Ladin, for example. What did he do? He went and murdered thousands of people in the name of Islam. Why, instead of killing innocent people and investing money in terror, doesn't he give money to the Palestinian people? Give them money, support them if there is a war, they can fight. But why does he just go and murder thousands of innocent people who never did anything to him? This is unacceptable. He has a lot of money and that's all.

Without his money he is nothing, a stupid man. People like him twist Islam. When you think about it now, the fact that many Americans don't like Arabs and Muslims and are afraid of Islam is a natural reaction to what happened on September 11th. If an American person came and bombed Arara, would I then like Americans? Of course not. I would say that they are terrorists, just like Bin Ladin is a terrorist. Why did he commit this act of terror in the United States? There are so many poor people in Afghanistan. Why didn't he spend the money on them? Why did he not give them money so that their lives would be better, instead of turning them into murderers? He could have given Afghan people money so that they could go and travel and study, even in the United States where there are many good educational institutions. The education facilities are known to be excellent in the United States. People like Bin Ladin have caused people to see Islam as bad, frightening and dominating. I know a man who went to the United States and immediately returned because he could feel the hatred towards him. Who knows? Maybe Bin Ladin is a fake Muslim whose job is to ruin Islam? I don't believe that a Muslim who is a Sheik and reads Qur'an would do such a thing. But regardless, it's people like him who are ruining the true meaning of Islam, which is peace.

These people like Bin Ladin are not religious at all. Islam doesn't call for the murder of innocent people. If you read the Qur'an you'll see that it's only permitted for soldiers to face soldiers in battle. Who told you that Bin Ladin was a Muslim? There are many people today who twist Islam and change its true meaning. And about the *shaheeds*, you shouldn't believe that someone who murders innocent people is sent to Heaven according to Islam.

Our Prophet Muhammad, peace and prayers be upon him, said that innocent people should not be killed. There's a religious Muslim man who says that Muhammad said that Muslims should fight whoever isn't a Muslim. This is completely false. Muhammad, peace and prayers be upon him, when he was conquering the Middle East, said that anyone who is converted to Islam is welcome. And if one didn't want to convert to Islam, that was okay. All they had to do was to pay the poll tax, which is like money for protection. That's exactly what he said, that people should not kill innocent people. Do you see how intelligent the leaders of that time were? Omar el Hatab, when he came to Jerusalem, was invited to a church for a visit. He declined the invitation because he knew that Muslims in the following generations would fight over this church because he had visited it. Look at the leaders we used to have in the past. I want to go to heaven, so what do I do? I do good things. I pray, I pay *Zakat*[103] and read several chapters of the Qur'an every day. Muhammad's neighbor was Jewish. This Jewish person left a mess in the Prophet's back yard. One day, some dates from the Jewish man's tree fell on Muhammad's lawn. He collected the dates and brought them to the Jewish man. He told the Jewish man, "These are your dates, They fell from your tree." Do you see how much he loved peace with everyone?

Come on, Smadar, when will you convert into Islam already? If you convert, you will be like a new woman, believe me. It's the only religion of true peace and the only religion that respects the other two. Try it, give it a chance and you won't be disappointed!

Q: Please tell me about your life here in Arara before and during 1948.

We lived here at the time but on the other side of the village. Arara was much smaller and there were fewer people here. Life was hard, especially for the women who had to work from early in the morning until late at night. We had to cook all day in the heat and bake bread. We had to walk quite a long way to get water for the family. I think it was a few kilometers from here, towards where Hadera is today. The women would walk together in big groups and bring whatever was needed. The men worked in the fields. We also had quite a few olive trees and we made our own olive oil. That was until 1948 when the Jews came. Life was hard, but it was also very good.

Q: What happened after that?

Well, the Jews came that year.

Q: What exactly happened? Did you see Jews or other Arabs?

Yes, I saw many Jews. Most of them were white skinned and European looking. As you know, Arara is situated between Haifa and Jordan. Many people who escaped from Haifa to Jordan because the Jews came stopped in Arara for a short rest, or even sometimes for a night. We used to cook food and give it to the people who were running away from the Jews. We made bread and sometimes meat and soup and we gave handed it out to whoever needed it. Of course, most of them didn't know if they would ever be able to come back although most of them thought they eventually would. I have heard of several massacres of Palestinians by the Jews, like the one in Dir Yassin and in several other places. It was terrible what they did to the women and children and even to the old people. Some of the Jews killed and raped Palestinian girls when they came. My father was worried that I would also get raped, but thank God I was not!

Q: How did most Palestinians escape?

Some of them were riding horses and donkeys, but many were walking on foot. There was also a pregnant woman whom I can remember well.

Q: Have you ever met any of these people again?

Well, you won't believe what happened. Last year, I went to Mecca with my husband and a few more friends from the village. For several years Israeli Arabs have been able to get into Saudi Arabia and visit Mecca. We receive temporary Jordanian passports instead of our Israeli ones. In Mecca, most people wear these special tags which say which country they are from. We had a tag which said Palestine because we would never put the name Israel on ourselves and besides, they would not allow us to walk around there with a tag saying we were from Israel. As we were walking around a man approached us and asked us exactly where in Palestine we were from. We said that we were from Arara Village. He then broke down and started to cry. In the beginning we were all amazed. We could not understand why he was crying. It turned out that he had passed through Arara in 1948, while he was escaping from Haifa, and that we provided him with food. He was only 12 at the time and I think I can remember him too, because not many 12 year olds came through our village. He said that he now lives in Amman, that he was never able to return to Haifa and that he's still indebted to us.

Q: Why did you not escape and instead stayed in your village?

My father was the one who decided to stay put and we accepted his decision. Most of the people who escaped ran away from cities because that was where most of the Jews went to when they came to Palestine. We stayed in Arara and have not moved since the Jews came.

Q: How do you psychologically and emotionally feel about the Palestinian people? Would you immigrate to the new Palestinian state if you had the opportunity to do so?

Personally, I would never choose to leave the place in which I was born. Wherever I was born is where I am going to stay forever. As you know, however, I might be relocated by the church and might find myself in Ramallah again, or even in Gaza. In that case, I will leave and go there because it is my job and my duty. My job is to care about people, wherever they might be. I work for people and not for politicians. Just like there are atheists who live without God, I live with God and with His help. I receive guidance from Him. As to the Palestinian people, I have to say that at different times I feel differently about them. Today, I am like a typical Israeli who doesn't really know what's going on in the Occupied Territories. I have been detached from those areas for a while now and have not identified with their suffering lately although I know that they are suffering. Sometimes I see things on television, like when that little boy was shot...what was his name? Muhammad al-Durrah I think. That made me very sad and even angry. Whenever I see a child killed, Jew or Arab, it makes me angry.

Q: If you had to take sides, whose side would you say you are? On the Jewish or the Arab side?

Sometimes I am more on the Arab side and sometimes less on their side. Regardless of whose side I am on, I am always angry about the stupidity of politicians on both sides. The stupidity and ignorance of our politicians is what really upsets me. I don't know exactly how to express my feelings about this, but a leadership in despair is very unpredictable. A functioning leadership should look at the general situation and not only at parts of it. The problem is that on both sides, in nearly each and every household, there is some kind of suffering going on because of the conflict. So many Jews and Palestinians have died in the last few years. The leaders have lost their minds. They are taking advantage of the situation because they want to hold on to their power. Sometimes, however, I try to put myself in the shoes of the leaders. How do you deal with a situation where each and every day someone is killed and an entire new household is grieving because it was hit by terror? What do you do when you have a constituency that demands retaliation? On the other hand, I would like to see these leaders trying to work for reconciliation between the two sides in spite of all the pain and suffering people are experiencing. I want the Arab leaders to say to the Jews, "Come, let's talk and try to solve the problem." The Jews have the right to know that the Arabs acknowledge their existence and do not want to destroy Israel. When I put myself on the Jewish side, even though there's peace with Jordan and Egypt, the Jews know that there's a lot to be afraid of. The Jew who lives in Israel know that millions of Arabs in the world object to his existence as an Israeli. A Jew knows that one lost battle on the Israeli side might mean immediate elimination of the Jewish state. So, both sides are justified in their concerns.

Q: Do you view the Palestinians as one people entitled to a state of their own?

Yes, of course. And think about it. If they don't have their own country, I, as an Israeli will suffer even more. If they have their own country and we have a peaceful relationship with them, I will have psychological rest in Israel and they will have psychological rest in Palestine. It's like an American Jew. The Jew likes living in the United States and doesn't want to come and live in Israel. But this Jew knows that Israel exists and that it has its own flag and a national anthem. He knows that if he ever needs to escape from the United States Israel will accept him and provide him with protection. This connects the Jew to Israel. The Palestinian isn't connected to anything now and that's bad.

Q: What do you think abut Arafat? Do you think that he is the right person to lead the Palestinian people?

I think that the Israelis sure view him as the right person. They don't want to see someone else have his job, or they would have gotten rid of him a long time ago. When a leader survives for thirty or forty years, he already becomes a symbol, regardless of whether he was a good or bad leader. Who really wants to eliminate a symbol? And a symbol can never lose, no matter what is done in its name. I mean, Arafat can do bad things and people will not condemn his actions. I think that if there were a different leadership on the Palestinian side from the very beginning, things would be much better now. A person like Arafat doesn't just survive without a reason, do you understand? Even though some people criticize him, no one dares to touch him and change the status quo. People like us who live in Israel, however, want to see someone else who is more modern and who does not dress like Arafat. We want someone who wears a suit and a tie, not an army uniform. I don't know if that would change the person, but seriously, look at Arafat. The world is becoming more modern in many ways. We don't want someone who walks around with a machine gun and wears uniform all day. And besides, I always get angry when I see that one person alone determines the fate of an entire people. This phenomenon makes me very worried. Dictatorship in general worries me and Arafat, undoubtedly, is a dictator. Whether Arafat is the right person to bring peace I don't know. And I don't really think that it's so much a question of whether he's the right man. He is what we have at the moment. Who shall the Israelis negotiate with? You have to remember that we are dealing with a certain people, a certain culture that doesn't know how to handle democracy, or what to do with it. They have to first of all be educated as to the value of peace and respect. The problem is that if Arafat, or any other leader there, began to teach such values to the people, they would be viewed as weak by the entire Arab world. This is, therefore, a long process which can't happen in a year or two. Years of education have to pass before things change and people change the perceptions in their minds. Israel has already achieved a very high level of democracy because it aspired to be a democratic state from the very beginning. For example, I can criticize the state and speak against the injustices I see. I can see very well what the Arab states do to people who criticize them. We can't and must not even try to compare Israel to the Arab world. This is the main problem that the Arab world faces today—the lack of democracy and the fact that criticism is not allowed. In Israel the western culture dominates, although it's an eastern country with an eastern mentality.

Q: What do you think of Arafat? Is he the right person to bring peace to the region?

Arafat is a man of peace. He wants peace. The Israelis force Arafat to accept whatever they want, even when there are suicide bombings. Arafat has no control over suicide bombings and he wants peace with the Israelis. The Jews must be blamed for the continuation of the violence in the West Bank and the Gaza Strip.

I support Arafat because he's a man of peace and not a man of war. If he could find a man in Israel with whom he could dialogue and shake hands, there would have been peace a long time ago. And if this happened a long time ago, we could all finally sleep in peace without having to worry about being killed at any moment. Now we can't sleep because we are so afraid.

Q: Many people to whom I spoke said that Arafat doesn't care about the Palestinian people at all. What do you think about this claim?

This is completely false. It's simply propaganda against Arafat and his government. Arafat almost killed himself for his people, even though he's been sick for a long time now. He always works for his people and for bringing a more relaxed atmosphere to the Middle East. Arafat wants peace and all the Palestinian people all over the world want peace. We don't care about Bshara, about Asad or about Lebanon. We live here and we want peace. Our sons want to live in peace. A mother sees her son with her heart before with her eyes. When my son leaves the house, I fear for him. We want peace and without peace we can't live.

[In the background a woman said: I don't want peace, I want war so that I can shoot the Jews]

Q: If Arafat wants peace so much, what's the problem?

There's no peace with the Palestinians because of Israel. Israel entered the Palestinian Authority and tore down houses and electricity stations over there. Everything collapsed because of Israel. The Jews also killed Arafat's people, the children, the women and the old people too. Of course there's no peace when such things happen. This behavior leads to killing and when there's killing there's no peace and quiet. I wish that the political situation were similar to our situation right now. We are talking and having a discussion. If we don't let you come to us and speak with us, how are we ever going to have peace?

Q: How do you feel about Israeli Jews at the moment? Do you feel any resentment at all?

No, I don't feel any resentment towards them. If a Jew came here like you have, I would speak to them very calmly and express my feelings to them. I am happy to speak to you.

Q: Do you feel any connection to the Palestinian people?

Of course. This is the cause of the problem, but there's nothing I can do about it. I own a house and the Israeli authorities won't even give me a permit to extend it. So, when the Jews come and take my house, what can I do? I am not satisfied with this treatment, so of course I feel even more connected to the Palestinian people and their suffering.

Q: What do you think about the Palestinian people and about their desire for their own state?

They have the right to live in their own country. Where will they go? They went to Lebanon and got killed by the *Maronites*.[104] They went to Algeria and were also expelled from there. They went to Tunisia and were also kicked out. They went to Kuwait and were kicked out after the Gulf War. Where will they go to next? Where will they be safe? Not only did the Jews take their land but they are also compelled to become nomads.

Q: Many Palestinians all over the world believe that all of Israel should become a Palestinian state. Do you agree with this?

Not all of Israel should become Palestine. The Jews have the same right as us to live on this land. Everyone has the right for their own country, don't you think? The Jews and the Palestinians should both have their own country and they should both receive their rights. The problem is that the Jews don't behave in a just manner. During wartime, the Jews killed our sons in Jerusalem and in Nablus. Why do they come and kill our sons? We don't have our rights here in Israel. Why does a Jew receive a higher salary than an Arab? Yes, the Jews enter the Israeli Army, but we do all the construction work and all the other hard work the Jews don't want to do. The Jews don't like us here. They look at us in a strange way, as though they want to swallow us up alive. Sharon gave the fundamentalists in this country power and the legitimacy to shoot Arabs. Sharon wants to have a country without any Arab people in it. He likes the settlers who shoot Arabs. So maybe it would be better if all of this were to become Arab land.

Q: What do you think about the settlers who live in the West bank and in the Gaza Strip?

These are the real racists. They are the reason for this war. Everyone is suffering because of them. They all want war and support it without shame. All they say is, "We want war!" They hate Arabs. Wherever there is an Arab they want to kill him. They will tear down the Arab's house and settle in it if they get the chance to do so.

Q: Why do you think there are some Jews in places like Hebron?

They are criminals and they are the reason for this entire problem. They are the symbol of Israeli discrimination. They are killing Arabs and don't want any Arabs left on this land. Sharon gave the settlers permission to kill us and when he entered Al Aqsa he contaminated it. He himself is contaminated.

Q: Some Jews believe that there are some Jewish holy sites in Hebron. So you agree with this claim?

No, I do not. We know that the Jews do not have any holy sites on this land. This was always Arab land and the Jews came much later. If anyone has holy sites here it is the Muslims.

Your side, Smadar, is the side that doesn't want peace. You don't like peace and you only want war. Sharon doesn't want the Palestinians to have their own state. If he supported the creation of a Palestinian state we would not be going through this hell right now. Instead he lets settlers go to Hebron because they claim they have something sacred there.

Q: But Jews also believe they have a holy site in Hebron.

Nonsense. It's not true. Qur'an never said such a thing!

No, I will not leave here. I will not leave my home and my village. I was born here, my sons were born here and they live close to me. I will die here. The Palestinians are my family, my loved ones, but this is my land and my home is here. I am an Israeli citizen, so why should I leave?

Q: What, if at all is your connection to the Palestinian people?

Do you want me to tell you the truth? Sometimes I feel for them and sometimes I don't. Sometimes I am on the Palestinian side and sometimes I am on the Israeli side.

Q: When do you feel that you identify with one side and not with the other?

When the Palestinians carry out suicide bombings here in Israel and innocent people get killed, I don't feel any compassion for them. When something like this happens, I feel like strangling them. When I see Israeli planes dropping bombs on Gaza and children crying, I feel for the Palestinians. I think to myself, "What has this small child done to deserve this?" When that small child, Muhammad al-Durrah, was shot and it was shown on television, I felt very upset and helpless. I thought to myself, "This little boy is Arab and Palestinian, but what has he done to deserve this?" But again, when a Palestinian comes with explosives and kills people who have never even been to Palestine, I get very angry and even depressed about the whole thing. Sometimes I feel that I am going insane.

Q: Do you view the Palestinians as one people who are entitled to their own state?

I don't think that the Palestinians are ready for their own state at the moment. I don't know, maybe they will be ready sometime in the far future. Before the Second *Intifada*, the Palestinians were very close to having their own state. The election of Sharon as prime minister might have changed some things, but what do I care about Sharon? They needed more patience and they maybe then they would have had their own state. I think that even if they get their own state they shouldn't be given any weapons. If a country wants to live in peace, they don't need any weapons. Besides, I wouldn't trust them at all. Look at countries like Iran and Iraq. They can't be trusted because they randomly attack innocent people all over the Middle East. When I go to Jewish towns and villages, I never feel afraid. I know that nothing bad will be done to me there. I never held a gun in my life, even during the war. Even when I received the offer to go on a shooting course and become a certified gun holder, I refused. When I was working in Neve Ilan, I never held a gun either. My weapon was the flashlight. And there is one more thing I would like to say here. The Palestinian people have to change their mindset. It doesn't help just to have a state. People's perceptions have to change and at the moment it seems that the Palestinians will never change. Most of them are fanatic and they hate not only the Jews and Israel but also each and every other western country.

Q: So, from what I understand, your identification with the Palestinian people is nearly non-existent.

That is true.

Q: How do you feel about the Al Aqsa mosque?

I am a religious man and the mosque has significance for me. It's different than the significance it has for most other Muslims here in Israel.

Q: What do you think about the fact that some Jews, a small minority, believe that the mosque should be torn down?

Look, the Al Aqsa mosque does not belong to me or to anyone else here. It's not something private belonging to one person or to one nation. It belongs to a whole people, to Muslims. It's not just a house or something like that. It's a holy place. Just try to imagine what would happen if a group of crazy people came and tore the mosque down? It would be a catastrophe and it would ignite a huge war between the Jews and the Muslim world. I think it might even be the Third World War. I believe that both people, Jews and Muslims, have holy places and that all of them should be respected. All of them must not be harmed. The ideal situation for me would be that people from both sides would acknowledge the holiness of all the holy sites in Jerusalem. Just like in the Jewish religion it is forbidden for a non-Jew to enter a synagogue, Jews should keep away from the Muslim mosques.

Q: So you do see the importance of some holy sites to all Muslims?

Of course I do. Let me tell you something. During Ramadan, more than half a million people came to Al Aqsa in order to pray and worship Allah. Of course it's a holy place for all Muslims. And remember that it's not something new that was built just yesterday. I don't know much about history, I admit, but I know this mosque is very old and it has survived a lot.

Q: Do you think that Al Aqsa should be a part of the Palestinian state?

Look, regardless of Al Aqsa and Jerusalem, what Barak was willing to give to the Palestinian people, no one will ever offer them again. He was willing to give them East Jerusalem and so much more, but they denied it. Who knows? Maybe they don't deserve it.

Q: Do you think that Arafat is the right leader for the Palestinian people?

No, no, definitely not. I swear to God, I don't like this man at all. A leader needs to be respectful and he has to care about his people. Arafat promises things and never comes through. He is lucky that Israel has kept him in power thus far. He's lucky he hasn't been assassinated by Israel yet. One thing always surprises me about this issue. Arafat has caused pain to so many Palestinians all over the world. Because of him, for example, Palestinians were kicked out of places like Kuwait and Lebanon. The Palestinians, however, always blame someone else for their misfortunes and never Arafat. How can this be? Are people not able to see who this man really is? I sometimes feel that the Palestinian people always blame others and never themselves. I don't think they will get anywhere with such behavior.

Q: Do you think he cares about the Palestinian people?

I don't know what's important to him, but let me tell you one thing. Now the Palestinian's economic situation is worse than ever before. In the past, about 60,000 Palestinians worked in Tel Aviv and in other parts of Israel. At that time, they were making money and earning a living. They also established personal relationships with Israelis. Today, not even one Palestinian is allowed to work in Israel because of the suicide bombings. So, in the past, Palestinians could care about their everyday lives, about making money and about raising their children. Today, what does Arafat have? Millions or even billions of dollars, so why would he care about anyone? Why should he care about the Palestinian people? Tomorrow he can get into his private jet and fly to Libya or to any other country that would accept him. He has no need to live in Palestine. And who is paying for this? His people, the Palestinians, of course. I hate Arafat, and I don't feel any sympathy for him. I could care less if he died now.

Q: Do you feel for Arafat's people, for the Palestinians?

For his people? What I feel for his people is that they have to get rid of him because he has failed. It's like a father who takes drugs and ruins his entire family. It's a pity, really. There are many educated people who could take his place and be much more successful in bringing peace to the Palestinian people.

Q: What do you wish for the Palestinian people?

I wish them to get a brain and become wiser. They should leave their weapons and concentrate on earning a living. They should concentrate on educating their children, instead of letting them go out into the streets and throw stones. I wish their children and our children a better future.

Q: Speaking about children, how do you feel about how the Israeli Army treats Palestinian children?

Look, when the Palestinian children throw stones, the Israeli Army reacts without any remorse.

Q: Do you think it is fair that the Israeli Army reacts to the throwing of stones with guns and tanks?

What can I tell you? No, it's not fair. I am against killing children. When an adult is killed, it doesn't really affect me, believe me. But when a child is killed, I don't care whether it's a Jew or an Arab, I cry. What can I tell you? Both sides lack a sensitive and coherent mind. Many years ago, if someone talked to Arafat and saw him as a man of peace, like Abie Nathan[105], they would be thrown in jail. Today people are wiser and they choose to talk to one another. People come and people go, but the land always remains and what I see is that many people are dying for it. I hope that people on both sides will become wiser, and lead a better life.

Q: And what about all the lands that were taken from your family in 1948?

Look, everyone dies in the end and we can't take the land with us. I have given up the rights to my land. I don't believe that we will ever get our lands back because they [the Jewish Israelis] will never give them back to us. Should we go and fight our neighbors for this? It's not their fault and most of them weren't even born in 1948 when everything happened.

Q: If you had the opportunity to leave Israel and emigrate to the future Palestinian, would you?

No, no, I would never consider doing such a thing. I wouldn't even dream to do such a thing. You know, even if they give me a house in Palestine and billions of dollars, I will never leave and go and live in a Palestinian state. Here I feel at home. I love the people who live around me. What's bad in my life? I love this country and I love the Jews. But, as I have said before, sometimes they [the Jews] push us and remind us that we are different. Still, I have never hated the Jews and most of my friends are Jews. When I think about it, I don't really have Arab friends to whom I am close. Every day I get up and go to the Jews for work and at night I come back from the Jews. When I worked in Neve Ilan, I worked from morning to night with Jews, and it was a wonderful experience. And about the Palestinian state—I fear to think what kind of state it is going to be. In any case, I don't want to be a part of it and I know that life here is much better.

Q: Some Palestinians celebrate the Day of the Land. Do you identify with or participate in this celebration?

Yes, and I will tell you why. Before 1948 these lands belonged to us. Then the Jews took them from us. I feel that this is my country and that it was violently taken away from me by the Jews. The Jews took these lands from us and also, this day reminds me more and more of the extremism the Jews show towards us here in Israel. Do you know the Jewish village of Nataf? The land belonged to my family before 1948, did you know that? The Jews told my family that they would be paid a ridiculously small amount of money. They were also threatened that if they didn't give the land to the Jews, it would be taken from them by force. This is what I have been told by my family.

Q: The Palestinians also celebrate a day called Yom al Nakba [the Day of the Catastrophe]. Do you celebrate it too?

I have heard about this day, but I am not sure what it is all about.

Q: Basically it's a day of mourning commemorating the day the Jews came here and created Israel.

I have never celebrated it.

Q: Do you feel that in 1948, when the United Nations declared the State of Israel, a grievance was done to the Palestinian people?

Of course I do. Imagine—now the Jews can come and live here whenever they want and the Arab people can't. People who lived here for hundreds of years cannot come here and those who came in 1948 can bring their family without any restriction. This is a catastrophe. Imagine how you would feel if your family had lived here for generations and then suddenly, all their lands and rights were taken and they had to beg for them? Of course it hurts. It really hurts.

Q: Do you have some anger towards the Jews?

If we were respected and given our rights, I wouldn't be as angry as I am now. I wouldn't feel that I am different or less worthy than a Jew. Look at the Jews—they are bringing people from Ethiopia and who knows if they're even Jews or not. These Ethiopian people get more rights than we do and we have lived here for generations. Of course all of this hurts!

Q: Are you in favor of the right of return for Palestinians living all around the world?

Of course I am in favor of this. This was their land in the first place and there is enough room for all of them to come back, if they wanted to.

Q: Jews are afraid that Palestinian refugees will flood Israel and that Israel will not remain a Jewish state anymore.

So what if it will not stay a Jewish state anymore? This is not the important thing. The important thing is that the Palestinians must get their lands back.

Q: Do you think that if the Palestinians returned to their lands they would accept you, who have lived in Israel and accepted Jewish rule?

I would not be afraid of them. The Palestinians who would return would understand very well why we're here and why we had to accept the Israeli rule. Look, even today there are many Palestinians who would rather live here than in the Palestinian Authority.

Q: So you would vote for the Palestinian's right to return because the Jews have a right to come here whenever they want?

Smadar, it's their land. It's their country and it's their right to come back here! I want to ask you another question. You are living here with your family. Would you like it if someone forcibly took you to the United States, or anywhere else without you being able to ever return? I think this question perfectly answers your question.

Q: If you look back at history, many people and many nations changed their location. Isn't it natural that people come and go? After all, times change, don't they?

If there's an occupation, the people have to fight until they get back their land. Egypt, Britain and France conquered many places and they eventually had to withdraw because colonialism had some to an end. So here's it's exactly the same thing. The Israelis will eventually have to leave and let the Palestinians rule themselves. I support the Palestinian's fight, but I oppose terrorism, the suicide bombings. On the other hand, I think it is obvious that the Palestinians don't have another way to fight the Israelis. It is complicated.

Q: Do you condemn the throwing of stones by children?

Smadar, do you condemn the shootings by soldiers? Think about it. The children are throwing stones and the soldiers are shooting back. This is their war in response.

Q: To what extent do you support the Palestinian's resistance and to what extent, if at all, do you feel Palestinian yourself?

I think that the Palestinians have to fight until they get back their lands. I am not sure how much stones will help them now and I don't think it can be done using only the stone. As to how I feel—I am Palestinian, but I live in Israel.

Q: Suppose you are watching television and you see a situation in which a young Palestinian boy is holding a stone and facing an Israeli soldier holding a gun. On whose side would you be and what would you feel?

When I see such a situation, I feel sometimes that the Palestinian boy should not throw stones at armed forces because they might shoot and kill him, as they usually do. To be honest with you, I am angry at the parents who allow their children to do such things. But, at the same time, I feel that the Palestinians must resist in some other way in order to gain their independence.

Q: Had Palestinian children never gone out with stones, do you think that anyone would pay attention to them and their struggle?

No. I'll tell you something. These children are going out with stones primarily because they oppose the settlements. That's what I think anyway.

Q: What do you think about the settlers?

These are the people I hate the most in this world. I have never before felt such feelings of hate in my heart towards anyone. I feel so much hate towards these people, that I can't even really describe it to you.

Q: Why? They claim that this land has historically always been Jewish.

They are lying. It's for the Arabs. They are saying this because they want to stay there. They know that they will always be harassed by the Arabs, but they still want to stay there. They are the main reason why the Jews and the Palestinians are still fighting one another. I am very angry at people like Goldstein[106] who went and shot Arabs, among them children. And, unfortunately, many Israelis supported his act.

Q: Do you think that Goldstein's act was appropriately condemned?

No, not at all. Even the secular Jews who do not get along with the settlers didn't really condemn this act in an appropriate way. What I saw was that an entire society wasn't visibly touched or disturbed by what he did.

Q: But when there is a suicide bombing most Palestinians do not condemn the act.

It is not the same thing.

A: Why not?

The Palestinians are being occupied and the Israelis are occupying.

Q: What do you think should be done with the settlers?

They should be kicked out of where they are now, and the land given to the Palestinians.

Q: What about their claims that the Jews have holy sites in places like Hebron?

You are only thinking about the Jews' claims. What about the Palestinian's claims?

Q: What are their claims in your opinion?

Clearly, it's their land and the settlers should leave as soon as possible. You can see on television that most of the war is happening in the Occupied Territories.

Q: Do you think that if the Jews left the Occupied Territories they would still be able to go back and visit their holy sites there?

Come on, are there really Jewish holy sites there?

Q: I mentioned Hebron before.

Of course they won't be able to go there. I don't think that the Palestinians will let them go back and visit. And besides, this is a lie. The Jews have no holy sites there.

Q: But who can really determine and know whether it's the Jews or the Muslims whose claims are the right ones?

You are asking a very hard question. As a Muslim, I believe that the Muslims are right, because I believe in the Holy Qur'an and that it says that this has always been and will always be Muslim land.

Q: Do you feel that Islam restricts your freedom and the rights you have as a woman?

Islam gives me all the rights, but it is the Arab tradition and its customs which restrict me. It's not at all Islam. Islam has always allowed women to leave the house and go and study. Islam was the first religion that truly considered the rights of its women. It is truly a religion of peace and love.

Q: To leave the house covered and obey the wishes of men means to have independence and right?

Yes covered, so what? That's the way it should be according to the Qur'an.

Q: Why shouldn't men cover when they leave the house?

That's just how it is.

Q: So you think that a woman can be required to put on a veil and yet receive all her rights at the same time?

Yes, of course. What's the connection between the two? I am telling you that Islam is the most liberal religion which gave women the right to work and study and advance themselves. Islam isn't what restricts me and orders me, for example, to be back at home by ten p.m. It's the village and the customs within it which truly restrict me. Islam doesn't restrict me by telling me not to travel abroad alone. It's the tradition that does. Islam said that a woman has to protect herself by not going out with men like you Jews do. We can't date men before our marriage. We can't sleep with a man before we get married. It's very unacceptable to do such things in our society.

Q: And you don't feel that these things restrict you?

No, not at all.

Q: So it doesn't bother you that an Arab man can go out with girls, have sex with them and even rent an apartment in Jerusalem before he is married?

No. I know that I have to stay a virgin until my wedding night. Men don't have the same body parts women have, which is why we women have to remain virgins and men do not. Maybe that's why they can sleep with women before they get married. But about Islam again, Islam calls for peace. And I think this is the same for every religion where people believe in one God. If the Jews, for example, followed the Torah, instead of changing it, things would be better. Both Arabs and Jews, had they truly followed these holy books, the world would have been a better place. If the

Jews read the Torah, and the Muslims the Qur'an and really understood them, especially the Qur'an, this war would have never begun. And again, Islam doesn't restrict me. I can go wherever I want to go, but covered and respectful.

Q: What do you mean when you say that the Jews changed the Torah?

I mean that they changed some things within the text. The Torah that you read today is very different than the Torah God sent to the Jews.

Q: If East Jerusalem was to be given to the Palestinians and all the settlers returned to the borders of 1967, would there be peace in your opinion?

Yes. If the Jews admitted that there is a Palestinian state, gave the Palestinians their rights and gave Jerusalem to the Christians and Muslims too, then there would finally be peace.

Everyone has a son and this son is precious. On our side we raise our sons and invest in them. It's the same for the Jews. But why is it that when one Jew dies they [Jews] kill thousands of Arabs? Why? We are filled with fatigue when we raise our sons. Why is it that when one Jew dies in Hadera the Jews go into Nablus, kill thousands of Palestinians and then destroy their houses? And sometimes they even kill us here, in Israel. Why?

Q: When a Palestinian commits a suicide bombing do you feel happy?

No, we don't usually support such acts. We don't support the killing of children and civilians. Just as our sons are dear to us, your sons are important to you.

Q: Many Palestinians go out into the streets and celebrate the death of a Jew.

No, we don't support the killing, and we are not happy. We don't accept the murder of Jews or Arabs. God created both Jews and Arabs, didn't He?

When I see a suicide bombing on television, I become sad.

Q: Even if a Jewish child died?

Of course. We have the same feelings towards our children. On both sides, children are dear to their parents. God created them all.

I just want to say one thing: Get out of our land. That is all.

You can't imagine how hard our situation as Israelis Arabs really is. And this is not only because of how the Palestinians view us. They hate us because they say we're traitors and Jews. But it's also because of how all the Arab world views us. Let me give you an example. I was traveling from Europe to Turkey for a peace conference with some other Israeli Jews and Arabs. I was sitting next to a Syrian man who had nothing to do with the conference. I talked to him for a while and told him that I was an Israeli Palestinian and that in Israel we're called Israeli Arabs. He could not understand what I meant. He said to me, "How can you be an Arab, a Palestinian, but live in Israel and travel with an Israeli passport?" I explained to him the situation and how this happened to all the Palestinians who stayed on their lands in what later became Israel in 1948. Then one of the Jewish women I was traveling with me came up to me and asked me a question in Hebrew. I answered her. The Syrian man was asking whether I was talking to her in Turkish. Maybe he thought I could speak Turkish because this was a Turkish Airlines flight and there were many Turks on the flight. I answered that I had actually spoken Hebrew with her because we both know the language. He said to me, "I'm angry with you." I asked him why and he said, "How can you speak Hebrew? I think you're a Jew. Only Jews can speak the Hebrew language." I told him that I was a Muslim, thank God, but he didn't believe me. Whatever I said he would not believe me. He was sure that I was a Jew and that I was lying to him. This is something Israeli Arabs always have to face and deal with. In Israel we're not treated so well and people think we're Palestinians. In Palestine people hate us and think we're Israelis and Jews. And when we speak to Arabs who are not Palestinians we are a strange kind, not belonging to any place, but assisting the Jews and the State of Israel. What a curse.

I will never forget what happened to me once in Egypt. I went there for a vacation together with my brother and his family. You see, when we, Israeli Arabs, speak Arabic, we integrate into it many Hebrew words. For example, we have an Arabic work for "ice cream" but most young children don't know it because we automatically say "glida" which is the Hebrew word for it. So, to tell you the truth, we really speak a language called "Harabic" which is half Hebrew and Half Arabic. When we speak to each other in Arabic, we always use words such as "beseder," [O.K.] ""betach," [of course] and "iy efshar" [it's not possible]. And we use many other Hebrew words too—especially men and women who work with Jews and have gotten used to speaking more Hebrew than Arabic. When we travel to an Arab country, be it Jordan, Egypt or Saudi Arabia, we suddenly have to try and control ourselves when speaking to other Arabs who are not from Israel. During this visit, I was doing some shopping. While I was hackling with an Egyptian seller, I turned to my brother and asked him something. Apparently I was speaking "Harabic" and the seller, who was listening to what I was saying, said to me, "You are speaking Arabic and something else, no?" I didn't know what to say and I didn't want to lie, so I just said that I was a Palestinian living in Israel. He said to me, "Oh, so you're a Jew." I said that I was not a Jew and that, as he could clearly see, I was wearing a *hijjab*. Still, he did not believe me. To prove it to him that I was a Muslim, I recited the Fatiha, the seven first verses of the Qur'an which every Muslim knows and still he did not believe that I was a Muslim. I told him that I speak Arabic and that I read from the Qur'an everyday. I also told me that I believe in the Prophet Muhammad, peace and prayers be upon him. You know what he told me? He said, "You are probably a Jew who learned Arabic and is reading the Qur'an in order to vilify it, or in order to become a Mossad agent. I was shocked. There I was standing, with the full religious Islamic dress and he would still not believe that I was a Muslim just because I also spoke Hebrew and lived in Israel. Can you imagine the feeling you have when you understand that Muslims, just like you, don't accept you?

Once I was a guest in a hotel abroad and I was waiting for the elevator. There were many Jews and Arabs staying at the hotel and some of them were also waiting together with me. When we finally got into the elevator I was standing there, surrounded by Jews and by Arabs like myself. A Jewish woman, who was with me in the same flight, asked me a question in Hebrew. I answered her. I could see how the other Arabs, who were not from Israel, were looking at me—as though I had committed the greatest crime of all by speaking in Hebrew. When we got out of the elevator, one of the Arabs came up to me and asked me why I was speaking in Hebrew. I said that I know Hebrew and that I was trying to help a woman who did not know Arabic. They laughed at me and said, "So you're really an Arab Jew." I don't know what he meant by that exactly, but I had a feeling it was not good. Did he mean that I was a Jewish woman? Or did he mean that I was a Jew who could speak Arabic, like some Jews coming from the Middle East do? Whatever he meant, I could see that he didn't believe that I was a Muslim woman. It hurt.

Israeli Arabs are isolated from the rest of the Arab and Muslim worlds. I think that this alienation started when the peace talks between the Israelis and Palestinians began in the early 1990s. This was when Palestinians started talking about a Palestine and Israelis started talking about an Israel which would be separated from the Palestinians. So, in effect, each side was speaking about a country which would have distinct characteristics—either Jewish or Muslim, Israeli or Palestinian. We Israeli Arabs, however, stayed in the middle, with nothing. On the one hand, we are not Israelis but Palestinians. We are not Jews but Muslims. But still we live in a Jewish state, unlike no other Arabs in the world. So, we don't identify with Israel and don't really consider ourselves to be Israelis. On the other hand, we live in Israel, so that if there is ever a Palestinian state, we will never live in it. So, while the Israelis and Palestinians were planning real and concrete states which would represent their citizens we Israeli Arabs were kept outside of this process. What will happen in the end is that both Israelis and Palestinians will have their own state, but Israeli Arabs, who are really Palestinian and Muslim will stay living in a Jewish state which does not represent who they are, their religion, traditions and aspirations. Once you realize this, you really get depressed. You ask yourself "Who am I? Where do I belong? Am I Israeli or am I Palestinian? What shall my future and the future of my children look like?"

When I travel abroad, I have to think before answering the question, "Where are you from?" Depending on who poses the question I can decide what to say. Sometimes I say that I am Israeli and sometimes I say that I am Palestinian. I rarely say that I am an Israeli Arab because people get confused and they don't believe me anyway. Being faced with this kind of dilemma is not something easy. When someone asks me who I am and where I am from, I want to say that I am Palestinian from Palestine. But I can't always say that because then people ask where I live and I have to say that in Israel, just so that they understand geographically where my home is. If I say I live in Palestine they think it's in Jenin or Ramallah. When I say I am from Arara, some people know it's in Israel and others find out. So, I always have to think who I am talking to. Only then I can tell them who I am and where I am from. This is not easy.

I am an Arab living in Israel. I have gotten used to saying that I am Israeli because in a way it makes thinks easier for me when I speak to people who are not Arab. What can I do? This is reality, it's a fact. When I travel abroad, I am an Israeli, of I want it or not. Israeli gave me a passport, which is more that can be said for Arab countries which mostly did not provide Palestinian refugees with passports or even work permits. While millions of Palestinians are wandering around the world passportless, stateless and jobless, I can travel freely everywhere in the world. O.K., so I can't travel to Arab countries, but all Israelis can't. It's not only against me and besides, this might change one day. And today I can even travel to Saudi Arabia, with a temporary Jordanian passport, and attend prayers in Mecca. I am not saying that everything is perfect here and that I feel a hundred percent fine as an Arab living in Israel. What I am saying is that there are many advantages living here, advantages that many other Palestinians are only dreaming of.

Responses from Children

Q: What do you think about how the Israeli government treats the Israeli Arab population?

They treat us badly. I think that they treat us like guests and not like real citizens. They also don't want us to help the Palestinians who are fighting against Israel. They treat us as though we don't belong here at all. And as to the Palestinians, the Israelis want to kill all of them and these are our brothers and sisters. We are all Muslim. Between the Israelis and the Palestinians there is no peace. Between Muslims and Jews there is no peace. It is a terrible situation and I wonder when it will end. Maybe never.

Q: How do you feel about what's going on in Palestine?

I feel angry. And even when I am happy about something, I can't be completely happy because I know that my brothers and sisters in Palestine are suffering. They can't celebrate at all at the moment and we can't either.

Q: What connection, if at all, exists between Israeli Arabs and Palestinians?

The Palestinians are the same people as we are. We have the same blood. We are Muslims, just like them. And we also share the same land, Palestine. We are really one people, when you think about it. The Jews want to separate us, but they won't succeed because we know that this land is going to be Muslim.

Q: Who is a Palestinian?

We are all Palestinians. The difference between myself and the Palestinians in the Occupied Territories is that they have a harder life. They are under curfew all the time because of the Jews. And they are always afraid because of the Israeli tanks that go there and kill everyone.

Q: Who is the leader of the Palestinian people now?

Yasser Arafat.

Q: What do you think about him?

I think he's okay with us, but maybe it would be better to have someone else now. Still, I am sure that he is trying to do his best to help the Palestinian people gain their independence and live in freedom from the Israeli occupation.

Q: What are the Israelis and Palestinians fighting over?

They are fighting over Al Aqsa.

Q: Only over Al Aqsa?

They are fighting over Al Aqsa and over the Land of Palestine.

Q: To whom do you think Jerusalem belongs?

It belongs only to the Palestinians.

Q: Why?

We pray in Al Aqsa, and Jerusalem is holy to us and to Muslims all over the world. We know the truth about all this. The Qur'an promises us this land, maybe not now, but in the future. Muhammad, peace be upon him, even then already knew how the Jews faked their Bible so that other people would think that this is their land.

Q: So, Jews were never here before 1948?

Of course not.

Q: Who lives in Jerusalem?

Jews and Muslims.

Q: So why should Jerusalem be given only to the Palestinians?

We need to be able to go and pray in Al Aqsa and do everything for Allah. The Jews say that they have a holy site in Jerusalem too, but that's a lie, it's not true at all. According to the Holy Qur'an, Jerusalem has always been Muslim and it will be Muslim once again. So why do the Jews try and lie to us by saying that it's their holy place?

Q: So how can war be solved if everyone wants the same land?

Peace must be made between the two sides. The land and Jerusalem must be returned to the Palestinians and that will solve all the problems, Qur'an says.

Q: If you could, would you move and live in what is known now to be the Occupied Territories?

No, never.

Q: Why?

There is a terrible war there, I don't want to go and live there. Also, people are really poor there and they don't have any money.

Q: But let's assume that the war ended. Would you then move and live in the Occupied Territories?

Yes, I would very much love to. It's better than living under the Jews and their rules.

Q: So would you leave your village and move to Palestine?

No, never.

Q: Why not?

My village, Kefar Kara, is on Palestinian land, so I wouldn't have to move anywhere in order to be in Palestine. All of this land belongs to Palestine, it is Palestine. All this area should be included in what will be Palestine...well, it's already all Palestine.

Q: So only this area, *The Triangle*, is Palestine?

No, everything here is Palestine. Jerusalem, Haifa...everything is Palestine. The Jews took it away from our grandparents. One day it will be ours again.

Q: Who does this land belong to in your opinion?

To the Arabs.

Q: What do you know about the holy sites?

There's Al Aqsa, our holy mosque.

Q: Is there anything else holy there?

No.

Q: Do you know anything about the Western Wall?

Oh, that. Well, what about it?

Q: Isn't the Western Wall holy to someone?

No...well, the Jews say it's holy to them.

Q: Do you agree with that claim?

ISRAELI ARABS AND THE PALESTINIANS

[Laughing] Of course not. The Jews are all liars. It was from the days of the Prophet Muhammad, peace be upon Him, that they lied to everyone. You know, they rejected his prophecies. They *say* that the Western Wall is holy to them, but you know, the Jews, they forged the Bible, so you really can't trust anything they say. This land is all for us—Qur'an promises us this.

Q: What do you think about the Jews?

I hate them. I want to kill them.

Q: Who told you these things?

My parents and we also learned this in school.

Q: What do you think about how the Israeli government treats the Palestinians?

Like trash. This land is for the Palestinians, so why did the Israelis take it from them?

Q: What lands are you exactly talking about?

All of Israel. The Jews came and took all of it.

Q: Are you very angry about this?

Not very angry. I never left my land or my home, but I definitely understand the Palestinians. Their land was stolen by the Jews.

Q: When did that happen?

I think it was in 1948, or around that time.

Q: How do you define yourself?

I am an Israeli Arab.

Q: Who are the Palestinians? Where do they live today?

Some Palestinians live in Israel and some live in their lands, in Palestine.

Q: Where is Palestine?

Next to Israel.

Q: Do some Palestinians live in other countries?

Palestinians don't have money to live anywhere they want. They are poor wherever they are. I think most of them live in Jenin and in Gaza.

Q: What language do the Palestinians speak?

Arabic.

Q: What religion do they practice?

They are Muslims like us.

Q: What should be done in order for peace to come?

I hate the situation the way it is now and I don't know what to do. I don't like how things are going at the moment. The lands should return immediately to the Palestinians. Maybe then there will be a chance for peace. Until that happens there will be war.

Q: Would you rather live in the Palestinian Territories or in Israel?

In Israel. In the Occupied Territories there are a lot of problems at the moment. There's a big war there and people are getting killed every day. The people there don't have any money, the children don't go to school and their houses are torn down by the Israeli Army sometimes. I don't care very much what happens, though. Whether the lands return to the Palestinians or not, I will continue living here on my land, in my house. What do I need all this war for?

Q: Do you feel any kind of connection to the Palestinian people?

Yes, I do feel a connection to them. They used to come and work in Israel, but now because of the situation they can't come here anymore and they are starving because they don't have any money.

Q: But do you feel that you, as an individual who is not of age to work yet, have any connection to the Palestinians?

Look, I am a Muslim and the Palestinians are also Muslims. This is our land and we are fighting for it. The Palestinians want what was theirs and what is still theirs. And you have to remember that this is a small piece of land, not a big one. There isn't room for everyone.

Q: Do you think that there's a chance for peace between Israelis and Palestinians?

No, it's impossible when people like Sharon are in power. People like him don't want peace. People like him don't like Arabs and we know this. Sharon and his supporters don't like us because we're Arabs. That's how they think.

Q: When you say "they" to whom are you referring?

I am referring to the Jews.

Q: All the Jews?

Yes, all of them. Well, maybe not all of them, but most of them. We try to like them, but the Jews don't like us at all. They don't give us anything and they think that we don't belong to Israel, as though we're foreign, from another place. They also think we're not as good as they are and they always think they are better than us. So, they always give us the worse of everything. Then they complain when we support the Palestinians.

Q: Do you talk about the political situation in your school?

Yes, of course. The teachers usually start talking about it and then everyone jumps into the conversation. The teachers usually start the conversation by telling us what's going on in the Occupied Territories. A few months ago our teacher told us how the Israelis went into Jenin and Nablus and killed many people. He told us that the Jews were doing this because they want all of this land for themselves. He said that Jews want everything, without sharing it with other people.

Q: What are some of the things you can recall students saying when talking about the political situation in your class?

Students talk about the Jews. And, of course, they say bad things about them and about Sharon. They say that he is a man who loves to murder and do bad things to Arabs all over the world. They say that Sharon wants to have all of Israel for the Jews and kick out all the Arabs.

Q: Do the students also talk about the Palestinians?

Yes, of course. They say that the Palestinians are good people who have a lot of power and are not afraid of anything. Above all, they say that the Palestinians will ultimately win their struggle.

Q: Do you usually agree with what is said in class?

I either always or mostly agree with what is said in class.

Q: Do you think that the education the Palestinian children receive in the Occupied Territories is better or worse than the education you receive?

Of course the education in Israel is much better. In the Palestinian Authority they don't have much interest in learning. They are busy struggling against the Jews.

Q: What do you think the children in the Occupied Territories are learning about Jews, if at all?

I have never been to the Palestinian Territories, so I don't know for sure what they learn about the Jews there. But I am sure that they hear that the Jews are bad and that they don't like Arabs at all, which is true.

Q: What do you see and hear about the Occupied Territories?

I am sick and tired of hearing about what the Jews are doing to the Palestinians there. Sometimes I just feel like I would rather watch a soap opera. I am sick and tired of watching the crimes on the news.

Q: What crimes?

For example, when a tank comes and murders a little defenseless child like Muhammad al-Durrah. I also saw a terrible incident on television. There was a suicide bomber who wanted to blow himself up. A Jewish man came and prevented him from doing this. Then the bomber was stripped naked and a robot came and caused the bomb to explode on the man. It was terrible. He exploded on television.

Q: Does it bother you to see what both sides are doing to one another?

I like to see what the Palestinians are doing to the Israelis, but I don't like watching what the Israelis are doing to the Palestinians. What can the Palestinians do? The Israelis come to the Occupied Territories with tanks and other kinds of weapons. What can the Palestinians do against this powerful force? Of course they are throwing stones. And the Israelis are complaining.

Q: If a UFO came up to you and asked you, "Who or what is a Palestinian?" what would be your answer?

A Palestinian is a person who loves his country. We Arabs have a saying. We say, "The land is the person, the person is the land, and the land is the land." A Palestinian is wise, he has a lot of strength and he's not afraid of anything.

Q: But where did the Palestinians come from?

A Palestinian is from Israel...I mean from Palestine. He has always been here and it's his land. Today some of the Palestinians, like us, live in a land called Israel. The Jews came here, killed the Palestinian and took his land.

Q: Where do the Palestinians live today?

Some of them, like myself, live in Israel. Some live in the Occupied Territories. Others live in Lebanon and in Jordan in refugee camps and some live in Saudi Arabia too.

Q: Who is their leader?

Yasser Arafat.

Q: What do you think about Arafat?

Arafat is a very good leader. He loves his people. He wants to make his people's lives better. I know that many of his people think he's a bad leader, but I don't think he is. He's an honest man.

Q: So, do you see yourself as being Palestinian?

I love myself because I am Palestinian.

Q: But you hold an Israeli passport and you reside within Israeli borders, don't you?

Yes, maybe that's true, but my grandfather and his father were Palestinian. All of them were Palestinians, not Israelis. And here, we love the Palestinians because they are like our brothers and sisters. Yes, I have an Israeli passport and yes, I happen to live in Israel. And after all I love this place, it's where I live. But it's really Palestine.

Q: If you had the opportunity to do so, would you move to the Occupied Territories?

No, I like living in my country, in Palestine. I will never leave this place. I will not leave like my grandfather and his father were forced to do. My heart is here and will always be. I will never leave!

Q: What is the connection, if at all, between Palestinians and Israeli Arabs?

Our blood is the same. This is our country, just like it is theirs. We are all brothers and we support one another especially during this hard time. .

Q: Do you think that they should have the right to return to their lands?

Of course they should, it's their land, always has been. It's always been their country. All the Palestinians, wherever they are now, must have the right to return to the lands that were stolen from them in 1948. Just like you Jews want to come here because you believe it's your land, the Palestinians want to come back here because they *know* it is their land. It's the same thing exactly except we *know* it is ours.

Q: So, if both sides believe it's their land, what can be done?

I think that the Jews have to get out of here and give the land back to the Palestinians.

Q: Where will the Jews go?

They should go back to the place from which they came.

Q: And what if they are not wanted there?

Well, then I don't know where they should go. It's entirely their problem.

Q: From what you know, when did the Jews come here for the first time?

They came here in 1948.

Q: Before 1948 were there Jews here at all?

Yes, but only a few.

Q: What happened when the Jews came here in 1948?

They killed people and took their lands.

Q: Where did the Jews come from?

They came from all over the world, unfortunately.

Q: Why did they come here?

They didn't have a country of their own then.

Q: Do you think it's okay that they came here?

Of course not and they should leave as soon as possible and give us back our lands.

Q: Do you think that the Palestinians should have the right to return to the lands they left in 1948?

Eventually yes, of course. But with how things are here at the moment, it's probably better for them to stay elsewhere until things calm down a bit.

Q: If you had the choice, would you prefer living in Palestine?

I would rather live in Palestine. I would like to be with my people and not among the Jews. I am not used to them and I don't like their culture. It would be better for me to live with Muslim Arabs.

Q: What do you think the Palestinians think about the Israeli Arabs?

They don't like us at all because they think we aren't helping them enough. They are right, but what can we do from here? They also think that we love the Jews because we live with them in the same country. It is really hard for me to explain how I feel. I live here, but I do not belong with the Jews. I have no choice but to live with the Jews because they control this place. But if I could choose that I wanted, of course I would not want to live with or among them. The Palestinians have to understand that we are forced to live with the Jews. We all hope that this will change one day soon once the land returns to Palestinian and Muslim hands. But until that happens, with God's help, we have to sit and wait. God will help.

Q: How do you feel about the negative way in which many Palestinians view you?

I feel great sorrow. Here we identify with the Palestinians as much as we can, being citizens of Israel. It hurts me that many of them don't like us and view us in such a bad way. I think that we should try as much as possible to change their mind about this and to prove to them that we are on their side. They have to understand that we are on their side in this conflict and that we want to help them redeem the land from the Jews. We are not against them but with them. That's the main thing I am trying to communicate to you.

Q: Whose fault is it that Palestinians feel like this towards Israeli Arabs?

It's the Jews' fault.

Q: Why?

It's obvious. If the Jews didn't come here in 1948 then the Palestinians wouldn't have escaped. Then we would not have a situation where some Palestinians are Israeli and some are not. We would all be Palestinians and have a good and free life. Do you understand?

Q: Is there anything else you would like to add?

I hope that one day there will be peace between Jews and Arabs. Once we get back our lands, everything will be okay. With God's help, Jews, Arabs and Palestinians will all have a better life soon when there will be a Palestinian state and everyone will possess a Palestinian passport.

Q: If someone came up to you and asked you who you are, what would you say?

I am Palestinian.

Q: Are you sure?

Of course, why?

Q: Because you live in Israel and if you travel abroad, I am sure you would be traveling with an Israeli passport.

No, I am Palestinian, even if the passport says that I am Israeli.

Q: Why do you view yourself as Palestinian?

Because I *am* Palestinian and this is how I was born.

Q: Do you feel at all Israeli?

No way! I have never felt Israeli and I will never feel Israeli.

Q: If there were a war between Israel and Palestine on whose side would you be?

Of course I would be on the Palestinian side. If there were a war, I would join the Palestinians in the struggle. I would never join the Jews. Maybe if Israeli Arabs and Palestinians fought together, we'd already have all our lands back. The problem is that the Jews separated us and now we are weak and the Jews are fighting us with tanks and guns.

Q: So you would never protect Israel against the other Arab countries in the Middle East?

Never. The Arab countries are a part of us and we are a part of them. We are all against Israel.

3

Suicide Bombings and Shaheeds

Children in Paradise: Qur'anic Verses

There are five verses in the Qur'an which refer to the idea of *jihad*. It is generally accepted that there are two kinds of *jihad*. The first one known as "the greater warfare" (*al-Jihadu 'l-Akbar*) refers to the inner struggle against one's inner lust and temptation. Muslims are expected to struggle inwardly in order to live up to the expectations of their faith. The second one known as "the lesser warfare," (*al-Jihadu 'l-Asghar*) emphasizes the notion of continuous struggle against infidels, those who do not believe in God. It is not the Qur'an, but rather the *hadith* which transforms the concept of *jihad* into meaning an active military war against all non-Muslims, "infidels." What is found here could be viewed as a development in the perception of the *jihad*. This development was probably the reason for promoting the ideas of *al-Jihadu 'l-Akbar* and *al-Jihadu 'l-*Asghar. In order to elaborate on this idea, let us examine the following verses found in the Qur'an:

Surah ix. 5- 6:

And when the sacred months are passed, kill those who join other gods with God wherever ye shall find them; and seize them, besiege them and lay wait for them with any kind of ambush: but if they shall convert, and observe prayer, and pay the obligatory alms, then let them go their way, for God is gracious, merciful.

Surah viii. 39-42:

Say to the infidels: If they desist from their disbelief, what is past now shall be forgiven them; but if they return to it, they have already before them the doom of the ancients. Fight then against them till strife be at an end, and the religion be all of it God's.

These verses indicate that war should be waged against all those who do not accept the words of the Prophet Muhammad. On the other hand, they also emphasize the fact that those who convert to Islam and thus accept Muhammad's teachings and his prophecies, automatically become a part of the Muslim Ummah, nation.[107]

This declaration is from the days of the Prophet Muhammad, a time when Islam was being imposed on pagan tribes living around the Arabian Peninsula and was not yet a universal missionary religion crossing the boundaries of continents. Later, after the Prophet's death, interpreters took the Prophet's words and expanded their meaning to a more universal one: now it was legitimate to kill in the name of Islam, wherever it reached, no matter where that might be. As a matter of fact, the Arab conquerors who lived after the death of the Prophet forcibly imposed Islam on all the nations they conquered, in particular if these nations were not a part of *ahal-al-kitab*. People who were considered by Muslims to be *ahal-al-kitab* were called *Dhimmis* and had the option of either converting to Islam or paying the *jizya*, a poll tax guaranteeing them protection. *Dhimmis* were, and in some places still are, barred from public office, forced to wear distinctive dress and subject to restrictions on the building and maintenance of synagogues and churches.[108] Those who refused to either pay the tax or convert to Islam were a legitimate target and could be killed without the murderers being tried in court.

Surah ix. 29:

Make war upon such of those to whom the Scriptures have been given as believe not in God, or in the last day, and who forbid not that which God and his Apostle have forbidden, and who profess not the profession of the truth, until they pay tribute out of hand, and they be humbled.

This verse explicitly says, "Make war," and there is no doubt that this war is not an internal one occurring within a person who is fighting against temptation or against Satan. This is an active and bloody war, aimed at killing people who do not accept the Prophet and his prophecy, as detailed in the Qur'an, which is considered by Muslims to be the last one and thus the most important holy book given to mankind—the only one never to have been edited. When closely examining the text, however, there is a problem with this verse and specifically with the word "apostle" which is found in it. If it is indeed true that the Qur'an in its entirety was revealed and recited by the Prophet Muhammad, why is he referred to in the third person? Why does he not simply say "I," indicating himself? One might suggest that as early as fifty years after the death of the Prophet, when the Qur'an was being edited, these words were attributed to the Prophet, even though he might never have said them.

Now let us examine the remaining two verses in the Qur'an where *jihad* is discussed and the idea of *jihad* is presented:

Surah iv. 76-79:

Let those then fight on the path of God, who exchange this present life for that which is to come...They who believe fight on the path of God, and those who believe not, fight on the path of Tagut: Fight therefore against the friends of Satan. Hast thou not marked those to whom it was said, 'Withhold your hands a while from war; and observe prayer, and pay the state's alms.' But when war is commanded them, lo!

Here, unlike in the previous verses, the description is not of an active military war, but rather of an inner war within a person who is fighting against evil and temptation, an idea also found in Judaism and Christianity, and striving to enter Paradise on the Day of Judgment. The prime responsibility is, therefore, to purify oneself, to pay *Zakat* and pray and resist straying away and becoming an unbeliever. When one is called to a holy war, however, one must go and participate, although the verse does not state that this is necessarily an active and bloody war or struggle against the infidels.

Surah ii. 216- 217:

They will ask thee concerning war in the Sacred Month [of Ramadan]. Say: To war therein is bad, but to turn aside from the cause of God, and to have no faith in Him, and in the Sacred Temple [the mosque in Mecca]...is worse in the sight of God;

and civil strife is worse than bloodshed. They will not cease to war against you until they turn you from your religion, if they be able...But those who believe, and fly their country, and fight in the cause of God may hope for God's mercy...

This verse states that it is not allowed to fight and spill blood in the month of Ramadan. It is very important, however, to note that this law was not observed throughout Arab and Muslim history. When Sadat attacked Israel in 1973, he ignored not only the fact that he was desecrating Yom Kippur (the Jewish Day of Atonement, known to be the holiest day to Jews) but also Ramadan, the holiest month for Muslims. The verse also stresses the fact that fighting is only permitted if Muslims are being tempted to change his or her religion, or if the way to the Holy Mosque in Mecca is blocked. Therefore, the possibility that a Muslim might convert to another religion is considered more terrible and destructive than the act of killing.[109] This notion of the Crusades [*Salibiyyah*] comes from a more general notion many Muslims and Islam as a religion, have always had. Islam has always assumed that Muslims are in constant danger of being converted and that people from different religions, especially Christians, have the primary aim of converting them. Saudi Arabian textbooks for primary school students which are exported to Muslim schools all over the world, for example, also emphasize this fact, and warn Muslims about the West and its intentions to eliminate Islam and convert all Muslims to Christianity:

An unhurried pause may be put in front of you the truth that is hiding behind the fog spread by your enemies to conceal it. Annihilating you and your nation is the goal. This is a war—be it overt or covert—against your religion. To this end your enemies have gathered, while there is no[other] bond or relation among them. *Reader and Text, Grade 7, pt.* 2 (2000) *p.* 69 [110]

According to verses 216 and 217 found in Surah II of the Qur'an, a Muslim must fight against this phenomenon of being converted, but it does not explicitly say what kind of struggle this must be; either a military one or an inner one. In a later Surah (Surah ix) it specifically says that the struggle is a military one, against all non-Muslims.

According to a rule known as *Al-nasih wal mansuh*, which determines that if in one recitation the Prophet said one thing and in another recitation he said another, the latter should be followed. Therefore, Surah ix, which calls for military war, should be followed and *not* the former one which calls for an inner struggle within the believer. The best example of this law is in the verses concerning the drinking of alcohol. Surah iv. 43 says, "O you who believe! Approach not *As-Salat* [the afternoon prayer] when you are in a drunken state until you know of what you utter..." This verse, although forbidding prayer under intoxication, does not forbid drinking per se. Later, in Surah v. 90, the believer is told, "O you who believe: intoxicants and gambling are an abomination of Satan's handiwork." Here, for the first time, all kinds of intoxicants are strictly forbidden. Here the rule of *Al-nasih wal mansuh* fully works, because Islam, following the latter Surah, strictly forbids the drinking of alcohol. Likewise, regarding *jihad* and its functions, Surah ix was followed rather than the earlier surah iv.

Is it possible that the Prophet Muhammad changed his ruling concerning *jihad* once he saw the reality of his times and the fact that many rejected his teachings? Oral traditions after his death emphasized the concept of *jihad* to be a violent struggle against all those who either militarily opposed Islam or ideologically rejected it—all those who opposed the Prophet and his message. Here we come to the issue of interpretation and its usage. After all, it is the interpretation of the text that seems to be more important and influential and not the source from which it comes, in this case the Qur'an.[111] Muslim religious clergy were and still are able to explain to other Muslims that the rule of *Al-nasih wal mansuh* should be applied only at certain times, or not at all. Liberal Muslim clergy could and still can emphasize the fact that *jihad* is explicitly the struggle within the believer to walk in the right way and not stray away from their belief. Although some clerics do this out of genuine belief, most do not. Islam, therefore, is in a desperate need for moderate religious leaders who are courageous enough to openly speak about the crisis of Islam and to teach Islam in a different way, a more liberal and accepting one. Islam is also in desperate need of Muslim leaders (both religious and non-religious) who are willing to unconditionally and firmly condemn terror against innocent civilians. This view is supported by many Muslims in Irshad Manji's website "Muslim Refusnik" (http://www.muslim-refusenik.com).The idea of a believer's struggle within him or herself can be found in Judaism, Christianity and Zoroastrianism, the other monotheistic traditions, as well as in Hinduism and Buddhism. In any case, since the widespread belief is that the Prophet Muhammad was an honest, gentle and peaceful man who strove for peace and social justice, it seems logical that the Qur'an should be interpreted in this way—that killing innocent people is a sinful act which is strictly forbidden and which is not rewarded with celestial benefits. Unfortunately, there are many Orthodox branches of Islam whose clergy, in their interpretations, stress that *jihad* according to the Qur'an, is a violent military war against all non-Muslims who reject Muhammad and his message of Islam. This destructive notion, propagated by the Saudi Arabian Wahabbi school of Islam, is widespread nowadays and has reached nearly each and every community in which Muslims live.

In ancient Islam, the concept of *jihad* was probably interpreted in a more liberal way: it described mainly the inner struggle (against Satan and temptation) within the heart and mind of the Muslim believer. The Prophet Muhammad, when faced with reality, might have changed his religious philosophy upon realizing that many opposed Islam and preferred their own religions. It might be that he then changed the meaning of *jihad* when he advocated for armed struggle against all those who did not accept his new religion. Later, when Islam began to spread (during the days of Umar, 13 h., 634 C.E.) the Muslim conquerors met, for the first time, a world very different from their own. A world full of pagans, who did not believe in the existence of one God and Jews and Christians who believed in their own prophets and did not accept Islam and its message. Interpreters of that time emphasized the teachings in Surah ix in order to justify the wars they fought against the pagans on whom Muslim conquerors violently imposed their religion. As for Jews and Christians, since Islam accepted them as people of the Book, they were forced to pay the poll tax in order to be spared from being killed. This did not prevent the Prophet Muhammad from massacring two Arabian Jewish tribes which had lived in peace among the Arabs until the emergence of Islam. Once Muhammad realized that the Jews did not want to adopt Islam as their religion he changed the direction of the Islamic prayer from Jerusalem to Mecca and started persecuting both Jews and "infidels."

I will now shift perspective to the Israeli-Palestinian struggle and specifically to the situation of the Israeli Arabs. I was always welcomed with open arms by most of the people of Arara. It wasn't until a suicide bombing took place in Tel Aviv that I felt any form of tension. One evening I was sitting with my Arab host family and we were all having a big dinner in a restaurant. We were talking and laughing and I was conversing with one of the family's members in English because he wanted to improve his ability to speak in this language. We were busy planning a trip in which he and my host sister Susu would come and visit me at my college in Maine. The television was on, but no one was paying too much attention to it as they were busy talking to one another about family and business matters. Suddenly, someone said, "There was a suicide bombing in Tel Aviv. I am not sure how many people were killed." Everyone stopped talking and there was complete silence in the room. The channel was quickly changed to one of the two Israeli news stations and everyone was waiting to hear what had happened. I immediately grabbed my cellular phone and called anyone I thought might have been in the area when the suicide bomber exploded. I suddenly felt very nervous and agitated as well as outraged. I was not afraid of being in Arara and I was not afraid of being surrounded by Arab people. I met there some of the best, most honest and most welcoming people I had encountered in my entire life. I knew and know now that some of these people will stay my friends for a long time, no matter how the political situation between the Israelis and Palestinians develops. I felt nervous because I was sad and I was angry and all I wanted to do at that moment was to scream, "Those bastards did it again. How can they kill innocent people? I hate them so much!" I couldn't do that and this made me feel so helpless. I didn't feel that I could completely express myself or my feelings towards the suicide bombers, the murderers, while being in Arara, surrounded by Israeli Arabs, some of whom either condoned the bombings or sympathized with the motives behind them. I think that it was then that I understood that despite the friendships I formed with some Israeli Arabs, our ideas about these critical issues would always remain fundamentally different. When I feel angry and sad about a suicide bombing in Jerusalem or Tel Aviv some of them might feel sympathy for the suicide bomber. When they feel sad and angry about an extra judicial assassination carried out by the Israeli Army in the West Bank or in Gaza, I might feel relieved. There seems not to exist a meeting point between the ideas, beliefs and attitudes most Israeli Jews and Arabs currently hold. With this reality affecting each and every Israeli citizen as well as each and every Palestinian the prospects for peace seem even more elusive.

In my conversations with Israeli Arab school children, the nouns *jihad* and *shaheed* recurred. I was especially surprised to hear quite a few students express their desire to become a *shaheed* and I decided to try and understand where this willingness and desire came from. Firstly, after listening to the children, I understood that the media played a major role in this issue. Israeli Arab children were exposed on a daily basis to news from *Al Jazeera* in which coverage of Muhammad al-Durrah and his fate was constantly repeated. He was glorified in all of the Arab television channels and was declared by several important Imams (religious leaders) as a holy *sha-*

heed who had sacrificed himself for the liberation of the Palestinian people. Most of the children who expressed their willingness to become a *shaheed* said to me, "I want to be like Muhammad al-Durrah." It is important to remember that it has still not been determined who actually killed Muhammad al-Durrah and that both sides, Israelis and Palestinians, accuse one another of causing his death. In spite of this fact many of the parents and children whom I interviewed were certain that the Israeli Army was responsible for al-Durrah's killing and that he was now residing in Paradise, with all its implications. Secondly, Israeli Arab children see the humiliation of the Palestinians and the bad conditions under which they live on television. They see the mothers and children who come from the Jenin area to Arara and Arra to beg for money and sell small gadgets and matches and identify with them. Thirdly, many of the mothers and several of the children pointed out the poverty that can be found everywhere in the Palestinian Authority. The poverty, according to many people with whom I spoke, explained some of the motives behind the suicide bombings. Although some of them identified suicide bombings as being fundamentally wrong, it was the poverty they believed that pushed people who were in utter despair into becoming *shaheeds* and committing these horrific and hideous crimes. It is true that people living in the Occupied Territories are subject to poverty, diseases and hunger. These are the consequence of the Israeli occupation and of Yasser Arafat and members of his government, who blatantly ignore the needs of their people by spending most of the money on themselves.

Although I am aware of the fact that the media plays a major role in the Israeli-Palestinian conflict and in Jewish-Arab relations, especially in its influence on children, I strongly believe that we must also look into and reexamine the religious perceptions to which some Israeli Arab children are exposed. Here, we must ask an important question: How are these perceptions communicated to the students? Israeli Arabs do have, as a part of their curriculum, general Qur'anic studies in their classrooms. Whatever the classroom does not provide for the students, because Israeli Arab schools work according to the Israeli secular education system, the *Madrasa*, the religious school, does. These religious schools, which are not attended by all Israeli Arabs, are run by the local municipalities or by the *Waqf* and do not receive money from the Israeli Ministry of Education. In some of the *Madrases*, Israeli Arab children hear completely distorted religious interpretations of the Qur'anic text and *hadith*. Some of the religious teachers emphasize the social discrimination against Arabs, which most definitely exists, but is at times exaggerated and blown out of proportion. They emphasize the necessity of being a good Muslim and that being a good Muslim means accepting Muhammad's mission. Unfortunately, what some of these children are taught is that *jihad* is not the inner struggle a Muslim must fight in order to reject evil and temptation, but rather an active war against non-Muslims, in this case the Jews. The Israeli rule of this land is obviously one of these non-Muslim forces, something which is unacceptable in Muslim belief. Islam has always emphasized that a Muslim must not be ruled over by a non-Muslim, that Islam is the superior religion and the only true one, and that Muhammad was in fact the last prophet.[112] The concept of *Jihad*, if taught and used incorrectly, can support this claim that Islam is the superior religion and that all non-Muslims should be either converted or killed.

The false interpretations of the Qur'an can probably be found in some Israeli Arab houses, as well as in some Israeli Arab schools, just as false interpretations of other religious texts can be found in some Jewish and Christian institutions. However, I must once again stress the importance of the difference between the education Jewish and Arab children in Israel and Palestine receive in their homes and schools. Most of the Muslim children I spoke to, whether religious or secular, were very much bound by their religious tradition and by the interpretations of the Qur'and to which they were exposed. Many of them did not acknowledge the right of Jews to the land, did not believe that Jews had holy sites in Israel (and some explicitly said that the Jews lied about this issue), believed that the Qur'an did not approve of non-Muslims, supported suicide bombings and emphasized the historical conflict between the Jews and Islam. It seems that only when Israeli Arab schools and households (as well as many Arab and Muslim schools all over the world) minimize the number of pseudo interpretations of the Qur'an that their children learn, will there be a chance for a real and honest dialogue between the two sides. Although official Israeli education does not propagate religious hatred towards Arabs and Muslims, the education some Jewish children receive within their households should also be re-examined and changed. Jews also have an equal responsibility in bringing change—they must even initiate it. We must get to the point where children condemn any killing of innocent people and do not support such acts according to pseudo-religious interpretations.

Responses from Adults

Q: Why do you think that suicide bombers decide to become *shaheeds*?

People think that the suicide bombers do it because their parents want them too, but this is not true at all. If a mother knew that her son was planning to become a shaheed, do you think she would let him do it? I don't think so.

Q: Then why can the suicide bomber's mother usually be seen dancing and praising her son after the suicide bombing?

The mothers are scared to death. Scared, scared, scared. Here in Israel, if a politician says something outrageous about the government, are they automatically taken to jail? Of course not. But in the Occupied Territories and generally in Arab countries, these people who speak out are killed and silenced immediately, no questions asked. These women have to come to the television screen after a suicide bombing not as normal mothers who would undoubtedly deny the money given to her from a terrorist organization or accuse the government, but as mothers who have to look happy and proud. These women can't cry out, "Why did my son die, why did he do this?" If they dared to look unhappy on the television screens, their families will be outcast and no one will speak to them, or help them. Five days a go, a Palestinian mother came on television and said, "What do we need from Arafat and these people? All the money he gets goes to his wife Suha in Paris and London and to his own bank account. We, the Palestinian people, are the poor ones and are becoming even poorer because of this war with Israel." People are starting to speak up, but this is still very rare because people are generally scared to do so; they fear for their lives.

Who said these mothers are really happy? I lost my uncle and I still cry into my pillow at night. The Palestinian mother who is on television must look happy in order to send Arafat and the leaders of the terrorist organizations the message, "We are with you!" That's why you can see mothers dancing and singing after a suicide bombing in which their son became a shaheed. There's no other reason. Pain is pain. I think that also forgetting is a process, not something that suddenly happens.

A child decides to become a shaheed because of the economic situation in Palestine. The child looks around and sees that his dad is unemployed and that his school is always closed. A child sees that he has no chance of becoming someone and having a good life. He then decides to sacrifice himself and help to liberate Palestine form the Jews. If this child had food and money he would never resort to such actions. It is against Islam to kill indiscriminately. But Islam also gives people the right to defend themselves and the land, especially if the land is being occupied by non-Muslims.

A mother can be happy that her son or daughter became a shaheed. What life would her children have in Palestine anyway? At least this way her child was not killed in vain but for an important cause. This is serious business that we're talking about—the liberation of the land. The Jews have caused so many problems in this part of the world, an in other parts too, that the only way to fight them is by turning to extreme measures.

Q: How do you feel when you hear about a suicide bombing in which many Jews were killed?

No one here likes to hear about a suicide bombing. It hurts me to hear about a suicide bombing, and when people are killed. It also hurts me to here when people are killed in the Occupied Territories.

I was in Beer Sheva the day the double suicide bombing happened. It was a horrible week. A few days before the bombing, I was driving around with a friend when a jeep suddenly hit us. All I can remember is that I saw the jeep coming towards up and then waking up in the hospital. Thanks

God nothing too serious happened to me. I was in terrible pain and stayed in the hospital for a few days, but I was alive. The day I was discharged I was driving back home with a friend when suddenly I heard a blast and I saw that there was a huge traffic jab. I also saw smoke. I was not sure what happened. In the beginning I thought that there might have been a really bad accident. I called my husband and he told me that there had been a bombing in Beer Sheva. I couldn't believe it. I was just discharged from the hospital and I was in the middle of the chaos after a bombing. I could see the bus and the smoke coming out of it. I wanted to get out of the car and help people—I could see people bleeding and hear them screaming. But I could hardly move because of the accident I had been in and also because I was so shocked and overwhelmed. What can I tell you? I was terrible. Actually, words can't really describe what it was. I feel pain when I see these things happen to innocent people, just like I feel pain when I see what's happening to people in Gaza and in the West Bank. It's all so terrible. I will never forget what I saw or heard that day in Beer Sheva.

Q: The interesting thing is that you are almost the first person who has so strongly spoken against suicide bombings. I spoke to a young boy this morning, and he not only told me that he understands the suicide bombers, who become *shaheeds*, but furthermore, that if Israel continues to abuse the Palestinians, he would consider becoming a *shaheed* himself. What do you think about this?

The children here said this? Are you sure?

I find it hard to believe that children here said such a thing. This only happens in the Palestinian Authority where they are told that if they blow themselves up they will become *shaheeds* and go to Heaven. The religion of Islam does not call for the committing of such acts, no religion does. In Islam it is written that in war, only soldiers are legitimate targets. In Islam, according to the Qur'an, it is not even allowed to hurt a tree in war. Even a tree can't be touched. I love Islam, it is such a gentle religion.

We don't teach such things in our villages. Maybe the Palestinian children are exposed to such things, but not here.

Q: Can you understand the young boys and girls who become *shaheeds*?

Look, the children in the Occupied Territories can see how praised they will be after committing a suicide bombing. They are taught these things on the streets, I have also seen the television broadcasting in Gaza. It's pure propaganda that penetrates into a person's heart, especially if they are young. Combined with the fact that they are poor, this becomes fatal.

Our children here in Arara are exposed to the suffering of the Palestinian people each day. They can see the children who come from the Jenin area to sell small thing in our junction in order to take back home maybe 10 shekels a day. So, our kids here hurt for the children in the Occupied Territories and they feel guilty for having more money. They know exactly what the situation in the Occupied Territories is. When there was an earthquake in Turkey we also watched television all day. And the children in Arara felt pain for the children over there.

You tell me, Smadar, what other option do the people in the Occupied Territories have? They see the Israeli Army every day and they suffer because of this army. They know that the army represents Israel and since they hate Israel they hate the Israeli Army. What can a person do in order to change things when he has no weapons? The only thing he can do is become a *shaheed* and sacrifice himself. This way, he will also redeem his people and will also go to Heaven and live an eternal life there. Believe me, you would do the same if you were in the situation the Palestinian people are in at the moment. This is their only option. I don't necessarily think that a suicide bombing is a good thing, but when it's the only option, that's exactly what it is.

Q: What, in your opinion, makes a child decide to become a *shaheed*? Is it only the fact that he and his family are poor?

I think that what influences the children in the Occupied Territories and also to an extent the children of Arara, was the death of Muhammad al-Durrah. The children saw him dying and wrote songs about him, because they realized that their lives could also be in danger. The children here in our village saw and continue to see, that Palestinian children are dying in this conflict. The children in the Occupied Territories are going through extreme suffering. They are poor and can't study like other children in the world. They can't go to school and learn so they ruin their lives.

The entire current atmosphere contributes to this phenomenon. Before the Second *Intifada*, things were much better and calmer. Since the beginning of this *Intifada*, things have gotten worse, and the people in the Occupied Territories have become much poorer. The poorer they get, the higher the chances of Palestinians becoming *shaheeds* are.

People say that things were better in the past, but I don't think this is necessarily right. It is the leaders who have always brought and continue to bring all of this pain upon everyone. They are fighting for power, for who will be the next prime minister, or president and who will rule the Palestinian people. They don't care about the simple people who are getting at home, caught in this mess. They are creating this big mess, but they are not suffering from it. It's the people who are suffering. Have you ever seen a member of Hamas or Ariel Sharon loose heir son or daughter to an act of terror? Of course not.

Q: What do you think about Arafat?

I think that maybe originally he was the right person to lead the Palestinian people. In the beginning, he did everything he could for them. But I think that now his hands are tied and that there's nothing else he can do at the moment. Things are out of control now.

Arafat wasn't okay even when he came back to Palestine. When he came back here, he should have lived like other Palestinians, even in a tent if necessary instead of giving millions of dollars to Suha in Paris and London where she lives in a luxurious palace. He should live like the poorest Palestinian people. People in the Occupied Territories are poor because of Arafat's fat bank accounts. He is always whining to Saudi Arabia to send him money and give donations to the Palestinian people. And what does he do once he gets the money? He puts all the money in his bank account and distributes it to the rest of his close family members. In the past, Palestinians could come to Tel Aviv or Holon and to many other places, in order to work and make money. Now, they can't come anymore and there's no money in the Occupied Territories. There is no food, so what will they do? What *will* they do?

Q: So Arafat is not the one suffering?

Of course not. Maybe now he's suffering because he is being pressured by everyone to finally be a real leader who cares about the Palestinian people. The Palestinian people have finally woken up. Maybe.

Q: What realization, if at all, do you think the Palestinian people have reached?

Realization? The Palestinian people know exactly what's going on, but they can't express themselves. What can they do? If they dare to say something bad about Arafat, he will kill them together with their families. Only a democratic election can change the status quo.

Q: But the prediction is that if the Palestinian people go to the ballots Arafat will be chosen again.

Yes, he might get elected once again, but you'll see, I think that the only reason why he would be elected again is because the United States and Israel demanded his replacement and said that he was not the right leader for the peace process. If they choose him again, it will be only to defy the United States and Israel.

Q: Which factors are created by the occupation?

The Palestinian people are buried. They can't leave their houses most of the time and they can't work properly and earn money. Their only option is to sit at home and this naturally strengthens their anti-Israel sentiments. If they had money and could go to work, their attitude would immediately change. Poverty only increases their hatred towards the Israelis.

There is another thing which is created by the occupation. Some Palestinians have lands on which they are not allowed to build. They become very frustrated when they see the Israeli government build houses for settlers on their lands. Many olive trees were also stolen form the Palestinians. When this happens the Palestinians tell themselves, "Hey, this is my home and you are building thousands of houses on it. It's my land, I have the right to do whatever I want on it."

Q: What do you think about the settlers? Do you think that they must leave the Occupied Territories in order for peace to be possible?

I think that they should leave all parts of the Occupied Territories. Once they are gone, the war will end. I can promise you this.

No, not necessarily. This is something that is up to both sides. I think that each person should be able to live wherever they wish. If these people don't mind living as a minority in a Palestinian state, why should they move somewhere else? They will have to pay taxes and behave as is acceptable in a Palestinian state. The Muslim rulers always allowed the Jews to stay on Muslim land as long as the paid taxes. If the Jews choose to do so, it's okay for them to stay. As I have said before, the human being is more important than religion, land and holy places. Fanatics from both sides should realize that everyone [including themselves] is suffering because of their stubbornness.

Q: You touched on an interesting thing when you were speaking with Amal before. You said that the politicians in the Palestinian Authority never send their own children to become the *shaheeds* they always speak about and praise on television. What do you mean? Why is this important?

Yes, this disturbs me very much. It disturbs me because the children who go and commit these acts are poor people who have experienced the hardship of living in a refugee camp where most people are poor. So, from the very beginning, these people might view death as a better option. They are being taken advantage of by the Palestinian leadership because of their status in life. Do you think that Yasser Arafat would send his own children to die in a suicide bombing? Do you think that Suha who praises the suicide bombings would send her child to die in such a way? Do you think a member of Hamas would send his daughter to do such a thing? I have never heard about a politician from the Palestinian Authority who has become as *shaheed* in order to liberate his country. It's always the poor people who have already experienced so much suffering who die in the end.

Q: A few days ago I read an article about a Palestinian girl who, at the last moment, decided not to carry out a suicide bombing to which she had committed herself. She was interviewed by Binyamin Ben Eliezer,[113] and she told him that after she changed her mind, the pressure on her to carry out the suicide bombing was immense. She said that she was practically dragged back in order to commit the bombing.

About a month ago, I heard about a similar girl who was also questioned by the Israelis. They asked her who sent her, and she said that it was her own decision. The Israelis asked her what would happen to her daughter without her and who would take care of her. She said, "God will. I have God."

Q: Many Palestinians don't acknowledge the right of Jews to any land, not only in the Occupied Territories, but also in Israel. They view all this land as being conquered by the Jews, by the Israelis. Do you think that the Palestinians should have a right to return to their lands, even if they feel this way?

Those who want to come back should be able to come back. I would like to see my family.

Q: But many Israelis, and definitely the Israeli government, doe not want the Palestinians to return to this land. They see it as a demographic disaster which might ruin the Jewish state.

Who told you all these people will come back? Some of them might not even want to come back anymore. If I am a person who has lived in Syria for the last 50 years and I have all my family here and also a job, how would I leave everything and go to a place that has changed so much, and that isn't what I left? The lives of most of the Palestinians who left in 1948 is elsewhere now, not where they left 50 years ago, even if they miss it very much.

Q: What would you tell a Palestinian who says that Jews should go back to where they came from? Just this morning I was speaking to a boy here in Arara, and he said to me, "The Jews should go back to wherever they came from!" This is a widespread notion among Arabs around the world, isn't it?

The children here in Arara, like the adults too, would ideally like to have the Jews leave. They would even find money to compensate them, if only the Jews would leave. I think, however, that both Arabs and Jews can live together, or at least one next to the other with love and friendliness, if only we tried to understand one another. If we don't listen to one another, life will continue as it is now, and we won't know anything else. On both sides, Arab and Jewish, we as parents must educate our children not to hate.

Q: You are both religious women. You, Samia, have told me that you read the Qur'an each and every day. Is there anywhere in the Qur'an that might say, or insinuate, that if you become a suicide bomber you will go to Heaven and live an eternal life? Does it say anywhere that if you kill women and children, you will be rewarded with seventy virgins in Heaven?

I have to tell you one thing. There is a problem in the world at the moment. Many people in Israel and in the world as a whole view Islam as a very dangerous and intimidating religion. Some people even look at Islam as the greatest threat to the world. This is not true at all. Islam is a religion of peace and justice. Not of war and injustice. People who think that Islam calls for killing are complete fools.

The terrorists say that they are carrying out a suicide bombing in the name of Allah, but this is completely false. Allah never asked people to go and kill and to do terrible things to other people. I don't know what Jewish people, or many other non-Muslim people, say as to whether our Imams preach to us that we have to sacrifice ourselves for Allah. Have you heard people talk about these things?

Q: Many think that in order to protect holy sites Islam permits killing. What do you think about this?

Our holy sites are of major importance and they must be protected, yes.

Q: On the one hand, you condemned the suicide bombings when I spoke to you earlier. On the other hand you say that killing should be forgiven in the case of holy sites. The *shaheeds* also claim that they are dying for Al Aqsa and for the land.

No, this is not the same. I am not going to carry out a suicide bombing among innocent civilians. But, if Sharon came to Al Aqsa, I would be there to protect and defend it from him. The citizens living in Hadera, for example, did they come and invade Al Aqsa? They didn't, so why would I go to a bus full of people who are innocent and might even hate Sharon and kill them? No, I will not do such a thing under any circumstances. But, if Sharon came, I would do what the people in Al Aqsa in October 2000 did. In the same manner, I think that if an Arab who had bad intentions went to the Western Wall, I, together with the Jews, would help them defend it. Why? Because it's a holy place and I accept all religions and people.

Q: Do you think that potential suicide bombers and Hamas members are tried in the Palestinian Authority?

Yes. Several Hamas members have been tried by Arafat, but he does not do this because they want to kill Jews, but because he doesn't want them to take his job, his chair. That's all. It's nothing to do with justice.

Q: So, is the Muslim obliged to respect all people and religions?

Yes. However, I don't believe in the Buddhist religion. We don't acknowledge them as a religion that worships God. We don't have any connection to their religion and tradition—they believe in many Gods and this is a sin.

Q: But do you respect them?

I respect them as people, but definitely not as a religion. I don't care about them. If I see a Buddhist, I'll say hello and be polite, that's all. You know, when a Buddhist dies, they don't respect the body like we do in our religion. I think they burn the body or something like this. It is awful.

Q: In your religion, can a Jew get to heaven?

Why not? Why not? Everything is from Allah. If the man or woman did good deeds then yes, even a Jew can reach heaven. If a Muslim does bad things, no one guarantees that he'll get to heaven. One has to be good and then later, Allah decides everything. I pray, I read the Qur'an everyday, I love peace and I hate wars. Even if I hurt someone, I can't fall asleep at night and even when I am exhausted I try not to yell at my kids. But, who knows? Maybe I won't make it to heaven. We people should not judge others. It's not in our hands.

Q: Can a Muslim marry a non-Muslim according to Islam?

Yes, it's possible, if the woman converts to Islam. It's possible for our men to marry Jews and Christians, and I know several men who have, but it's better if the woman becomes a Muslim. But for me as a woman, I can't marry a non-Muslim man, unless he converts to Islam. We can't marry Jewish and Christian men, it's against our religion. You see what a wonderful religion we have? Can you see the beauty of Islam? Everyone is welcome to join and there's no problem at all.

Q: So, if a Jewish woman were to convert into Islam, would she be accepted?

Yes, of course.

Q: If a Jewish woman were willing to convert into Islam and marry your son, would you accept her?

Why not? If she converts and dresses appropriately and accepts Islam, she is even better than a Muslim girl who is only Muslim because she was born to a Muslim father and might not even be a real Muslim. A woman who is Muslim by birth might have read Qur'an. She might have never dressed modestly and might have never respected her parents. So, I would accept a Jewish woman who converts and genuinely came into the religion because she believes in it. She doesn't have to necessarily cover, but she should behave like a Muslim woman and accept our tradition and way of life.

Q: I have heard that some Imams condone suicide bombings and some don't. But many people think that in extreme Muslim and Arab countries Imams perpetuate a lot of the existing hate and violence. Many people say that this usually happens in the mosque, after the Friday prayers.

The religion of Islam is very far from this, Smadar. The religion of Islam gives equal rights to all people. In the Ottoman Empire, for example, the Jews got equal rights and the right to return to Palestine. The Qur'an says that we have to treat the Jews and the Christians equally. The call for violence does not come from the Qur'an, so how are you telling me that people think that our religion calls for violence? Our Prophet, Muhammad, peace be upon Him, never said that terror was a good thing. He was a gentle man who loved and respected everyone. He never even hurt a fly. Islam as a religion does not call for terror and destruction. I never learned that Islam supports terror or that people should use terror to gain their human rights. I have never heard of this, I have to tell you.

Q: Then why do you think that there are people all over the world who are terrified of Islam, in a way that they are not terrified of any other religion?

To tell you the truth, I really don't know. But I will tell you one thing: Islam is a good religion. Believe me, if everyone were Muslim, the world would be a better place.

The Qur'an speaks of nothing of this kind. The children who become *shaheeds* are poor and desperate and brainwashed by their parents and by their teachers. They are not brainwashed by the Qur'an because it does not say to do such horrible things to other human beings.

Q: Do you think that a person who carries out a suicide bombing is a religious person?

Of course he or she is not. In our religion, it's not allowed to commit suicide for any reason whatsoever. Many religious Muslims even say that a person who commits suicide is doomed to eternal Hell.

A person who does such a thing is not a Muslim.

Yes, why not? Only Allah can judge whether a person is a Muslim or not.

What else can these poor people do? Of course they are Muslim, whatever they do.

Of course they are. They are some of the best Muslims.

Responses from Children

Q: What do you think about the suicide bombings and about the people who carry them out?

When I grow up, I am going to gather all my friends and do you know what we're going to do? We will create an army that will unite and fight all the Jews. We will fight the Israelis and then we will return Al Aqsa and Palestine to the Arabs. I know several friends who are willing to participate in my army.

Sharon is a pig. I wish I could become a suicide bomber and kill him and all of his family. Pigs like him don't deserve to live. I would take explosives and put them on myself and then I would go to the Knesset and jump on him and then explode. And then I will die, but that's OK, I don't care. It's not really dying, it's just living somewhere else forever. And how bad can that be?

The suicide bombings are bad. But you know, the Palestinian people don't have any other option, but to do this. I would never become a *shaheed*, but you know what I saw on television? I saw Muhammad al-Durrah. Did you see how he was shot by the Israeli Army? And did you see the honor he received from everyone. His family was also praised. So I think that if I were living in the Occupied Territories, I might have chosen to do the same thing.

If someone approached me and asked me to be a suicide bomber, I would immediately agree. Think about it. You do something to help other people and you get to go to Paradise. You know that little boy who was shot? He sacrificed himself for the Palestinian people too.

So tell me, what else can the people living in the Occupied Territories do? Should they just sit at home and ignore what is being done to them by the Jews? Of course not. They should do something and show the Jews what they can do. And then maybe the Jews will understand that the Palestinians are not weak and that they can fight for what is legally theirs. And besides, why are the Jews complaining? Don't they send tanks and things like that into the refugee camps? And what do they expect? Do they want the people there to just shut up and not do anything? It's stones against tanks, so is this fair? Is this just? I don't think so.

I don't know if the bombings are good or not. I mean, I think that they are the only thing the Palestinians can do. At the same time, I once saw a suicide bombing on television and it was so disgusting. There were limbs scattered everywhere and I felt like I wanted to throw up, or even worse. I think I am torn between supporting the bombings and opposing them. But then, when I see what the Israeli Army is doing in Jenin, I say to myself, "Good, we should kill as many Jews as we can!"

I want to blow up and kill Jews.

Q: What do you think about the fact that some Palestinians are killing Jews in suicide bombings?

Some of the Jews are good and some of the Jews are bad. Those who are bad deserve what they get.

Q: But there have also been Israeli Arabs who have also died in suicide bombings too. Do you think that is O.K.?

Well, no, it's not OK. I think that the suicide bomber has to first check and see that there aren't any Arabs or Muslims on the bus. You have to understand, the Israeli Arabs and the Palestinians do not want all this mess. It's the Jews, they started all of this, so why are you so surprised that there are suicide bombings? If you do something bad to someone, don't you get something bad in return?

Q: But it doesn't seem that the suicide bombers try to find out if there are Muslims in the bus. What do you think about that?

It's not good that they don't try to distinguish between the people.

Q: What do you think about the suicide bombings?

The Palestinians commit suicide bombings in order to kill Jews. There is a war between the Jews and the Arabs at the moment.

Q: Why do the Palestinians carry out suicide bombings?

Because the Jews are killing the Palestinians.

Q: Do you think the suicide bombings are good?

On the one hand I think they are bad, because innocent people are dying. On the other hand, the Jews are killing the Palestinians so what can they do?

Q: To you, who is a Palestinian?

All of us here are Palestinians.

Q: What do you know and think about the Palestinian people?

The Palestinians are Muslim and Arab, like us.

Q: Where do they live?

They live in Palestine.

Q: Where do you live?

I also live in Palestine. All of this is Palestine.

Q: But you live in Israel, don't you?

No, this is really Palestine, not Israel. The Jews stole it from the Palestinians many years ago.

Q: So to whom does the land belong?

Only to the Palestinians. I also know this because Qur'an says that this is Muslim land.

Q: So what would happen to the Jews if the Palestinians ever take over this land?

We will kick the Jews out.

Q: Where should they go?

I don't know. They should go to wherever they came from. This land is not for them.

Q: What do you think Jews and Arabs are fighting over?

We are fighting over Jerusalem.

Q: What is there to fight about over Jerusalem?

The Jews claim that the Western Wall is holy for them. But it is not true because Al Aqsa is holy for us, for the Muslims. This place is not for the Jews, it doesn't belong to them. Don't you think it's ridiculous how the Jews always make things up? Like, they say this land is theirs.

Q: But the Western Wall was there before Al Aqsa, no?

That is not true and even if it were, it doesn't matter at all. The place still belongs to the Palestinians. The Jews didn't live here before 1948 and this place has no connection to them whatsoever. They came here and invented all sorts of stories so that other people believe the land belongs to them.

Q: Why did Jews come here?

They came when the English were here. But I am not sure exactly why they came.

Q: What happened when the Jews came here in 1948?

The Jews came here, killed the Palestinians and took their lands.

Q: What, if at all, do you feel your connection with the Palestinians is?

The Palestinians suffered because the Jews came here and took their lands. I am Palestinian as well, so the Jews took my lands too. My family stayed here, but many Palestinians escaped to the Occupied Territories and still live there. But really, we are the same people and our lands were taken from us by the same people. We are the same and we have to support one another.

Q: Who is the current leader of the Palestinian people?

Yasser Arafat.

Q: What do you think about him?

He's very good for the Palestinian people and their cause.

Q: Why?

He protects the Palestinians who live in the Occupied territories and wants to create a country for them, without Jews.

Q: As far as you know, how is the current situation for the Palestinian people in the Occupied Territories?

The situation is not good at all because the Israelis are continually invading Ramallah, Jenin and other towns.

Q: Who is the ruler in Israel at the moment?

Sharon.

Q: What do you think about Sharon?

He's a very bad man. He hates the Arabs and especially the Palestinians and he wants to kill all of them.

Q: How do you think that the Israeli-Palestinian conflict can be solved, if at all?

Sharon must leave the government and all the land should be returned to the Palestinians. Maybe the Jews can stay, but only as guests. We will rule them and not the opposite.

Q: And then there will be peace?

Yes.

Q: Do you think that the fact that the Israeli Army is in the Palestinian Territories condones suicide bombings?

Yes.

Q: Why?

Because they don't have any other choice.

Q: What do you think about the education system in the Palestinian Authority?

In Ramallah, students learn to read Charles Dickens and Shakespearean plays such as *Romeo and Juliet* from the age of eleven years. This is why they leave school with a very good education.

Q: But you are speaking about a very select group of people, aren't you?

Look, now because of the *Intifada* things are different. A few weeks ago I met a guy from a village near Jenin. He told me that before the *Intifada* they used to study as usual. He said, however, that when the Israeli Army entered the camps, they couldn't go to school as they used to before. Of course they can't go to school with all these tensions and with tanks rolling down their streets.

Q: What do you think Palestinian children living in the Palestinian Authority learn about Jews?

In their schools they don't talk about Jews.

Q: But I have seen many documentaries which portray the strong anti-Israel and anti-Jewish sentiments taught in Palestinian schools. Sometimes the teachers even ask them to draw suicide bombings and attacks on Jews.

Listen, I'll tell you exactly what it is. It's got nothing to do with what teachers teach the children in school. Each and every child has his or her own views about the political situation between Israelis and Palestinians. The teacher told them to draw what they thought was appropriate.

Q: And what about when teachers encourage children in class to draw suicide bombings and the killing of Jews?

I really don't think these things happen in Palestinian schools. When a teacher asks them to do such a thing, he's not teaching them, but he's asking them to express themselves so that he can see what they think about the situation. Every child has their own views. And what do you expect? Sharon comes to the place where they live and kills everyone. A child is sitting in his or her house and suddenly there are soldiers all around. What is this?!

Q: But do you believe that there is anti-Israeli and anti-Jewish propaganda taught in Palestinian schools?

Listen, if someone harms me, it's just natural that I will hate this person back, do you understand? So, those who harm these children are hated by them. If you go to a class in one of the schools in the Occupied Territories, you will see that in a class of thirty pupils each and every child has lost a mother, a father, a brother or a sister. Do you understand what this means? This is why these children are so filled with sorrow and hatred and obviously, the teachers are the same for they have experienced the exact same reality.

Q: What do you think about the suicide bombings?

The suicide bomber wants to explode and kill Jews because the Jews are killing the Palestinians.

Q: Do you think the suicide bombings are good or bad?

I think they are bad, because people are dying. But I also think that the Jews shouldn't kill Palestinians. We are permitted by our religion to do this, because our land is being occupied.

Q: Where do you live at the moment, in Israel or in Palestine?

In Palestine.

Q: Are you sure?

Yes, I am sure. This land belongs to the Arabs. We must kick the Jews out of here.

Q: Where should the Jews go?

I don't know.

Q: **What are Jews and Arabs fighting over?**

They are fighting over Jerusalem.

Q: **What's in Jerusalem to fight over?**

We are fighting for Al Aqsa. The Jews say that there's something under our mosque that is holy for them, but it's not true. Jerusalem is not for the Jews, it's for the Arabs.

Q: **But the Western Wall was there before the Al Aqsa mosque, wasn't it?**

That's not true at all. The Jews came from Europe, and they don't belong to this place. They made all of this up. They are new to the area.

Q: **Why did they come from Europe?**

I don't know.

Q: **What happened when they came here?**

When the Jews came here, they massacred the Palestinians and took all of their lands.

Q: **What, in your opinion, has to happen with the land now?**

It has to be given back to the Palestinians, and then everything will be okay, and there will be no more war.

Q: **Can you understand why some people decide to become *shaheeds*?**

Yes, I can understand them.

Q: **Why?**

The person who becomes a *shaheed* knows that the Jews killed many Palestinians and he wants to avenge their death by becoming a *shaheed* and fighting for their cause.

Q: **Would you become as *shaheed*?**

I am not sure, but maybe I would.

Q: Do you condone the suicide bombings?

Well, it's not necessarily a good thing.

Q: Why not?

Because there might be Arabs or Palestinians in the bus.

Q: But let's say there are only Jews on the bus, would you then support a suicide bombing against them?

Yes.

Q: Do you support the suicide bombings?

I don't support the suicide bombings at all.

Q: Why not?

Because when there's a suicide bombing, Israel responds with more force. I think the suicide bombings only make things worse and strengthen the occupation of Palestine.

Q: So you think that the suicide bombings should be stopped?

I think that if the suicide bombings are stopped, there will finally be peace between Israelis and Palestinians.

Q: And what do you think about the occupation?

I think that the soldiers must immediately leave the Occupied Territories.

Q: What do you think about the suicide bombings?

If the suicide bombings stop, then maybe there will be more chances for peace.

Q: Do you understand the people who become *shaheeds*, or do you think that suicide bombings are a bad thing, regardless?

I think it's not a good thing regardless.

Q: Why?

Every time there's a suicide bombing, the Israelis invade Jenin again and Palestinians are killed. It brings out the worse from the Jews. But there's still a problem here.

Q: What kind of problem?

Why should only the Arabs stop with the suicide bombings? First the Jews have to stop killing Palestinians. A while ago, Sharon said he wants peace for Israelis and Palestinians. When the Palestinians heard this, they stopped the suicide bombings. But the Israelis never stopped and the Israeli Army continued its terror in the Occupied Territories. Of course the Arabs started the terror again, why shouldn't they? First the Jews have to stop and then, believe me, the Arabs will stop too.

Q: Do you understand the people who become *shaheeds*?

Yes, I do.

Q: Do you think that it is okay that people blow themselves up?

Well, it's not okay, but it's okay.

Q: What do you mean?

I mean, it's not okay, but it is okay because the Jews are killing the Arabs.

Q: Do you believe in peace between Israelis and Palestinians?

I don't think there will ever be peace between the two sides.

Q: Why not?

Because each side wants what they think is theirs and no one is willing to listen to the other side and compromise. I think that only when there is democratic rule all over the world will there be peace here. In the Arab countries there is no democratic rule at all. The Prophet Muhammad, peace and prayers be upon him, said that there must be democratic rule all over the world. At the moment, the Arab countries don't want democracy and that's a very big and serious problem.

Q: What do you think about the United States?

Bush and Clinton don't like the Arabs. They only like the Jews. I think I know why they feel this way.

Q: Why?

The Arabs are always ruled by kings who were not chosen by the citizens of the country. The Americans aren't interested in people who are not chosen in a democratic way. They are interested in prime ministers who are chosen by citizens in democratic elections.

Q: Do you think that the Arab world cares about the Palestinians?

I think they do, but they are afraid of the United States, so they can't speak out and show their support.

Epilogue

My childhood in Israel was no different than that of most Jewish Israeli children and seemingly, there was nothing unique about it whatsoever. I was born in Haifa while my parents were living on a *Kibbutz* located along the Israeli-Jordanian border. When I was three we moved to Neve Ilan, a small *Moshav* (a cooperative agricultural village) in the Judean Hills near Jerusalem. I attended a primary school, Alon, for children coming from a *Kibbutz* background and then transferred to the Givat Brenner High School, where I completed my education. I then joined the Israeli Army in April of 1995 and served in Givati, one of the army's infantry units, for nearly a year and a half. While I was in the army, my unit moved from southern Lebanon to the Golan Heights and then to the Gaza Strip. On completion of my army service I worked for a few months in a local restaurant and as the assistant of the Neve Ilan hotel's housekeeping department manager. I then left for the United States with the sole purpose of traveling around for a month or two. Two months turned into six years!

What was very similar between my childhood and that of most other Jewish Israeli children was the lack of contact I had with Arab people. This lack of contact was not intentional and my mother and father did occasionally take us children to the neighboring Arab village, Abu Ghosh, in order to meet with the local population. In spite of this fact, I never had the opportunity to befriend an Arab girl, for example, or to have her come over to my house. On the way to and from school our school bus used to pass through Abu Ghosh and I remember always looking at the Arab children and wondering what their life was like. Although I knew that most of them could speak Hebrew, I was also aware of the fact that I could not speak any Arabic. We were not required to study Arabic in primary school at that time and we could not put together a sentence in that language had our on it. Only one time, during all my primary school years, did our school encourage us to meet with Arab children and organized a meeting between its students and the children of Abu Ghosh. We went to the village, spent a few hours in their school and then dispersed to their homes to enjoy a traditional Arab meal. That was it. After that visit, there was no follow up and we never again visited an Arab school.

I can remember an incident that happened to me many years ago and which threw my own ignorance right in my face. The father of one of the Arab men who worked with my father at that time came to our house to extent the patio in our garden. In the very beginning he asked some questions about exactly how he should build the extension and later what we thought of his work thus far. Since he was an older man, and was from the village Katane (situated in the West Bank) he could not speak any Hebrew. My mother, my father and I stood outside our house for a full ten minutes, using our hands desperately, trying to explain to him what we wanted. The man could not understand us and we could not understand him. He went on rambling in Arabic and we went on rambling in Hebrew. There was no meeting point between us and the more we all went on talking, the more we understood that we would not get anywhere. It was then that I understood for the very first time that I had a real disability. I was living in a country where a big part of the majority group could not speak the language of the minority group—although the latter group was quite big and definitely visible. I was living in a country where Arabs and Jews interacted daily but where I, an average Jewish person, was not able to speak Arabic and prove, at least to myself, that there was another language worthy of knowing in Israel. Language can bring people together, but it can also serve as a barrier—I was stuck way behind this barrier and I had not yet attempted to cross it.

In high school, we were required to take only one year of written Arabic. No one in class wanted to learn Arabic and definitely not a form of Arabic we would never use in a conversation. Maybe if we had learned vernacular Arabic, we would have taken the class more seriously, but by the end of the year it was clear that nearly all of the students were going to fail this subject—no one took it seriously from the very beginning. And maybe, if we had learned vernacular Arabic, I would have been able to at least attempt to converse with one of the Arab children who came to our community's swimming pool on the weekends. The cultural and linguistic separation was so big by the time we graduated from high school that I never thought I would ever have Arab friends or know how to utter more than "Salam" in Arabic. It was only later in life that I took the first step and made some sort of effort to learn Arabic and interact with Arab people.

The separation between Jews and Arabs in the army was maybe the most evident one. Most Israeli Arabs (with the exception of the Druze and the Bedouins) do not serve in the Israeli Army and those who do are accused of treason and betrayal by other Arab people in Israel and in the Middle East. At the time I was interviewing people in Arara I was informed about a family whose son had decided to join the Israeli Army. He and his entire family were ostracized by other Arabs living in the village— it was not a comfortable situation for anyone. "How can he go and fight against the Palestinians?" they all asked me. In the army we never learned to hate the Arabs, neither those living in Israel nor those residing in the West Bank and the Gaza Strip. Even in boot camp, which is where we attended classes every day, we were never taught to hate Palestinians, Arabs or Muslims. Yes, we were told that we had to defend our country against anyone who seeks to destroy it, but we were not taught that we could indiscriminately kill whoever opposed us. Sadly, although some of us were about to be sent to Gaza Strip or to the West Bank to stand in checkpoints and interrogate Palestinians, we were never required to learn a word in Arabic.

A scene which haunts my mind and is related to the issue of the inability of most Jewish Israelis to speak Arabic is one from the movie *Promises* where [Palestinian] Sanabel's family is standing at one of the checkpoints between Israel and the West Bank. The soldiers working at the checkpoint are not able to utter a word in Arabic and one of them, questioning Sanabel's family, is continuously yelling, "Does someone here speak Arabic and Hebrew?" and "Can anyone here translate what they are saying?" The separation between the two peoples is so evident in this scene and is undoubtedly targeting and criticizing Israel for not demanding that at least soldiers learn basic Arabic. In spite of the fact that the army as an organization didn't teach us to hate Palestinians, it was there that I encountered hatred towards the Arabs (coming strictly from individuals) for the first time. The army was the first place where I met people coming from completely different backgrounds from my own. I met men and women from the city and from towns located in the Negev (the Israeli dessert). I also met men and women from Moroccan and Yemenite families and those from poor and needy ones. And, of course, for the first time, I met people who held different political views from my own—I was definitely a *Kibbutznik* in my political beliefs. I remember one of my fellow women soldiers once telling me, "You want to know what my solution to the situation is? It's actually very simple. I think that we have to develop a drug which, when injected into a person, kills him or her instantaneously. Then, we should use it on the Arabs, until we get rid of them all. It won't hurt them or anything, it'll just put them to sleep for a very long time."

The idea of doing a project about the Israeli Arab population was born in a small diner at Bates College, the college in which I studied for my Bachelor of Art degree in English. It was my sophomore year in college and I was about to apply for a grant that would allow me to undertake a project in whichever field I chose. Initially, I thought of undertaking a project related to my major, English. I was thinking of going to a small village in China and teaching the children basic English skills. It just so happened that my mother was visiting me from Israel that week and it is largely thanks to her that I am writing this book today. When she heard about my idea of going to China, although she supported it (my parents have always supported whatever I choose to do) she looked at me and said, "How about finally doing something in your own country for a change?" It was at that moment, in that place, that the idea of interviewing Israeli Arabs was born. I wrote the project proposal and two weeks later was notified that I was chosen as one of the Phillips Fellowship recipients. When I started my project, the last thing I thought I would be doing two years later was writing a book.

I went back to Israel at a chaotic time when suicide bombings frequently occurred, and Jews and Arabs were more separated from one another than ever before. It was in the airport in Newark, when I was returning to Israel to undertake my project, when I realized for the first time how severe the situation in Israel really was. As I was standing in line to board the plane, I overheard a conversation between two Jewish men. One of them was saying to the other in a very ironic tone, "Oh great, I see we're going to be seated next to our cousins." It took me a moment to understand that he was actually referring to an Arab family that was also waiting in line. The Arab family didn't hear this comment, but its members also seemed quite unhappy at the possibility of being seated next to Jews. In the plane I was seated next to a Palestinian mother and daughter from Ramallah and was happy to converse with them. The daughter, who was seventeen years old and was about to marry an American Palestinian from Houston, Texas, told me about life in Ramallah, the difficulties they went through getting to the airport when flying to the United States and her future plans. According to her, she was marrying in order to get out of the Palestinian Territories and hopefully ensure a better future for herself and her family. When the flight was over, a Jewish woman who was sitting behind us looked at me said, "Well done. I wish there were more people like you on both sides." I then understood how rare it was to have Jews and Arabs (whether Palestinian or Israeli Arab) sit and have a calm and engaging discussion. Little did I know at that time that this kind of conversation was becoming rare in Israel because of the worsening of the political situation.

Once in Israel, I wanted to find out how Israeli Arabs felt towards Israel and towards Jews as a whole. I also wanted to learn to what extent Israeli Arabs were willing to meet with Jews and hold discussions with them, as well as to what extent they were still interested in being Israeli citizens and contributing to the state. The best indicator came from responses I received from children among whom the problem seemed much more evident. What I found out, especially among young children living in *The Triangle*, is that a big part of the future Israeli Arab generation does not view itself as Israeli and does not want to contribute or become an integral part of the society in which it lives. Although there were some voices calling for integration and cooperation with the Jews, these voices were so rare, that at times they completely disappeared. People who publicly called for integration with Israeli Jewish society were usually viewed as "strange birds" that were missing the point of being an Arab and a Muslim and were, therefore, at times afraid to publicly voice their opinions.

The responses I received from many of the children I interviewed troubled me and to an extent even surprised me. Although I was aware that a problem existed with regard to the treatment of Israeli Arabs by Israeli Jewish society and that many of them did not feel that they were an equal part of Israeli society, what I discovered was at times overwhelming. I never before thought of Israeli Arabs as wanting to become or viewing themselves as Palestinians. I never thought of them as having such feelings of resentment towards Israel and the Jews living in it. I always believed and was taught while I was growing up—that in 1948 Arabs accepted the Israeli government and honored their Israeli identification card and passport. For me, a Jewish woman growing up in Israel and going through the Israeli school system, the Israeli Arabs were Israeli, regardless of whether or not they were justified in their claims of being discriminated against. In head, I viewed them as unquestionably being on our side in the Israeli Palestinian conflict and in case of war, I believed they would support Israel. What I found out when speaking to many Israeli Arabs was quite to the contrary. It seemed that years of living abroad strengthened my naïveté in regard to the relationship between the Israeli Arab and Israeli Jewish communities. Many of the children (and some of the adults as well) stressed a sincere desire to separate themselves from Israeli Jewish society and to even actively fight against it. It was evident that many of the ideas these children communicated to me were instilled in their minds by the education they received both at home and in their schools. It was very clear that many of them believed that they do not owe anything to Israel and that they are not required to contribute to it in any way. While they were geographically situated in Israel they mentally and emotionally viewed themselves as Palestinians. They were very explicit about the inequalities between them and the Jews, but they were not at all explicit as to the responsibilities they as citizens owed the state.

It seemed to me that instead of encouraging them to view themselves as Israeli albeit Muslim and Arab, many of them were encouraged to separate themselves and only define themselves as Muslims belonging to the Arab Ummah (Nation), while completely omitting the word "Israeli" from their vocabulary. Instead of calling for their rights as Israeli citizens while becoming more involved in Israeli social life, they were encouraged to stress their connection with the Palestinian people—this happened for many reasons. I would even say that in some cases the messages some of these children were receiving from their parents, as well as from other educators whose religious indoctrination is of major importance, were aimed at instilling in their minds hatred, suspicion and disrespect towards Jews and Israelis. Nearly without exception, they all believed that the Jews have no connection to the land, that they are a people who cannot be trusted, and that according to Qur'an, the land will one day become Muslim once more. The same sentiment can be detected in parts of the Jewish education system where religious indoctrination is twisted and aimed at educating people to long for a return to the borders of the "Promised Land" of Judea and Samaria. This religious indoctrination, although not actively calling for the killing of Arabs and Muslims, ultimately forces people to mistrust the Arabs and view them as a people who have no rights to the land whatsoever. In the last few years, Jewish extremists have become increasingly strong and influential and an increasing number of settlers are working very hard to give the Jewish religion a bad and destructive name—many of them actively call for murdering innocent Arabs and even Jews who support the Disengagement Plan [from Gaza]. The movie *Promises* features a religious Jewish boy living in a settlement in the West Bank who, after explaining that God had given all the land to the Jews, expressed his desire to see all the Arabs "fly away."

Can there be peace between Israelis and Palestinians, as well as understanding between Jews and Arabs in Israel, while such extremist religious indoctrination dominates the lives of so many people on both sides? I strongly believe that genuine peace and understanding will not be possible until people let go of some of the effects religious indoctrination has on their ideology and worldview. Until Israeli Arabs and Palestinians acknowledge the right of Jews to the land and stop claiming that Qur'an explicitly promises the land to Muslims (while it's the *hadith* which developed this idea), genuine respect towards Jews will never be possible. How can Jews be respected by the Muslim world if their country is viewed as a cancer within the Arab and Muslim worlds and groups such as Hamas continue to exist and call for its elimination? A famous Muslim *hadith* found in the official political platform of Hamas, tells:

Said the Prophet of God: The time will come when Muslims will fight the Jews and kill them to the extent that a Jew will hide behind a stone and a tree. And the stone and the tree will call the Muslim and say, "There is a Jew hiding behind me, come and kill him." Only the bramble tree will not call the Muslim, for it is the tree of the Jews.[114]

This extremely violent *hadith* is taught in many schools and mosques all over the Muslim world. How can Muslims all over the world genuinely open up to Jews and Christians (as well as to others such as Hindus and Buddhists who are defined in the Qur'an as "infidels") when many Muslims do not question Qur'anic verses such as:

O ye who believe! Take not the Jews and Christians for friends. They are friends to one another. He among you taketh them for friends is one of them. Allah guideth not wrongdoing folk.[115]

For Israel, the problem will not end once a Palestinian state is declared. Israel is surrounded by entities which overtly oppose its existence and by those (such as Egypt and Jordan) who covertly do so. Islamic hatred towards Jews (or towards the West in general) did not start in 1948, when the

State of Israel was established. It started much earlier, shortly after the emergence of Islam when entities such as Israel and the United States did not even exist. When Israelis are willing to compromise and allow the existence of a Palestinian state—hopefully very soon—the Palestinians and the Arab world surrounding them should also recognize the right of the Jews to their own sovereign land. They should then immediately terminate all forms of propaganda against Jews in general and the State of Israel in particular and start forming diplomatic relations with it. The Gulf states will probably be the first to sign trade agreements with Israel. Until anti-Israeli propaganda on Arab television channels completely stops, I do not see much hope for genuine coexistence between Arabs and Jews, whether in Israel or in other parts of the world.

In more general terms, one can also argue that there is a belief in parts of the Muslim world which views Jews as conniving beings who undermined the Prophet Muhammad and betrayed him. In the movie *Promises* a Palestinian Muslim boy expressed this "religious belief" when he said, "I don't like talking to Jews. I know them. They're mean. They are deceitful. Since the time of the Prophet Muhammad. They betrayed him in the battle and fought against him." This boy had never before met a Jew and was basing his opinion solely on what he had learned in his mosque or what he had read in the Qur'an and *hadith*. How can Jews be respected when they are systematically dehumanized in most Arab and Muslim societies? The fact that many Muslim and Arab states incite against Israel and against Jews has nothing to do with the Israeli-Palestinian conflict—the conflict is used as an excuse. The Israeli-Palestinian conflict started before 1948 and will probably continue also after the establishment of a Palestinian state. When Muslim Algerian and Moroccan men attack religious Jews in the streets of Paris or burn a synagogue in Brussels they always do it under the pretext of identifying with their suffering brothers and sisters in Palestine. In today's world, people can apparently commit anti-Semitic crimes and get away with it because it was done in the name of helping the Palestinian people. The World Conference against Racism which took place in Durban, South Africa, in 2001 was only one example where anti-Jewish and anti-Israeli sentiments were legitimized by the international community—the conference turned into an anti-Israeli rally and the main issue of racism and discrimination (which apparently did not exist in other parts of the world) was hardly discussed. On the same note, religious indoctrinating among some religious and orthodox Jewish sects should also be immediately re-examined. As long as some Jews believe that the borders of Judea and

Samaria should be maintained at all cost; that all of the land was given to the Jews by God and that there is, therefore, no room left for the Arabs, the fighting will continue. Individual Jews who are encouraged by their families and friends to hate Arabs by dehumanizing them are also a main obstacle for peace between the two peoples—they also have blood on their hands. And let us not forget that Yitzhak Rabin was murdered by a religious Jew. As long as both sides cling to certain interpretations of religious "holy" texts and divine promises, written so long ago and undoubtedly edited and manipulated, a solution to external problems—the Israeli-Palestinian conflict and to internal problems—the suspicion and hatred between Israeli Jews and Arabs—will not be found.

The problem with the term "Holy Land" must be thoroughly examined here because it seems to be the cause of many of the world's problems. Both Jews and Muslims believe that they are fighting for a holy land, ordained to them by no one else by God himself. Can a land in itself be holy? And if it is considered holy, is it then worth the lives of so many innocent people? Years ago in Israeli schools, students used to learn the slogan, "It is good to die for our country." This sentiment has changed throughout the years for it is obvious that it is better to live for one's country than to die for it—in order to effect change, one has to be alive. Yeshayahu Leibowitz, a Jewish Israeli religious philosopher, also occupies himself with the idea of the land's holiness (or rather the lack of its holiness) when he explicitly says, "Anyone who elevates a country, a nation or anything else one can find existing in our reality—is a true idol worshipper."[116] One of his main claims was that modern Jewish orthodoxy has largely become an idol-worshipping body because it stresses the holiness of the land before it does the holiness of a human being's life. This is also very true of Islamic orthodoxy where young boys and girls are persuaded by "religious" individuals and groups to give up their own lives in order to redeem a "holy" land—the "life" of the land is always prioritized.

Once land is believed to be holy problems inevitably begin because it seems that if an object is considered holy, then people's lives are automatically considered unholy or secondary. It then becomes an acceptable norm to kill innocent people in the name of the holy land or object. When a suicide bomber marches into an Israeli bus with the soul aim of killing as many people as possible, it is obvious that he (or recently, she) do not view those sitting in the bus as human beings created in the image of God—they are inhuman, deserving of death, "infidels." And, when this monstrous act is done supposedly to redeem the land, it is legitimized in the mind of the suicide bomber who is incited to believe that redemption can indeed come through terror and that eternal life in heaven can be achieved through murdering innocent people. It only takes a short glance into our world to see the destruction, hatred and death that have all been caused in the name of holy places and lands, as well as in the name of God or of a divine being. As long as both peoples, Israelis and Palestinians as well as Jews and Arabs in Israel, believe that their God gave them the very same piece of land and base their right to the land on religious texts (either the Bible or the Qur'an), a genuine compromise will never be possible. In this manner, religion and nationalism intertwined is one of the most detrimental combinations possible, one that dictates much of the hate and violence existing in today's world.

The more time I spent talking to people in *The Triangle*, the more I understood that the problem between Israeli Jews and Israeli Arabs was not always a social one, but rather political. Although many people pointed to the social injustices existing between Jews and Arabs, their resentment towards Jews stemmed also from the Israeli-Palestinian political situation and from a strong religious indoctrination that viewed Israel as an illegitimate entity. According to most of the children, the reason they hated Jews was not because their schools were less good, or because many Arab villages didn't have any paved roads, but because they did not believe that the Jews had any right to the land. There is no doubt in my heart, however, that the existing severe social and economic injustices strengthened the anti-Israel and anti-Jewish feelings many of my interviewees exhibited. The fact that their schools were neglected, that the sewage was still running through their village streets and that members of their family had great difficulties finding a job angered and even outraged them. I believe that had these problems been solved by paying more attention to their wants and needs at least some of their resentment towards Israel would have subsided throughout the year.

In my interviews, and in other conversations I had with Arabs in Israel, I detected several reasons why they were not satisfied with their social status in Israel and thus expressed feelings of animosity towards Israelis and Jews alike. Firstly, there is no doubt that there is neglect by the government of big parts of the Israeli Arab population. Israeli Arabs generally do not receive a budget based on their proportional representation in the Israeli population, which is approximately twenty percent. Thus many Israeli

Arab schools are often neglected in comparison to Jewish schools and this causes a situation where Arab children feel discriminated against from a very young age. Raging mothers spent hours detailing to me the inequalities Israeli Arab children experienced in their classrooms—inadequate buildings and lack of computers and other necessary facilities. The notion that many of my interviewees had, however, that all Jewish schools receive adequate funding and that there are no poor Jews living in Israel was also false. It is no secret that schools in towns such as Yeruham and Dimona[117] are unfortunately also being neglected by the Israeli Ministry of Education—most of them lack extracurricular activities and adequate facilities.

Many Arab villages do not receive enough funding to pave their roads and improve their sewage system—a large number of them have been purposely forgotten by the Israeli government. Arab villages are notably different from Jewish villages, where one never sees sewage water running through the streets. It took many years for Arara, for example, to receive funds for paving a wide and smooth road through the village and the residents claimed that if this were a Jewish village the funds would have been allocated much earlier. Israeli Arabs also find themselves behind in the work market—when Israeli shopkeepers put up a note saying, "Waitress wanted, Army experience necessary" they are really saying, "Jewish waitress wanted." It is obvious that not enough has been done by successive Israeli governments to change the unjust status quo and reduce the number of Israeli Arabs who are living in poor or even squalid conditions—this is a great challenge for the young Israeli state. Secondly, the fact that Jews were never really required to learn Arabic is also painful and disturbing to Israeli Arabs and simply contributes to the already existing separation between Jews and Arabs. It seems to me that Israeli Jewish society often looks down on Israeli Arabs and does not wish to associate with them or learn their language and traditions.

All my interviewees, without exception, were aware that their economic and social situation is much better in Israel and that if they were living in Palestine, they would not be able to speak against the government and about the abuses they might be experiencing under its control. Only one woman showed willingness to immediately move to a Palestinian state and even she was aware of the dangers she might encounter once there. Even when I asked people whether they would be willing to move to the Palestinian state if they could take their lands and property with them, they said they would not. It was obvious to them that the health care and education they receive in Israel would not be given to them in Palestine—there were many advantages living in Israel. Among the children I interviewed many said that they would like to become a Palestinian citizen, if their village becomes a part of Palestine. There is no doubt that the sense of wanting to become Palestinian was stronger in the minds of children.

The theme of one's identity recurred in my conversations with most of the Israeli Arabs I interviewed. On the one hand, most of them wanted to believe that they were still seen as a part of the Arab and Muslim worlds surrounding them. Emphasizing their shared religion and ethnicity, they supported the Palestinians and their struggle and viewed themselves as Palestinians who happen to be living within the Israeli political borders, following a catastrophe that took place in 1948. On the other hand, many of them are aware of the fact that the Palestinians view them as traitors who, for the last fifty-seven years, have been supporting the existence of the Jewish state by accepting its identification card and passport. Many of them told me that they wished that the Palestinians would understand the difficult situation they were in: Arabs living in a Jewish state. On the one hand they found themselves living within Israel and had to accept its rules and on the other hand, they did not genuinely want to be a part of it. Unfortunately, Arab states all over the Middle East do not encourage their citizens to support neither the Palestinians living in the West Bank and Gaza, nor the Israeli Arab population. On the contrary—Arab regimes work very hard to provoke more hatred towards the Palestinian people living in Syrian, Lebanese and Jordanian refugee camps.

It is important, however, to emphasize the fact that not all Israeli Arabs exhibited hostility towards Israel and detachment from it. Some Israeli Arabs did indeed identify themselves as Israelis, even if they could point to many cases of discrimination against them. The fact that they were Arab and Muslim did not contradict their sense of belonging to Israel, or their Israeli citizenship. Most of these people were also able to accept that what happened in 1948 had happened a long time ago and that the existence of Israel as a state could not be questioned. They defined themselves as an Arab minority living within the borders of Israel—an internationally recognized Jewish state that had a right to exist as such. Mostly, their feelings were strongly opposed or brushed away by other members of their family, who could not understand where they were coming from. I hardly ever heard an Israeli Arab saying, "I am Israeli." Israeli Arab men who chose to join the Israeli Army were looked down upon and their families usually suffered from harassment by other inhabitants. They were viewed as traitors who were actively supporting Israel against the Palestinian people.

When it comes to the Israeli-Palestinian and Jewish-Arab conflicts and tensions, there is an evident problem with how history is remembered. This problem is closely tied to the education both Jewish and Arab children receive. It is my belief that if the new generations of our world want to move forward and change the world for the better, they must at times be taught to forget, instead of being taught to remember. Remembering history, in the Israeli-Arab context in particular, forces us to remember hatred, wars, violence and destruction—things we must not allow to function as obstacles for peace in the present and in the future. Although we must remember events that happened in order to study them and place them within the chronology of history and in order to hopefully learn a lesson from the past, we must not remember them in order to fuel hatred which will then be spilled into the future. One can only imagine what would happen if Jews were nowadays taught to remember the Crusades or the Holocaust in order to incite hatred towards Christians and Europeans. A.B. Yehoshua speaks about this in one of his articles:

The description is of a "stuck" person/people/nation either because he [the person] was expelled and misses his lost Paradise, or because he can't escape from the situation in which he finds himself. Either way, in the novel the hero/nation is paralyzed and incapable of being active. According to the novel, this is a diseased situation which must be abandoned and dismissed, even if the price of doing so is the giving up of one's unrealistic fantasies, or the feeling of revenge against those who expelled him or stuck him in a horrible and intolerable situation.

It's as if the novel says: Look, similar situations to this don't have only one answer, but many, and you, the human being (or the nation)must choose the way which will help you get out of whatever situation you are in. Be smart, not only right. [118]

He then continues:

The real liberty/freedom, according to the novel, will only come when people let go of their dreams of the past. The physical liberation (autonomy, a piece of land or a Palestinian state) must be followed by a personal-spiritual liberation. The Jews, too, are not off the hook when it comes to drowning themselves in myths and they also must release themselves from them in order to approach a state of cooperation between Jews and Arabs. The desirable state of cooperation is one with defined lines, but where each side acknowledges their own value/worth and that of the opposite side.[119]

Most Arabs I spoke to were not able to forget the failure of the Arab armies to defeat Israel in 1948 and then again in 1967. They spoke about 1948 as being damned, catastrophic as well as traumatic. It was mainly because of this that they were unable to see a future in which Jews and Arabs could coexist within the same county, let alone if the country were Jewish. The fact that many Israeli Arabs find it hard to accept the existence of Israel should be theoretically understood by Israeli Jews, even if they do not agree with it and find it offensive or frightening. Israeli Jews should also be more sensitive to the feelings of Israeli Arabs because of the emotional and psychological trauma they have experienced since 1948 when many of them were separated from their families. Even if these feelings of automatic resentment cannot be condoned and accepted by most Israeli Jews, they must be heard and discussed because they are real. As I have claimed before, it is more important to find *why* people feel the way they do, even if *what* they feel is exaggerated, fictitious, or distanced from reality.

Many Israeli Arab children are encouraged to remember what they call *al naqba*, "the catastrophe" of 1948, which many Muslims around the world compare to "the catastrophe" in 1492 in Grenada where the Muslim Boabdil of Grenada was defeated by Catholic King Ferdinand and Queen Isabella. They are taught that Jews had no connection to the land previous to 1948. While children on both sides are encouraged to remember the past and elevate it to an extent that it is more important than the future, Jews and Arabs, in Israel as well as in the world as a whole, will never be able to coexist because they will not be able to reach the point where they genuinely respect one another as well as "the otherness of the other." Parents on both sides must look to the future when raising their children and teaching them ethics and morals and not only to a past which is frequently full of feuds, wars and pseudo interpretations of events. Only when this happens, will Jews and Arabs be able to look one another in the eye and not automatically see the other as an enemy.

In spite of the fact that many of the Israeli Arabs I spoke to support, or at least understand the motives behind suicide bombings and define themselves explicitly as Palestinian, the majority are not willing to consider moving to a new Palestinian state, if and when it is established. Some of them (especially Christian Arabs, but also many Muslims) are aware of and fear the uncontrollable corruption, poverty and civil abuses existing within the Palestinian Authority. Others do not want to leave their lands and relocate and instead claim that they are already living in Palestine. It was evident to me, therefore, that many of the people I interviewed were caught between living in a country where they do not feel equal to others and to which they do not want to belong, and an Arab and Muslim world that also rejects them, sees them as foreigners and at times even views them as "Jews." They, therefore, prefer to introduce themselves as Palestinians living in Israel, thus situating themselves in the middle. This identity conflict can also be seen in Palestinian poetry such as that of Tawfiq Sayigh who in his poem "To enter a Country" explicitly says that he, a Palestinian, is caught between the Jewish state and the often hostile, abusive and inconsiderate Muslim and Arab worlds.

In the last few years, the Israeli state has found itself increasingly clueless as to what must be done about the Israeli-Palestinian and the Jewish-Arab conflicts. Israel, falsely wanting to believe that it is a Western country, has always looked towards Europe and the United States as a role model. Within Israel, it was mostly the European elitist culture that dictated Israeli culture and tradition. Because of this fact, Israel as a country forgot long ago (or at least attempted to forget) that it is a Middle Eastern country, situated in the heart of Arab and Muslim territory. This issue was discussed in a small conference I went to in Jerusalem where the Egyptian ambassador to Israel at that time, Muhammad Basyunni, questioned whether Israel considered itself a part of the Middle East or of Europe.

When I came to the United States, something struck me. It was obvious that most of the money was concentrated in the hands of a few, that race was still definitely an issue, that people of different colors and ethnic groups were not treated equally and benefits such as health care were not equally distributed. However, nearly everyone I met (with an exception of only a few) considered themselves to be American. American Indians, who were abused and even exterminated by the European newcomers, also mostly referred to themselves as American. When I asked a white person, a black person, or an Asian what their nationality was, they said, "I am American." When I asked Jews, Muslims and Christians what their nationality was they said, "I am American." During the war in Iraq, I asked some people who were in favor of the war who they were and they all said, "I am American." I then asked people who opposed the war who they were and they also said, "I am American." There was some common desire to be

American, regardless of political views (national and international), or social inequalities. Those who wanted to stop the war in Iraq, wished to do so in the name of the United States and the freedom it should in theory, but not by force, transmit to other countries which have not adopted democracy. Others wanted to do it as Americans who did not believe the United States had the right to intervene in the internal status quo of another nation. Those who wanted to continue the war wanted to do so because they, as Americans, believed that the United States should use its power to help those who are suffering around the world. Others desired, as Americans, to economically benefit from the war and its outcome. Regardless of the wide range of political views, all people (perhaps with a very small exception) still viewed themselves as Americans, were calling for changes as Americans, and were willing to defend their nation. I was amazed and even in awe of how people of all colors, backgrounds, religions and ethnic groups cherished their American citizenship and were not ready to give it up.

In Israel, things are very different from the United States. Within Israel exists an Arab minority (composing nearly 20% of the Israeli population) of which many do not identify themselves clearly as being Israeli. They identify themselves as Palestinian, or Muslim, or Arabs living in Israel before identifying themselves as Israeli. Their loyalty to Palestine, to the Arabs and to the Muslims often comes before their loyalty to Israel. Clearly, there exists a situation where a large group of people, living within an internationally recognized state, does not feel that they are part of it. Some of the reasons they give for feeling this way are legitimate, as I have tried to explain. Israeli Arabs have the right to defend their rights. The question is: should they do this as Israeli citizens who accept the existence of their state, or is it in their interest to do so as Palestinians who happen to live in Israel?

The dreams held by many Arabs around the world, as well as some in Israel, that the State of Israel will evaporate and disappear from the face of the earth, is too farfetched and will probably never happen. The Palestinian dream of seeing a Palestine from Eilat to Kiryat Shmona and from Tel Aviv to Jordan will most probably never materialize either. Israeli Arabs will probably always reside within Israel and most probably within a Jewish state (although this is debated by many). Some people from both sides have called for the exchange of land and citizens. They have suggested that areas such as *The Triangle* (which is predominantly Muslim Arab) should be exchanged for areas in the West Bank, where there are big Jewish enclaves, such as Maale Adumim.[120] It seems to me, after speaking to many Israeli Arabs, that most of them will not want to become a part of the Palestinian state to be as much as they call themselves Palestinians. Jews and Arabs are 'stuck with each other', whether they like it or not.

All the voices you have heard in this book, whether calling for love or for hatred, for reforms within the Israeli or Palestinian governments, for war or for peace, for friendship or for separation, for the importance of the future or of the past, are the voices of people. People I have met. People I have spoken to. People with whom I have laughed and cried. Some of them are people I love and will love forever. Some of them are people whom I will always visit when returning home. Some of them still call me when there is a suicide bombing in Jerusalem, to see if my family is okay. Others are people I will most probably never see again. All of these voices, without any exception, are the voices of people living in a harsh reality, filled with pain and grief—most of them just want to live a normal and calm life. No matter what their political and religious views or how much they believe they are being discriminated against in Israel, they are all grieving over innocent Israelis; Arabs and Jews alike, and Palestinians who are being killed. They also realize that as the conflict worsens, the relationship between Jews and Arabs in Israel worsens too.

When I last went to Umm el-Fahem, I visited the local art gallery. One of the enlarged photographs being exhibited was of a bathtub, full of fresh blood. Over the image it said, "Israel-Palestine 2000-2001." Is this what we want for both people? Is this how we want our children to grow up? Is this what we have always envisioned for ourselves and for our fellow human beings? There is no doubt that both sides must compromise, in the Israeli-Palestinian, and Israeli-Jewish and Israeli-Arab conflicts, if a solution is ever to be reached. This *can* be done. We can, and we all have the right, to live in a place where we feel safe. We have the right to live in a just society where people do not feel that they are second-class citizens, or that they simply do not belong. We have the right not to fear for our lives every second of the day. We have the right to happiness and security. Only when both sides are willing to compromise and to listen to the concerns and pains experienced by others, will Jews and Arabs, Israelis and Palestinians be able to look into each other's eyes and realize that at the end of the day, with all of our differences, in spite of the past, the present and the future, we really are all the same.

Notes

1. Rewriting history has always been a part of the general religious view in Islam. This was done in order to prove that Islam was indeed the origin of all other existing traditions and that the Qur'an was the only true and perfected word of Allah. Among other things, Islam claims that Ibrahim (Abraham) was not a Jew and not a Christian, but a Hanif who had submitted himself to Allah. This Qur'anic verse emphasizes the fact that he is the first Muslim and thus that Islam is the first religion the world had ever known. According to Islam, the Prophet Muhammad's genealogy is traced back to Ismail (Ishmael), Abraham's son. Thus, Prophet Muhammad is a direct offspring of Abraham and his family, and the claim that Abraham was a Muslim, the first Muslim, is supported and proven. Islam never experienced destruction of a holy place or dislocation of people (excluding the events in Catholic Spain). Because of this fact, the messianic idea of the end of the days is not well developed in the Islamic religion. The reward a person receives is by the mere fact that they are Muslim and that they follow the teachings of the Prophet. A Jew or a Christian who return to the only true faith are maximally rewarded because Islam claims that every child was born a Muslim and was later converted to either Christianity or Judaism. Yet, when Muslim scholars look at the end of the days and the way Islam is to become the only tradition (religion) on earth, they view it as a big procession where the grand Imam followed by Jesus Christ arrive in the Church in Seville, where Jesus will lead the people in prayers. In order to prove that the Qur'an is Umm al Kitab (Mother of all Scriptures) the text par excellence claims that Jewish and Christian sages have forged the true writings containing the word of God and thus, the Torah and the New Testament are not genuine books, but fake ones.
2. This term dates back to the partition of Palestine into Trans-Jordan and the State of Israel by the UN in 1947. That day, Israel was attacked by all its neighboring Arab countries. These countries urged Arabs residing on the Israeli side of the new border enter Arab countries as refugees. These refugees were subsequently referred to as Palestinians. Those Arabs who opted to remain in

Israel were awarded Israeli citizenship and are generally referred to as Israeli Arabs. Today, many Israeli Arabs refer to themselves as "Palestinian citizens of Israel", "Local Palestinians," or simply "Palestinians".

3. The Israeli parliament located in Jerusalem.

4. On September 29, 2000 Ariel Sharon, then Israel's opposition leader, entered the Temple Mount in the Old City of Jerusalem. By tradition, the Mount is the biblical site of Abraham's binding of Isaac. Therefore, it is the holiest site in Jewish traditions; the First and Second Temples, built respectively by King David and King Solomon, were erected there. For the same reason, the Mount is also holy to Muslims and Christians. It is the third holiest site in Islam, after the Ka'abah in Mecca and the Prophet's Mosque in Medina. It is one of the most contested religious sites in the world.

Subsequent to Sharon's visit, serious violence and bloody clashes erupted both in the Palestinian Authority and later in several Israeli Arab villages. Many Palestinians and Israeli Arabs who started and then participated in the Second Intifada claimed that their violent actions and resistance to Israel were a response to Sharon's visit to their holy site. Others claim, however, that Sharon's visit was not the actual catalyst, but that the violence and desire to resist Israel existed earlier and would have erupted regardless of Sharon's actions. In any case, Sharon's visit became the pretext for what would later be called the Second Intifada, which in 2005 has entered its fifth year and claimed the lives of countless innocent Israelis and Palestinians.

5. A language school located in Netanya, a town on the Mediterranean coast. Since the Second Intifada (uprising) broke out in October 2000, Ulpan Akiva found it hard to recruit sufficient students to open Arabic language courses. Due to the situation, many Israelis no longer wanted to learn Arabic; Palestinians who used to come to study Hebrew also stopped participating in Hebrew language courses.

6. An Israeli cooperative which operates bus lines throughout Israel.

7. http://news.bbc.co.uk/2/hi/middle_east/3241884.stm

8. A geographical area, located east of Hadera, a Jewish town, and west of Jenin, a Palestinian town. It is predominantly Muslim Arab and is known to politically identify with the Palestinian population. The name derives from its geographical shape.

9. An Israeli Arab village in the Judean Hills, about 15 kilometers from Jerusalem which bases most of its economy on internal, Israeli tourism. In 1948 the village decided to stay loyal to Israel and did not cooperate with the invading Arab forces. The local population did not join in either the intifada or in the October 2000 riots.

10. An Arab village in *The Triangle* located east of Hadera.

11. A predominantly Jewish town situated near *The Triangle*.

12. A scarf which some Muslim women wrap around their head, and which covers their hair and ears. It is worn for purposes of modesty because Islam, like Judaism, considers the woman's hair to be very sensual and attractive to men. There is no indication in the Qur'an that Muslim women should wear such a garment.
13. *Na'amat*, Hebrew acronym for "Movement of Working Women and Volunteers," is an organization and a movement striving to enhance the quality of life for women, children and families in Israel, the U.S. and around the world.
14. An Arab dish containing mostly chicken, rice and spices.
15. A large Arab Israeli town within the borders of Israel but very close to the West Bank. Many of its inhabitants have family in the West Bank, especially in Jenin.
16. A Palestinian Arab town in the northern part of the West Bank.
17. Celebrated by women, the henna party takes place the night before a wedding. Young and old, the female family and friends of the bride get together, play music, dance and decorate their hands and feet with henna. This custom is also practiced in Jewish families originating from the Middle East and Northern Africa.
18. Although some religious Muslim and Christian women cover their hair too, here I am referring exclusively to Muslim women.
19. A port of entry located between Israel and the Gaza Strip where different goods coming from Israel cross the border into the Palestinian Territories. This port of entry serves as the only trading artery from which medication, food and other necessities can reach the Gaza Strip. When I was conducting my interviews, this was one of the only places where Jews, Israeli Arabs and Palestinians could still be found working together.
20. A small private liberal arts college in Lewiston, Maine, U.S.A.
21. The Israeli organization equivalent to the American CIA and FBI.
22. Committee of enquiry established in order to investigate the events occurring on October 2000 and the subsequent shooting of thirteen Israeli Arab men. Its conclusions and recommendations were published in 2003.
23. The former editor of the of the Arab Communist party's newspaper *Al Itihad*
24. "An Impersonal Story," *Eretz Aheret*, issue no. 16, May-June, 2003, p. 19
25. Most of my interviewees were Muslim and not Christian because my initial and later contacts were with Muslims.
26. Religion Law and the Role of Force: A Study of their influence on Conflict and on Conflict Resolution. Edited by J.I. Coffey and Charles T. Mathewes, Transnational Publications, 2002, p. 32.
27. The reader should note that the Shar'ia and the *hadith* were written after the days of the Prophet Muhammad. Although based on the Qur'an, these texts should not be considered as divine in origin or as supreme in their impor-

tance. Problems usually start when these texts, written by men, are considered divine and indisputable.

28. The Encyclopædia Britannica describes the Protocols as a "fraudulent document that served as a pretext and rationale for anti-Semitism in the early 20th century". The *Protocols* shows an alleged plan of a worldwide "Jewish conspiracy" to take over the world. It was published throughout Europe during the 20th century. This document is one of the most widely sold and read documents in most Arab and Muslim countries and is once again regaining popularity in Europe. "Protocols of the Learned Elders of Zion." *Encyclopedia Britannica* from Encyclopedia Britannica Online.
http://www.search.eb.com/eb/article?tocId=9061621
[Accessed January 18, 2005].

29. The first of several waves of secular Zionist Jewish immigration to Israel, which began in 1882 and ended in 1903. During this period, the land later partitioned into Israel and Trans-Jordan belonged to the Turkish Ottoman Empire

30. Ben Kaspit, *Ha'aretz*, November 30, 2004.

31. Israeli Arab villages located very close to the future border between Israel and Palestine.

32. The entire text of the *Orr Committee's* conclusions and recommendations can be found on the *Ha'aretz* web site www.haaretz.com.

33. People of the Book: Muslims, Christians and Jews. Zoroastrians were also considered to be a part of this group by some Muslims.

34. Wistrich, Robert S., *Muslim Anti-Semitism*. The American Jewish committee, 2002, p. 9.

35. Although the Israeli Ministry of Education determines the curriculum taught in Israeli Arab schools, many children told me that the issue of the Israeli-Palestinian conflict and of Jews in general is often raised in the classroom. It seemed to me that these classroom discussions were a source of many of the ideas, assumptions, and prejudices that Israeli Arab students held regarding Israel and Jews in general. This is also where their views, assumptions and stereotypes regarding the United States emerged and were developed.

36. Islamic religious school.

37. Muslim religious education also comprises the sermons and prayers taking place in mosques, especially the Friday afternoon sermons. There, Friday prayers (Juma prayers) are traditionally known to encourage rioting against non-Muslim Arab leaders, as well as against other 'infidels,' meaning those who are not Muslim. Since Juma prayers are traditionally considered the most important, many people who might not attend mosque during the week attend them. Translations of Friday sermons in areas administered by the Palestinian Authority may be found at:
http://memri.org/bin/articles.cgi?Page=archives&Area=sr&ID=SR2403

38. A martyr; an individual who sacrifices themselves for a certain cause. Some of the children even expressed their desire to become a 'shaheed', meaning to martyr themselves for Islam. The concept is defined in the Qur'an, Surah iii. 163: "Count not those who are killed in the way of God as dead, but living with their Lord." These children genuinely believe that the Holy Qur'an promises a shaheed an eternal life in Paradise.

39. It is interesting to note that many verses in the Qur'an indicate that the Jews are God's chosen people, and that the land currently in dispute belongs to the Jews, and will in fact be the place where the Jews will gather once again (Qur'an 2:47, 2:122, 7:137, 17:104)

40. Wistrich, Robert S., *Muslim Anti-Semitism.* The American Jewish committee, 2002, p. 9.

41. Waqf is a legal term which signifies the appropriation or dedication of property to charitable uses and the service of God. An endowment

42. The reader may note that Jews who immigrated to Israel from Middle Eastern and North African countries do speak Arabic. Many of them, however, have not passed the Arabic language on to their children and grandchildren who were born in Israel.

43. The Movie 'Promises' was directed by B.Z. Goldberg and Justin Shapiro in 1995. It tells the story of 7 Israeli and Palestinian teenagers living in and around Jerusalem. Although they live only fifteen minutes from each other, their life experiences are all very different and unique.

44. The Jewish holy scripture known by Christians as the Old Testament.

45. "An Impersonal Story," *Eretz Aheret*, issue no. 16, May-June, 2003, p. 14

46. The Iraqi minister of information during the Second Gulf War (2003).

47. Although in some Arab countries people do have access to western media through satellite and the internet, some countries prohibit it or strictly limit it.

48. A group of elderly American women who get together and sing anti-war songs.

49. When using the term "liberal" in this context, I am not referring to the political liberal left. I refer to a liberal concept of education which exposes students to a wide variety of ideas from which they can choose. (According to this definition, the liberal left is, in fact, no longer liberal, since it constricts the individual to a narrow range of ideas and beliefs).

50. This term refers and describes the Israeli upper class residing in the northern part of Tel Aviv, especially in the wealthy suburb of Ramat Aviv.

51. The historic Sea of Galilee, which is the major fresh water source of Israel.

52. A Palestinian city in the West Bank.

53. One of Tel Aviv's suburbs, inhabited primarily by orthodox Jews.

54. A wedding hall in Jerusalem. The Versaille Tragedy refers to the night when the Versaille wedding hall collapsed killing dozens of people and injuring hun-

dreds. It was later discovered that the building collapsed due to the constructor's negligence.

55. Ehud Barak was the Israeli Prime Minister between July 1999 and March 2001. He was defeated by Ariel Sharon in special elections held in February 2001.

56. A Jewish town on the banks of the Sea of Galilee.

57. A pre-military training facility.

58. An Israeli Arab village located near Jerusalem.

59. An Israeli Arab village located near Jerusalem and situated within the Green Line.

60. Rabbi Meir Kahana, author of various publications on the rise of anti-Semitism in the Western world and the danger of another Holocaust, and the founder of the Israeli extreme right Kach party (which was later banned by the Israeli government). He was assassinated in New York by a Muslim.

61. Pardon, forgiveness, reconciliation. 'Sulha' is also used to describe a formal meeting which effects a reconciliation of conflicting parties or family members.

62. A hospital located in Jerusalem.

63. A Member of the Knesset since 1973, Namir has served as a member of the Committees on Education and Culture (1974-77), Public Services (1974-77) and Public Audit (Control) (1977-81), as well as chairing the Committees on Education and Culture (1977-84) and Labor and Social Welfare (1984-92). From 1992-1996, Namir served as Minister of Labor and Social Affairs. She was appointed Israeli Ambassador to China in 1996.

64. Israeli Jewish villages located near Jerusalem.

65. A Jewish town located in the Judean Hills, very close to Jerusalem.

66. Made of Lawsonia leaves, henna is used to produce a dye traditionally used to decorate women's hands and feet, usually before their wedding.

67. The Israeli secret service agency.

68. Before 1948, Christian Arabs inhabited these two villages. In 1948 they took refuge in neighboring towns, within Israel's political borders, and were therefore given Israeli citizenship. In 1955 their lands were expropriated for establishing Jewish settlements. They have appealed to the Israeli Supreme Court to be allowed to return to their original location. They have not yet been allowed to do so.

69. The Druze are one of the minority groups living in Israel. They separated themselves from mainstream Islam and developed their own religion between the years 996 and 1021 A.D. They are persecuted by Muslim rulers and religious leaders who view them as heretics guilty of distorting the one and only true religion. Due to this, the Druze religion is secretive and kept from outsiders; the Druze people themselves were compelled to settle on mountains where they could more easily protect themselves. The Druze believe that they have existed

ever since the creation of the world. The main principles of the religion are the belief in one God and in reincarnation.

70. An Arab village in the Galilee. During the October 2000 riots, two 22-year-old men from Sahnin were killed by Israeli police forces.

71. Anwar Sadat, president of Eygpt, 1970 -1981. He signed a peace treaty with Israel in 1979, for which he was awarded the Nobel Prize, and was subsequently assassinated by a Muslim fundamentalist in 1981.

72. Community center where adults and young people go in order to participate in extracurricular activities such as drama, art, sports and preparation classes for one's college education.

73. One of Tel Aviv's suburbs, where Jews and Arabs still live and work side by side.

74. (ne-'vé shal-'om / 'wah-at i-sal-'am: Hebrew and Arabic for Oasis of Peace. A village in Israel established jointly by Jews and Palestinian Arabs of Israeli citizenship and engaged in educational work for peace, equality and understanding between the two peoples.

75. Givat Haviva is center for education, research and documentation, founded in 1949. Today, Givat Haviva's mission is help Israeli society cope with major social issues and to foster educational initiatives, research and community work in the fields of peace, democracy, coexistence, tolerance and social solidarity.

76. A night club in Tel Aviv where a Palestinian suicide bomber detonated himself, killing a large number of teenagers who were attending a party.

77. Official Spokesperson for the Israeli Army during the first Gulf War; today a commentator on current events.

78. A Palestinian town in the West Bank, site of biblical Shechem.

79. A month in which Muslims are religiously obligated to fast from sunrise to sunset.

80. A Palestinian boy, who was caught in crossfire between the Israeli Army and Palestinian gunmen and was killed.

81. *Mifal ha Payis* is an Israeli organization that runs the state lottery. Mifal ha Payis uses the proceeds from the lottery for community development projects, such as sponsoring the construction of community cultural centers and sport facilities in Israeli towns and villages.

82. In 1976, Israel's practice of expropriating Arab land in northern Israel to build Jewish settlements provoked Arab residents in the Galilee town of Sakhnin to protest. On March 30 they marched to repudiate the Israeli Defense Ministry's confiscation of a parcel of farmland on the outskirts of the town. Six Arabs were killed during the violent protests. Since then, Israeli Arabs have commemorated March 30 as "Land Day" and turned the day into a general protest against what they view as discriminatory practices by the government.
http://www.jewishvirtuallibrary.org/jsource/Society_&_Culture/landday.html

83. Arabic word meaning that which is strictly forbidden.

84. Husni Mubarak, Egypt's president at the time I conducted my interviews.
85. A nightly Israeli news program broadcast in Hebrew.
86. Since my interviews were recorded, Bshara has been tried in an Israeli court and acquitted. It was concluded that his words fell within the definition of free speech, and were not a clear incitement for the Arab world to physically wage a war against Israel. In spite of this fact, many Israeli Jews felt that he was a traitor against Israel.
87. Although Israel does not have a constitution, its Declaration of Independence (1948) rules that all citizens, including minorities of all religions and ethnic groups, are to be treated equally. Therefore, by law, Israel does provide all minorities with equal rights and opportunities.
88. In Arabic: "Day of the Catastrophe." The term refers the day in which the State of Israel was declared in 1948.
89. Most Israeli Arabs have historically refused to join the Israeli Defense Forces, with the exception of some Bedouin and Druse clans, as well as a small minority of other Israeli Arabs. The main reason for this is that they do not want to find themselves in a conflict against their own families living in the Occupied Territories. Since this is a valid reason, they are exempt from serving in the Israeli Army. Jewish Israelis, both men and women, are drafted at 18.
90. Israel's Declaration of Independence states, [Members of the people's council, representatives of the Jewish community of Eretz Israel] "Hereby declare the establishment of a Jewish state in Eretz Israel, to be known as the State of Israel." It is, therefore, clearly a Jewish state, established for the Jewish people. It is one of the only countries (together with several Muslim countries) in the world that has the name of a religion in its definition. Creating a bi-national state, as Dr. Gnam suggests, would mean that Israel would not be defined as a Jewish state. There are also some Jews, many of whom live outside of Israel, who believe that Israel should not be defined as a Jewish state per se.
91. *Ha'aretz*. Sunday, June 29, 2003
92. This word means "return" in Hebrew and refers to the right of return of Palestinians to their lands.
93. Three towns in Israel that were inhabited predominantly by Arabs before 1948.
94. "An Impersonal Story," *Eretz Aheret*, issue no. 16, May-June, 2003, p. 12.
95. An Israeli Arab movie director.
96. "I am the Arab-Palestinian-Hebrew-Israeli," *Eretz Aheret*, issue no. 16, May-June 2003, p. 54.
97. An Arab village in Wadi Arra.
98. In Arabic, an acronym for 'Harakat Al-Muqawama Al-Islamia' -- Islamic Resistance Movement, Hamas was formed by Ahmed Yassin in late 1987 as an outgrowth of the Palestinian branch of the Muslim Brotherhood. A fundamental-

ist Muslim terrorist organization, it has been outlawed by the United States and the U.N.

99. Traditionally a holiday of the Moroccan Jews, celebrated on the last day of Passover. It is usually celebrated out in nature, particularly in public parks.

100. Founded in 1951, Oranim College provides training for teachers and childcare personnel.

101. A refugee camp in Lebanon, where Palestinian refugees were massacred by the Lebanese Falanj in 1982. It is widely claimed that this massacre was executed with the knowledge of Ariel Sharon who was Israel's defense minister at that time.

102. This literary genre developed in Arabic literature from the 8th century onward, where Biblical stories as well as post-Biblical stories of both Jewish and Christian may be found. Among the most famous authors of the Israiliyyat were Abu Kaab al-Ahbar (rumored to have accompanied Umar on his first visit to the Temple area) and Abu Rihana (said to be related to the Prophet by marriage). I do not know of a prayer called Israiliyyat, and the interviewee is probably referring to a text found in the Israiliyyat.

103. Compulsory alms donated to charity; one of the five pillars of Islam. Unlike Christian charity or Jewish 'tzedaka' (Hebrew for charity), Zakat must be donated to Muslim charities alone. Zakat is given by Muslims to needy Muslims inside their own society. Practices vary enormously throughout the Muslim world. Zakat is generally 1/40 of a person's income.

104. Maronites are Christians who believe in the doctrine of Monothelitism; that Jesus had one will but two natures, one divine and one human. They follow the precepts of the fourth century priest Maron. The Lebanese Maronite community has historically been known to clash with the Druze.

105. An Iranian Jew who for many years had a pirate radio station in the Mediterranean which advocated for a dialogue with the Palestinians. The station, **The Voice of Peace**, started airing in March 1973 and was shut down in October 1993.

106. Dr. Baruch Goldstein, a physician and resident of the extreme right-wing Kiryat Arba settlement murdered 29 Palestinian Muslims during Friday prayers, on February 25th, 1994, in the Cave of the Patriarchs, a site in Hebron holy to both Muslims and Jews. Goldstein was beaten to death by the survivors. 26 Palestinians and 2 Israelis died in rioting immediately following the massacre. Goldstein's actions were condemned by the Israeli government and by the Israeli populace in general. All organized denominations of Judaism denounced his act as immoral and as terrorism. However, he became a hero to some Israeli right-wing fringe extremists. Members of the outlawed Kach organization, to which he belonged, justify his actions by claiming that he pre-empted the mass murder of Jews by Arabs.

NOTES

107. Nation, incorporating all Muslims. The idea of the 'Umma' was preached for the first time by the Prophet Muhammad who wanted to bring all Muslims under one rule. The importance of the 'Umma' is clarified in several of the Qur'anic stories

108. Dershowitz, Allan. *The Case for Israel*, New Jersey: John Wiley & Sons, Inc., 2003, p. 59.

109. Several branches of Islam permit the killing of a man or woman who converts to another religion, unless the individual recants and reverts back to Islam within three days. Islam also assumes that every person was born a Muslim and then converted to another religion. This is why converts to Islam are considered to revert to Islam and not convert to Islam. Among other people Islam believes to have been Muslim is Jesus Christ.

110. Jews, Christians and the West in Saudi Arabian Textbooks.

111. The reader should note that the Shar'ia and the *hadith* were written after the days of the Prophet Muhammad. Although based on the Qur'an, these texts should not be considered as divine in origin or as supreme in their importance. Problems usually start when these texts, written by men, are considered divine and indisputable. A professor of Islam in one of the universities in Nablus (known to Jews as Schem) fell victim to the inability of many Muslims to accept criticism of Islamic texts. When he dared to insinuate in his class that the Qur'an might have been edited some thirty years after the death of the prophet Muhammad and challenged the accuracy of several central hadiths his students forcefully carried him and threw him out of the class's window. During a lecture honoring Gideon Libson's new book on Jewish and Islamic Law: *A Comparative Study of Custom During the Geonic Period*, the author stated, "The difference between how Judaism and Islam evolved is quite clear. Let me illustrate it for you in a simple manner. Let's assume that Islam is indeed a God given religion which was given to human beings from the sky. The problem is that although it was given to people from the sky it never truly reached earth but instead stayed in the sky. It never really came down to the people so that they could debate it and help it fit modern days. It stayed up there, untouchable and undebatable. Judaism, assuming that it is also a religion given to human beings by God, did not stay up in the sky. Instead, it was given to human beings who have for thousands of years debated and criticized it in Jewish Bible schools and pointed at problems and contradictions it might exhibit. One religion is still up in the sky and the other in here on earth. The implications of a religion still being in the sky are clearly evident in today's world."

112. This is why Muslims have persecuted other religions, especially those which are still awaiting the coming of a Prophet—an ideal which is abhorred by Islam.

113. Israel's Defense Minister between March 2001 and November 2002.

114. Tafsir Jalalin.

[115] Qur'an 5:51.
116. Leibowitz, Yeshayahu, *I wanted to ask you, Professor Leibowitz.* Jerusalem: Keter Publishing House, pp. 248, 1999.
117 .Two Jewish towns located in the Israeli Negev whose inhabitants are predominantly Jews from Middle Eastern and North African countries as well as new immigrants from Russia and the Former Soviet Union.
118. Yehoshua, A.B. "The Liberating Bride." In Alei Siah, Issue 47, Ha-Kibbutz Ha-Meuchad (summer 2002), pp. 9-20.
119. Ibid.
120. Maale Adumim is one of Jerusalem's suburbs, built on land which is supposed to return to Palestinian hands once a peace agreement is signed between Israelis and Palestinians. Some people have suggested its inclusion in a land swap that would enable areas populated predominantly by Jews to remain in Israel and areas populated predominantly by Arabs to remain in Palestine.

Select Bibliography

Books

Caspi, Mishael and Jerome Weltsch. *From Slumber to Awakening.* University Press of America, 1998.
Cook Michael. *Muhammad.* New York: Oxford University Press. 1983.
Crone, Patricia, and Michael Cook. *Hagarism. The Waking of the Islamic World.* Cambridge: Cambridge University Press. 1997.
Dershowitz, Alan, *The Case for Israel*, 1st edition (New Jersey: John Wiley & Sons, Inc., 2003).
Esposito, John L. and Francois Burgat (ed.). *Modernizing Islam.* New Brunswick,
  New Jersey: Rutgers University Press. 2003.
Farah, Caesar E. *Islam.* Woodbury, New York: University of Minnesota. 1970.
Goitein, S.D. *A Mediterranean Society.* Berkley and Los Angeles: University of California Press. 1967.
Hourani, A. *A History of the Arab People.* Cambridge, Mass: Harvard University
  Press. 1991.
Lapidus, I.M. *A History of Islamic Societies.* Cambridge University Press. 1988.
The Glorious Qur'an, text and explanations by Muhammad M. Pickthall, Tahrike Tarsile Qur'an, Inc., Elmhurst, NY, 1999

Encyclopedias

1. *Encyclopedia Judaica*, 1ST edition., s.v. "Israel."
2. *Encyclopedia Judaica*, 1st edition, s.v. "Palestine."
3. *Encyclopedia Judaica*, 1st edition, s.v. "Islam."
4. *Encyclopedia of Asian History*, s.v. "Jihad."
5. *Encyclopedia of Islam*, 6th edition, s.v. "Islam."
6. *Muslim Peoples: A world Ethnographic Survey*, s.v. "Jihad."

Index

ahal-al-kitab, v, 56, 234, 332
al Aqsa, iii, 89, 146, 151, 153, 189, 217, 247, 262, 295, 302
Al Aqsa *Intifada*, 82, 84, 131, 231
Al Jazeera, 66, 74, 170, 198, 282
al-Medina, vi
Al-nasih wal mansuh, 279
Annan, Kofi, viii, ix
Arafat, Yasser, vii, xlviii, 126, 152, 217, 223, 225, 228, 240, 242, 247, 285
Arara, vii, xxx, xxxi, xxxii, xxxv, xl, xli, 58, 83, 106, 107, 125, 127, 149, 150, 159, 178, 179, 214, 215, 216, 232, 233, 235, 237, 238, 281, 282, 288, 289, 294, 313
Atatürk, l
banat al-hur, vi
Banu Qaynuqa', vi
Banu'l-Nadhir, vi
Bar Kochva, xlv, xlviii
Barak, Ehud, lii, 152, 247
Bashir, Abu bakr, vi
Basyunni, Muhammad, 326
Ben Gurion, v
Bible, xxvi
Bshara, Azmi, xxvi, 140, 143, 144, 158, 206, 336

dajjal, xiii
Dershowitz, Alan, 65
Dhimmis, 276
Druze, 112, 190, 227, 313
Durrah, Muhammad al-, 169, 191, 239, 245, 268, 282, 289, 299
France, iv, 251
Givat Haviva, 131
Ha'aretz, 140, 205, 210
Hadith, xiii, xliv, 56, 275, 283, 317
Hamas, iii, 221, 290, 292, 295, 317, 337
Herzel, Theodor, 209
Hizballah, 66
Hussein, Saddam, 65
Islam, 165, 191, 233, 234, 235, 254, 255, 276, 278, 279, 280, 283, 286, 294, 296
Israel, xii, xxvi, xxviii, xxix, xxxi, xxxiv, xxxvi, xxxvii, xxxviii, xl, xlii, xliv, xlv, xlvi, xlvii, xlviii, l, li, lii, 56, 57, 58, 60, 61, 62, 66, 69, 70, 72, 74, 77, 79, 80, 85, 87, 88, 89, 91, 93, 94, 96, 97, 99, 102, 103, 104, 107, 109, 112, 115, 117, 118, 120, 121, 122, 123, 124, 126, 133, 136, 137, 138, 140, 142, 143, 144, 145, 150, 151,

153, 155, 158, 160, 171, 179, 180, 181, 182, 183, 184, 187, 188, 191, 192, 195, 197, 198, 199, 201, 205, 206, 207, 208, 209, 210, 213, 214, 215, 220, 222, 224, 228, 229, 231, 232, 233, 239, 252, 256, 265, 266, 267, 268, 269, 273, 278, 284, 285, 287, 289, 291, 293, 294, 302, 306, 308, 311, 313, 314, 315, 317, 318, 320, 322, 323, 324, 325, 326
Israeli Arabs, xxvi, xxxvii, xlv, xlvi, xlvii, xlviii, 59, 61, 69, 124, 205, 207, 209, 210, 211, 213, 281, 314, 321, 325
Israiliyyat, 234, 337
Jerusalem, iii
Jesus Christ, xii, xxxix, 181, 182
kibbutz, 71
Knesset, ii, vii, xxvi, 206, 299, 334
Leibowitz, Yeshayahu, 319
Mahsom Carney, 182
Majli, Nazir, xxxvii, 63, 211
Milosevic, 142
Mossad, xxxvi, 258
Muhammad, xxxviii, 56, 128, 276, 277, 279, 280, 281, 309, 318
Na'amat, xxxii, xl
Natur, Salman, 212
Neve Shalom, 122
Nimrodi Case, 140
Orr Commission, xxxvii, l, lii, 155
Palestine, vii, xlix, 58, 89, 107, 153, 209, 231, 238, 243, 248, 257, 260, 269, 284, 286, 297, 322, 327

Protocols of the Elders of Zion, xliv
Qur'an, vi, ix, xiii, xxvi, xxxix, 55, 57, 62, 86, 128, 155, 156, 157, 235, 236, 244, 254, 255, 262, 263, 264, 275, 277, 279, 280, 284, 288, 294, 296, 297, 302, 316, 317, 320, 331, 333, 339
Qur'anic, xliii, 275, 283, 338
Qurayza, vi
Rantisi, Abd al Aziz, iii
Sabra and Shatila, 234
Sachedina, Abdulaziz A., xliii
Sadat, Anwar, 18, 278
Sahnin, 116
Shafik, Munir, vi
shaheed, 57, 147, 173, 197, 236, 282, 285, 286
Shari'ah, vii
Sharon, Ariel, vi, xxvi, 88, 89, 134, 152, 153, 219, 234, 243, 245, 295, 299
The Triangle, vii, i, xxix, xxxi, xxxii, xxxix, xlviii, xlix, 66, 263, 315, 320, 327
Tiberias, 71, 94
Tibi, Ahmad, vii
Umm el-Fahem, vii, xxxi, xlii, xlix, l, 82, 95, 161, 202, 206, 219, 328
Wahabbi, 280
Waqf, 59, 283
Wistrich, Robert S., 56
Yassin, Ahmad, vii, 100
Yaum al Nakba, 207
Yehoshua, A.B., 323
Yavetz, Zvi, x
Zahrani, Nasar al-, iii

About the Author

Smadar Bakovic was born in Haifa, Israel. She was raised in the *moshav shitufi (*cooperative village) of Neve Ilan, located in the Jerusalem foothills. After her military service she left for the United States where she spent six years traveling the country, including living on the Flathead Indian Reservation in Montana. While in the USA, she attended Salish Kootenai College in Montana, Northwest College in Wyoming and Bates College in Maine. She served as the Middle East columnist for all three colleges and participated in numerous panel discussions and conferences about the Israeli-Palestinian conflict. She graduated with a B.A. in English from Bates College in May 2003.

Smadar has worked for the United Nations in Geneva, Switzerland where she served as a researcher for the Committee on the Status of Women and the Working Group on the Girl Child. In May 2001 she began her research on the Israeli Arab population, thanks to a Phillips Student Fellowship she received from Bates College. In March 2004 she moved to Eastern Turkey where she researched Kurdish women and Turkish Sunni Islam in the ancient city of Mardin, on the Turkish-Syrian border. Smadar now lives in Jerusalem and serves on a multi-disciplinary team implementing a major initiative on behalf of Israel's Druze population with the American Jewish Joint Distribution Committee (JDC). She is also a Board Member in the Young Israeli Forum for Cooperation, an organization involved in Israeli-Palestinian dialogue in Europe.

Tall Shadows: Interviews with Israeli Arabs is her first book.